Politics and popular opinion in East Germany 1945–68

MANCHESTER
UNIVERSITY PRESS

Politics and popular opinion in East Germany 1945–68

MARK ALLINSON

Manchester University Press

MANCHESTER AND NEW YORK

DISTRIBUTED EXCLUSIVELY IN THE USA BY ST. MARTIN'S PRESS

Published by Manchester University Press
Oxford Road, Manchester M13 9NR, UK
and Room 400, 175 Fifth Avenue, New York, NY 10010, USA
http://www.man.ac.uk/mup

Distributed exclusively in the USA by
St. Martin's Press, Inc., 175 Fifth Avenue, New York,
NY 10010, USA

Distributed exclusively in Canada by
UBC Press, University of British Columbia, 6344 Memorial Road,
Vancouver, BC, Canada V6T 1Z2

British Library Cataloguing-in-Publication Data
A catalogue record for this book is available from the British Library

Library of Congress Cataloging-in-Publication Data applied for

ISBN 0 7190 5554 7 *hardback*

First published 2000

06 05 04 03 02 01 00   10 9 8 7 6 5 4 3 2 1

Typeset in Garamond with Chianti
by Northern Phototypesetting Co. Ltd, Bolton
Printed in Great Britain
by Bookcraft (Bath) Ltd, Midsomer Norton

CONTENTS

FOR MY PARENTS

ACKNOWLEDGEMENTS

This work would not have been possible without the support of many people over a number of years, to all of whom I feel greatly indebted. The initial years of the project were financed by the British Academy, and Bristol University's Arts Faculty Research Fund kindly financed an additional research trip to Weimar. Once in Thuringia, I was fortunate to enjoy expert support from various sources: Dr Wolfgang Geist granted me unparalleled access to the SED's former *Bezirksparteiarchiv* in Erfurt while it was still under PDS management; the Thuringian State Archives in Weimar – particularly Frau Johannes and Frau Bock – ensured I was never short of files; and the staff of Erfurt city library – particularly those in the local history department – answered many queries.

I might never have travelled to Erfurt at all without the friendship of Jürgen, Brigitte and Julia Benedikt who helped with accommodation problems and introduced me to much of the splendid Thuringian landscape. Steffen Kachel – a fellow postgraduate student of twentieth-century Thuringian history and then a member of the Thuringian *Landtag* (regional parliament) – has provided much practical support, background information and stimulating discussion about the issues covered in this book.

I have been fortunate throughout my time in Thuringia to have met many people happy to help and talk about their experiences in the GDR (East Germany) and their outlooks since unification. These informal conversations have helped me to corroborate the archival records. In particular I should like to thank the following people for their time and patience: Dr Klaus, Ursula and Thomas Kachel, Anka Sommer and her family, Gerlinde Plotzke, Martin Weidauer, Dr Rosemarie Collet, the staff of Intertext Berlin and Erfurt, Karin Becherer and family and – at the PDS – Knut Korschewsky and Elke Pudzuhn, among many others.

In England, I owe debts of gratitude to Andy Hollis at Salford University – who originally sent me to the GDR – Dr Elizabeth Harvey for her advice before I started this project, Dr Nick Stargardt who encouraged me with the transformation of the work into a book, my colleagues in the German department at the University of Bristol – particularly for permitting me an essential sabbatical term – and the helpful staff at Manchester University Press. Dr Keir Waddington, Dr Neale Laker and Jon Telfer supported me at various stages with their unremitting patience, as did my parents throughout, not least when they let me fill their house with communist literature. Finally, this project could never have been started or completed without the dedicated support of my thesis supervisor, Professor Mary Fulbrook, to whom I am greatly indebted. The shortcomings which remain are all my own work.

ABBREVIATIONS AND GLOSSARY

AfI
: *Amt für Information*
Information Office (of *Land Thüringen*)

BDS
: *Bund demokratischer Sozialisten*
League of Democratic Socialists

BdVP
: *Bezirksbehörde der deutschen Volkspolizei*
Regional police authority

Bezirk
: county (GDR administrative region, 1952–90)

CDU
: *Christlich-Demokratische Union*
Christian Democratic Union
(unless specifically stated, reference is being made to the CDU in the GDR and not the West German party)

CPSU
: Communist Party of the Soviet Union

DBD
: *Demokratische Bauernpartei Deutschlands*
Democratic Farmers' Party of Germany

DFD
: *Demokratischer Frauenbund Deutschlands*
Democratic Women's League of Germany

DSF
: *Gesellschaft für Deutsch–Sowjetische Freundschaft*
Society for German–Soviet Friendship

DWK
: *Deutsche Wirtschaftskommission*
German Economics Commission (proto-SBZ government)

East Germany
: same as German Democratic Republic (see GDR)

EKD
: *Evangelische Kirche in Deutschland*
Evangelical Church in Germany

FDGB
: *Freier Deutscher Gewerkschaftsbund*
Free German Trades Union League

FDJ
: *Freie Deutsche Jugend*
Free German Youth

FRG
: Federal Republic of Germany (also called West Germany)
Bundesrepublik Deutschland (*BRD*)

GDR
: German Democratic Republic
Deutsche Demokratische Republik (*DDR*)

gleichgeschaltet
: 'co-ordinated' (see *Gleichschaltung*)

Gleichschaltung
: 'co-ordination': term often used to describe the co-ordination of state, political and societal structures with the NSDAP in the Third Reich

HSB
: (*Betrieb mit*) *halbstaatlicher Beteiligung*
semi-private firm

Jugendweihe	the socialist coming of age ceremony, introduced in 1954
Junge Gemeinde	'Young Congregation' informal parish grouping of Protestant youth
Junge Welt	FDJ newspaper
KGB	Committee for State Security (USSR)
KPD	*Kommunistische Partei Deutschlands* Communist Party of Germany
KPKK	*Kreisparteikontrollkommission* District party control commission
Kreis (plural *Kreise*)	district
Kreistag	district council
Land (plural *Länder*)	province/state/region (administrative unit of SBZ/GDR 1945–52)
Landrat	senior district administrator
Landtag	regional parliament
LDPD	*Liberal-Demokratische Partei Deutschlands* Liberal Democratic Party of Germany
LPA	*Landesparteiarchiv Thüringen der PDS* PDS Thuringian Party Archive
LPG	*Landwirtschaftliche Produktionsgenossenschaft* agricultural production co-operative
MdI	*Ministerium des Innern* Ministry for the Interior
MfS	*Ministerium für Staatssicherheit* Ministry for State Security (also known as the *Stasi*)
MTS	*Maschinen-Traktoren-Stationen* farm equipment stations
NATO	North Atlantic Treaty Organisation
ND	abbreviation of *Neues Deutschland*, the official SED newspaper
NF	*Nationale Front des demokratischen Deutschland* National Front of Democratic Germany
NKVD	Soviet People's Commissariat of Internal Affairs, the Soviet secret police (until 1954) and forerunner to the KGB
NSDAP	*Nationalsozialistische Deutsche Arbeiterpartei* National Socialist German Workers' Party (Nazi party)

NVA	*Nationale Volksarmee* National People's Army (GDR)
Oberschule	high school
Oberstaatsanwalt	public prosecutor
Ostpolitik	'eastern policy': here, the western European policy of building bridges to the socialist states of eastern Europe introduced during the late 1960s / early 1970s
PDS	*Partei des demokratischen Sozialismus* Party of Democratic Socialism (successor party to the SED, founded 1989–90)
Pfarrjugend	'Parish Youth' informal parish grouping of Catholic youth
PGH	*Produktionsgenossenschaft des Handels* Commercial Production Cooperative
Politbüro	politburo, the supreme policy-making committee of the SED
POW	prisoner of war
RdB	*Rat des Bezirkes* regional council
RdK	*Rat des Kreises* district council
RdS	*Rat der Stadt* town/city council
RE	religious education
Republikflucht	fleeing, or leaving, the republic (i.e. the GDR)
SBZ	*Sowjetische Besatzungszone* Soviet Zone of Occupation
SED	*Sozialistische Einheitspartei Deutschlands* Socialist Unity Party of Germany
SMA(D)	*Sowjetische Militäradministration (in Deutschland)* Soviet Military Administration (in Germany)
SPD	*Sozialdemokratische Partei Deutschlands* Social Democratic Party of Germany
Stasi	unofficial term for the MfS
ThHStAW	*Thüringisches Hauptstaatsarchiv Weimar* Thuringian State Archives, Weimar
Thüringen	Thuringia
TVZ	*Thüringer Volkszeitung* Thuringian People's Newspaper (KPD 1945–46)

USPD	*Unabhängige Sozialdemokratische Partei Deutschlands* Independent Social Democratic Party of Germany (1917–22)
USSR	Union of Socialist Soviet Republics, or Soviet Union
VdgB	*Verein der gegenseitigen Bauernhilfe* Association for Mutual Farmers' Assistance
VEB	*Volkseigener Betrieb* state-owned enterprise
Volksaussprache	public debate (particularly prior to the adoption of the 1968 constitution)
Volkskammer	People's Chamber (GDR parliament)
VVN	*Verein der Verfolgten des Naziregimes* Association of the Persecuted of the Nazi Regime
Wende	'change', term often used to describe the autumn of 1989 when the SED's old guard fell from power
West Germany	same as Federal Republic of Germany (see FRG)

MAP I   The GDR and its *Bezirke*

Source: W. Oswald, ed., *Die DDR im Spiegel ihrer Bezirke* (Berlin, Dietz Verlag, 1989), p. 91.

MAP 2   Thuringian *Kreise* and *Bezirke*, 1952–90

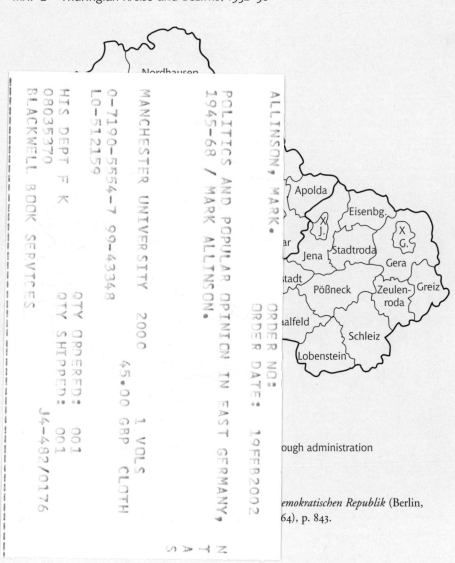

... ough administration

... *emokratischen Republik* (Berlin, ...64), p. 843.

1

Introduction

Perhaps the most frequently asked question about Germany's twentieth-century history is not 'what happened?' but 'how could it have happened?'. Usually this question has referred to the national socialist dictatorship, a period of history which seems impossible to comprehend within the normal framework of historiographical analysis. More than half a century after the end of the Second World War the spectre of German neo-Nazism still fascinates and terrifies the world, while similar political groupings elsewhere are relatively ignored. Perhaps underlying this perception is the memory of German national socialism as, at least initially, a genuinely popular mass movement. Western perceptions of state and society in the formerly socialist countries of eastern Europe, however, assume a form of rule imposed on the masses by a small minority with no popular or democratic legitimacy. Hence, the peoples of the former Soviet Union are generally not expected to feel collective responsibility for the millions of victims of Stalin's purges, while Germans, even two generations later, are still expected to bear the guilt of the Nazi holocaust against the Jewish people.

This peculiar contrast between the origins of two systems – in shorthand at least 'fascism' and 'communism' – which in their most extreme forms – Hitler's Third Reich and Stalin's Soviet Union – produced arguably similar results, is of direct relevance to the history of the postwar East German state, the German Democratic Republic (GDR, or East Germany), whose population was urged within a few years to fight both for the *Führer*'s final victory over the Soviet Union and for the victory of socialism at the side of the Soviet Union. For forty-four years, from the arrival of Soviet troops in 1945 to the 'peaceful revolution' of autumn 1989, East Germans lived mainly quiescently under 'real existing socialism'. 'How could it have happened?', one might well ask. Analysts have offered two principal schools of thought to answer this question.

First is the Marxist argument, proffered mainly during the GDR's existence, that socialism was an inevitable historical development and the natural positive response to the horrors of Nazism. The division of the German working-class movement during the Weimar Republic was overcome by joint action by communists and social democrats to ensure that fascism never returned. Thus the Socialist Unity Party of Germany (SED) was created and legitimised as the leading political force in the postwar Soviet Occupation Zone of Germany (the *Sowjetische*

Besatzungszone, SBZ), in which territory the GDR was created in 1949. The SED's legitimacy was accepted, in this explanation, not only among the working classes but also among other sections of the population who, after a period of 'class struggle' against both internal opponents and western 'imperialist agents' in the Cold War, embraced and allied themselves with socialism, embodied in the SED, as the rightful, majority societal and economic order. Marxists emphasised the USSR's roles as Germany's liberator from national socialism and the leading global force in socialism, but in the spirit of internationalism rather than of military force.[1] This official party line was largely unable to explain the internal opposition which occurred in the GDR, even long after the initial 'class struggle' should have been won. Nor, for instance, did it explain the SED's tendency to appeal to elites in society more than to the traditional working class, on whose numerical superiority the SED's legitimacy supposedly rested. However, the role of institutions such as the *Stasi* – the 'popular' name for the GDR's Ministry of State Security (MfS) – and the single-list electoral system in maintaining socialism in the GDR was legitimised in this argument by the need to prevent fascism from re-emerging and individuals or small groupings from overthrowing socialism for their own personal vested interests to the detriment of the greater good. In the Marxist view, this greater good was 'scientifically' proven to lie in socialist and ultimately communist rule, as defined by the SED at the Soviet party's behest.

The contrary argument is that socialist or communist systems are imposed on the population by a small minority and possess no legitimacy, democratic or otherwise. It is argued that east German socialism and quiescence were the product of Soviet tanks, of the barbed wire and 'shoot to kill' policy at the Berlin Wall, and of the notorious *Stasi*. This view is, perhaps understandably, predominant amongst the many who suffered under the GDR state, but also in western Germany, reflecting both the Cold War and a nationalist bitterness at Germany's division after 1945. As the western occupation zones of Germany merged into the Federal Republic of Germany (FRG, or West Germany) and developed along conservative, capitalist lines, it became important in the western state to legitimise the FRG's own political course, particularly at a time when the political and economic non-viability of 'real' socialist or Moscow-aligned communist systems was still unproved. Nationalist and conservative, capitalist appeals were deployed in the FRG's diplomatic and propaganda offensive against the GDR, particularly during the iciest period of the Cold War before the advent of *Ostpolitik* (see Glossary on p. x) in the early 1970s.[2]

Since the GDR's collapse, many western German politicians and historians, as well as east German opponents of the GDR, have been at pains to continue the battle, perhaps still perceiving the need to legitimise the FRG's political and economic system to the state's newly acquired eastern citizens. Thomas Neumann's 1990 history of SED rule, for instance, attempted to discredit Marxism per se and write off the GDR's history as simple Stalinism.[3] In 1994, an enquiry by the parliament of united Germany, the *Bundestag*, concluded that the GDR was 'a dictatorial system based on violence and injustice'.[4] The conclusion was unsurprising, as the commission's aim before the investigation had been to 'ensure that those forces which were decisive in organising the repression of people in the GDR never again receive a political chance in united Germany'.[5]

This policy has effectively led, since 1989, to the FRG's retrospective reversal of the diplomatic and legal recognition it had accorded the GDR since the early 1970s. The FRG's courts have witnessed trials of the GDR's political hierarchy and officialdom, among them the former leader Erich Honecker and other members of the SED's *Politbüro* (the policy-making committee), concerning actions taken within a state now defunct and under a very different legal framework. Strangely, the offensive against the GDR relaunched in late 1989 by those who rejected the GDR's very legitimacy as a state sharply contrasted with the memories of millions of east Germans, and in particular with the wide and enduring wave of nostalgia for numerous aspects of the GDR (not least job security and a sense of solidarity, but also for particular brand names), and to the relatively strong showing of the Party of Democratic Socialism (PDS), the SED's successor.[6]

Clearly, the GDR could not have functioned as a stable entity if only a small number of fanatical communists had existed to coerce the entire population. Large numbers of people actively supported the state system, whether as members of the GDR's political parties or mass organisations, or as managers of a factory or business. By the late 1980s much of the GDR's stability was no longer attributed to the presence of Soviet troops, but to the omnipresent, omniscient *Stasi*. This meant that possibly hundreds of thousands of people were working directly or indirectly for the *Stasi* to defend and preserve the system. Beyond this, the vast majority of the remainder of the population had to be prepared to tolerate passively the system that the smaller, but still large, group of people were working to uphold. On occasion, as on election days, this vast, normally passive, majority had to be prepared to vote actively for the candidates of the 'National Front' (NF), the 'governing coalition' of the GDR's constitutional political parties.

That this situation of overwhelming active or passive support of the system existed for almost forty years is a historical fact, however uncomfortable that might have appeared after 1989 in either eastern or western Germany. The continued allegiance of many east Germans after 1989 to some, if not all, aspects of the GDR state – and the refusal of most to condemn it entirely – means that an understanding of why this state of affairs evolved and persisted is both essential to understanding eastern German society after 1989 and a prerequisite for a true unification of Germany which accommodates the differing experiences of Germans in both parts of the country. It is important to establish how far East Germans supported, accepted or tolerated the GDR's system of government, and to determine the extent to which East Germans themselves created their society or had it imposed by Soviet intervention. As the number of committed communists in 1945 was relatively small, they alone could not have ensured the country's transformation to a stable socialist society. How and to what extent were they able to co-opt the rest of the population? What in any case is meant by the term 'SED rule'? By 1968 the party counted over 1.8 million members, approximately one adult in seven,[7] but it would seem unlikely that these large numbers formed a homogenous political mass. It is hard to reconstruct the range of personal motivations for party membership, but it is possible to gauge the degree of members' dedication to the cause and thus to determine the real extent of the SED's political hegemony at different stages of the GDR's development.

Beyond these questions' specific relevance to Germany, there is potentially wider significance for a case study of the methods used by one group in a society, in this case the SED's communist core, to acquire active and passive support throughout society. After all, the GDR was one of several socialist states established throughout eastern Europe in the wake of the Second World War and operated principally as a satellite of the Soviet Union to satisfy Moscow's foreign-policy imperatives in the postwar era. Though this work considers just the GDR, it can be seen partly as a case study of developments which were common to the founda-tion of new political and societal forms in much of eastern Europe during this period, notwithstanding the specific factors which characterised the East German socialist state.

This work takes as a central assumption that the GDR was for most of its his-tory a stable state. This assumption is based on the general absence of popular uprisings and political adventurism, the only notable exception being the events surrounding 17 June 1953 (discussed in Chapter 3). This absence is striking when compared to the instability in some eastern European states (particularly neigh-bouring Poland) in the postwar era. The GDR's history was not marked by repeated, mass attempts to overturn the SED's hegemony until the late 1980s, despite the existence of active, if tiny, openly oppositional minorities. Alongside the questions of how this stability was achieved and whether the GDR's population principally supported, accepted or tolerated SED rule, this book also addresses the question of how long it took to achieve stability for the GDR's socialist order and to identify the key turning points in this process. I aim to demonstrate that the GDR had essentially stabilised in terms of the population's outward behaviour by 1968, but that a number of existential questions remained which may have con-tributed to the system's ultimate collapse. The year 1968 is a useful cut off point as it included two seemingly contradictory developments, namely the population's mainly negative reactions to the GDR's involvement in repressing Czechoslovakia's 'Prague Spring' of 'socialism with a human face', but also the adoption of the GDR's first socialist constitution at the end of a prolonged period of relatively open popular debate and after a referendum not run in accordance with the GDR's normal intimidating election procedure.

In postulating a history of stability, I am immediately at variance with an important stream of historical thought on the GDR, according to which the state was doomed to failure virtually from the start, or at least after the apparent failed uprising of June 1953. This viewpoint has been expressed most clearly in *Untergang auf Raten* (literally 'Downfall by Instalments'), in which Armin Mitter and Stefan Wolle examine a range of public opinion reports, mainly collated by the *Stasi*, which appear to tell a tale of inevitable decline.[8] In some senses their thesis is correct: clearly the GDR did collapse in 1989–90, and did so chiefly because its population was no longer prepared to support or tolerate the political and economic system which the SED imposed. However, it seems simplistic to view the GDR's history exclusively in terms of decline, as the title of their book suggests. I hope to demonstrate that the SED succeeded in creating an essentially stable polity out of chaos and on the ruins of a state in which organised communism had been illegal. Further, the SED managed to convince some that its cause was right, and to co-opt many others in support, while neutralising effective opposition until the late 1980s. Viewed in this light, the GDR's history becomes one of the construction and advancement of the party's power and influence until at least the early 1980s. Thereafter the internal difficulties and contradictions and a changed international climate conspired to reverse the process, events which are beyond the scope of this work.

Chapters 6 and 7 of this book show how decline and collapse became less rather than more likely as the 1960s progressed, even though the foundations of the SED's power were far from secure even by this point. The continuing lack of ideological certainty in the 1960s among many of those upon whom the system ultimately rested and amongst many of the younger generation may be seen as pointers to the system's later collapse, yet the reasons which encouraged or compelled so many people to carry the system during the 1960s, even against their own personal preferences, should not be overlooked, as they contributed greatly to the SED's overall stability. In enabling the system to solidify in the 1960s, functionaries and non-functionaries alike were laying the foundations of political longevity which itself became a stabilising factor.

In order to provide a focus for this analysis of popular reaction to SED rule and motivations for its perpetuation, I have concentrated on one particular geographical region rather than considering the entire GDR, since the country's general political history in a domestic and international framework – as well as the methods used by the SED to assert its power – are well documented. Such histories are extremely useful and informative in establishing the essential contours, but they tend not to reveal how well the SED was able to exert power in the localities nor the specific effects on the population of national political developments. How were policies decided in Berlin actually implemented in the localities? How were they experienced by real people? Which sections of the population supported or opposed particular measures? The answers to these questions are as important in recording and understanding the GDR's history as issues relating to the country's political developments at the macro level.

The GDR was a highly centralised state, and there have therefore been relatively few regional studies produced outside the country (though this is being gradually remedied). The GDR was often perceived abroad as a largely homogenous state, and most attention was paid to its capital, Berlin. However, those who knew the country before 1989 were well aware that life in Berlin was very different from that in Rostock or Dresden. This book is intended in part to rectify the longstanding monotone view of the GDR by demonstrating, for instance, that events such as the uprising of 17 June 1953 took a rather different course in the regions than in Berlin, and that local factors such as religious heritage could be highly significant in determining responses to SED policies.

The region chosen for study, the Thuringian *Bezirk* (county) of Erfurt in the southwest of the GDR,[9] recommends itself for various historical and demographic reasons, discussed in greater detail in Chapter 2. However, this work does not aim to prove that Thuringia was either unique in the GDR, or necessarily typical of the GDR in every respect. While the administrative structures introduced by the SED were common to the whole of the GDR, Thuringia displayed certain specific characteristics (such as a strong Catholic minority, a border with the west) which posed unique problems for the party. Other areas had different issues to contend with, such as the existence of the Sorb minority in Brandenburg and Saxony, and the strong agricultural nature of the economy in Mecklenburg. The degree to which Thuringia was representative of the GDR will only be ascertainable once similar research is undertaken on the country's other regions. This work is to be taken as a record of one region's experience of the GDR, though I hope that its conclusions may shed more general light on the mechanisms employed by a party such as the SED in establishing its hegemony in a particular locality, and on the patterns of behaviour of a regional population away from the country's capital in shaping and responding to the local forms of the national political, societal and economic framework.

The limitations of this book do not permit a comprehensive account of politics and society in *Bezirk* Erfurt between 1945 and 1968. Rather than attempt such a project I have preferred to concentrate on several topics which I believe to be representative of developments in other spheres, discussed against a background of the wider developments between these dates. The aim has been to explore the interplay between the state and party authorities in *Bezirk* Erfurt, on the one hand, and the general population (including the grass-roots state and party functionaries and members), on the other. How well and by what means were the authorities able to control the region at different times during this period, and how well or badly did the population respond?

In order to pursue this line of questioning, I have divided this book into four principal sections, which are designed to tease out various strands before showing how they fitted together.

Chapter 2 presents a short introduction to Thuringia's social and economic structures. It also considers the rise and collapse of national socialism in Thuringia, and the region's temporary occupation by American forces between April and June 1945 to illustrate the immediate situation faced by the incoming Soviet occupiers and civilian rulers at the end of the war. There is a brief discussion of the emergence of the Thuringian communist and social democratic parties after the war – and their merger as the SED – but these topics are not explored at length here as much material on the subject has already been published.[10] Instead, the chapter devotes greater emphasis to the other political forces which emerged after 1945 and how these were fashioned into the SED's tools to prevent any challenge to the party's hegemony. Comparisons are made between the developments at national (GDR) level and their parallels in Thuringia to show how those elements of the regional SED which were loyal to the central party line secured an unchallenged hold on the region's political and administrative life.[11]

In Chapters 3 and 4 the emphasis shifts to popular reactions to the development of 'real socialism' (as SED leaders and propagandists often termed the form of GDR society) in Thuringia from the perspective of the ruled and the co-opted, and concentrates on the region at particular junctures in its postwar history. Some of these are the turning points traditionally emphasised in GDR histories, such as the creation of the GDR itself, the uprising of 17 June 1953, the impact of the Soviet invasion of Hungary and the erection of the Berlin Wall in 1961. However, consideration of other events – such as Stalin's death, the collectivisation of agriculture (1960) and the years which followed the erection of the Berlin Wall – place the headline-grabbing events in the context of ongoing trends and demonstrate that people's lives could be just as affected by domestic developments as by those with obvious national or international implications. In examining popular reaction to these events and to longer term developments in various parts of the population, this part of the book aims to demonstrate the progressive degree of stabilisation of the GDR's political system in the region, and to provide evidence for the sources of support, acceptance and opposition, as well as exploring the motivations for these varying reactions. Attention is paid not only to the reactions of the general population, but also to the degree to which functionaries and party members at the grass roots were capable of implementing the policy decisions taken higher up. Materials in the state and party archives suggest that filling district and local posts with the apparently loyal was not enough to secure full co-operation with the regional authorities.

As it would be impossible to cover all the aspects of life and development in Thuringia in which the regional authorities interacted with ordinary people and well established traditions to mould societal and economic forms towards 'real existing socialism', Chapter 5 interrupts the chronological flow to present a case study of how the system of control was deployed to influence the population's lives practically. The example chosen concerns relations between party and state and the churches in Thuringia / Bezirk Erfurt, and explores the SED's attempts to destroy organised religion as a societal force which challenged the party's hegemonic aspirations. The story of the churches' decline under the pressure of a well organised campaign stands as an example for the methods used in similar transformations, such as the nationalisation of private businesses and the overhaul of the education system.

Chapters 6 and 7 attempt to determine the degree of stability achieved for SED rule by 1968, particularly by examining popular reactions to both the constitutional debate and the invasion of Czechoslovakia by Warsaw Treaty troops with GDR participation. Chapter 7 draws conclusions about the course and nature of developments throughout the period under review.

Establishing the answers to the questions posed above is no straightforward matter. As I have indicated, much opinion and material on the GDR is heavily biased from one standpoint or the other. Material published in the GDR was not primarily designed to provide an historical record but to serve the cause of Marxism and the 'historical mission' of the GDR.[12] Meanwhile, much (though not all) historical or political material about the GDR published in West Germany was designed to present the socialist German state in a poor light. Some western reporting of the GDR was by individuals with particular reasons to present essentially negative views. Karl Wilhelm Fricke's exhaustive accounts of political intimidation by the GDR authorities, for instance, should not be read without considering his own mistreatment at the hands of the *Stasi*.[13] More neutral or positive reporting which was not underpinned by a basic view of the GDR as a totalitarian state has been criticised by, among others, Jens Hacker.[14] These trends have continued beyond the *Wende* (or 'change', the autumn of 1989 when the SED's old guard fell from power). A good example of this is the unambiguously anti-SED standpoint adopted by Gerhard Besier in his otherwise informative text on the GDR churches.[15] There have also been renewed attempts to dismiss and decry the GDR as 'totalitarian', a highly politicised term which has little value as an historical concept.[16] The political orientation of the *Bundestag*'s historical investigation has already been noted (see pp. 2–3). In response to what they saw as history written by the victors, historians close to the PDS have sometimes tried 'to oppose from leftwing standpoints this attempt to claim the power of interpretation over a significant part of German history'.[17] As a British writer, I aim to report the GDR as dispassionately as possible and with no particular political axe to grind, least of all from a nationalist perspective. However, I make no apologies for approaching the GDR as a state which, between 1949 and 1990 had as much (or as little) right to exist as the FRG. It must be recognised that this in itself is a viewpoint which is controversial in certain quarters.

Another trend in GDR history-writing since the *Wende* has been the predominance of detailed studies on specific individual topics, often limited to a particular region or time span, and large volumes of original documents. In line with the political tendencies already outlined, there has also been a largely unbalanced flurry of publications about corruption, the repressive nature of the GDR and, in particular, the *Stasi*. By contrast, relatively few works have attempted to offer an interpretation of GDR society as a whole while also employing significant amounts of empirical evidence.[18] This book hopes to make a contribution to this area of GDR historiography by offering a history of GDR society and an interpretation of its dynamics from the perspective of Thuringia.

This work is principally based on extensive searches of two major archives: the *Thüringisches Hauptstaatsarchiv*, Weimar, and that of the SED *Bezirksleitung*, Erfurt. The latter has been incorporated into the former since the primary research was completed. The closely related nature of party and state in the GDR means that very similar materials are to be found in both archives, and that both (but particularly the Weimar archive) contain materials from a wide range of sources. This resulted from the tendency of the state organs – including the police and on occasion the *Stasi* – the various parties and mass organisations to report to the SED and each other. As there was also multiple reporting of the same issues by a range of diverse sources (party officials, state functionaries, local police officers, officials of the Free German Youth (FDJ) and many others), I was often able to corroborate events and opinions reported in one source with evidence collated independently by another.

Apart from files relating to internal functions of both the state and party apparatuses, one of my principal sources has been the records of public opinion kept by the various offices of the state, by the parties and by the mass organisations and held in both archives. However, these sources have often proved as problematic as the secondary literature. It has been difficult to gauge the veracity of such reports and to interpret their contents. While reports in the early postwar period tend to record very negative popular opinion on a wide range of issues, such reports are less frequent after the mid-1950s. Reporters seem to have preferred to relate a more positive account of life and popular reactions to developments in their particular locality or economic sector. Reports from the 1960s on reactions to specific developments regularly begin with several pages of individuals' positive comments, before hinting and finally admitting that a certain proportion (occasionally 'most') of the population was dissatisfied.

Given our knowledge of the ideological and economic problems facing the GDR's leadership at a macro level, and the ultimate collapse of the system in 1989, it is tempting to ignore positive statements and concentrate entirely on the negative. This in itself may produce a distorted picture. It also ignores the fact that the very existence of large numbers of people prepared to make positive comments about the system and its development is evidence of a growing acceptance of the GDR, whether born of conviction, pragmatism or other factors. In analysing these reports I have tried to take greatest note of consistency between different sources relating to the same event or topic, and to pay more credence to the 'many' or 'most' reported to hold one opinion than to the list of twenty (or perhaps far fewer) named individuals who hold the opposite viewpoint.

As I have indicated, in the case of specific incidents – such as the events of 17 June 1953 or reactions to the Soviet intervention in Czechoslovakia in 1968 – records from different sources tend to agree in their evidence of particular cases of protest or support. Police records also tend to provide quite precise and comprehensive reporting of specific incidents, from which the degree of unrest in the population as a whole can be deduced. Given the seeming accuracy of police reports, and the great controversy surrounding that of *Stasi* reports,[19] I have preferred not to include an evaluation of *Stasi* records.

Though we are dependent on the opinions, political standpoints and motivations of those who compiled the vast archives which the GDR bequeathed us in 1990, I have, informally, attempted to verify my understanding of the GDR in conversation with a large number of Thuringians who experienced the period under review, and have been pleased that my own view, formed from paper records, largely accords with their memories. Though many of those who lived through the period discussed here may have experiences which are at variance with parts of my portrayal, this book is also intended as an attempt to record a significant chapter of their lives from contemporary records.

Notes

1 See, e.g., G. Roßmann (ed.), *Geschichte der SED: Abriß* (Berlin, Dietz, 1976), pp. 5–7.

2 See D. Vorsteher (ed.), *Deutschland im Kalten Krieg 1945 bis 1963* (Berlin, Argon, 1992).

3 T. Neumann, *Die Maßnahme: Eine Herrschaftsgeschichte der SED* (Hamburg, Rowohlt, 1991).

4 Deutscher Bundestag, *Bericht der Enquete-Kommission "Aufarbeitung von Geschichte und Folgen der SED-Diktatur in Deutschland"* (31 May 1994), p. 20. German sources quoted in English in this work have been translated by the author.

5 *Ibid.*, p. 5.

6 Cf. H. Behrend, 'Inglorious German Unification', in H. Behrend (ed.), *German Unification: The Destruction of an Economy* (London, Pluto Press, 1995), pp. 26–7; G. R. Kleinfeld, 'The Return of the PDS', in David Conradt, *et al.* (eds), *Germany's New Politics: Parties and Issues in the 1990s* (Providence, Berghahn, 1995), pp. 221–54.

7 Landesparteiarchiv Erfurt der PDS (hereafter LPA), IV/B/2/5-190, 'Vergleich der Jahresanalyse der Mitgliederbewegung des Zentralkomitees und des Bezirkes Erfurt', 14 March 1968.

8 A. Mitter and S. Wolle, *Untergang auf Raten: Unbekannte Kapitel der DDR-Geschichte* (Munich, Bertelsmann, 1993).

9 The administrative *Land* Thuringia existed from 1945 to 1952, when it was divided into three *Bezirke* (counties): Erfurt, Gera and Suhl. It was re-established in 1990. The sections of this work which consider the 1945–52 period generally refer to all of Thuringia; those on later years generally only to *Bezirk* Erfurt.

10 This is referred to in the notes of Chapter 2.

11 In this book the term 'regional' refers to the *Land Thüringen* level before 1952 and the *Bezirk Erfurt* level thereafter; the term 'district' refers to the intermediary *Kreis* level, and the term 'local' to subordinate levels (towns and villages under the direct jurisdiction of a *Kreis*).

12 A. Dorpalen, *German History in Marxist Perspective* (London, I.B. Tauris, 1985).

13 See particularly Fricke's *Politik und Justiz in der DDR* (Cologne, Verlag Politik und Wissenschaft, 1979).

14 J. Hacker, *Deutsche Irrtümer: Schönfärber und Helfershelfer der SED-Diktatur im Westen* (Berlin, Ullstein, 1992), especially pp. 15–16, 458.

15 G. Besier, *Der SED-Staat und die Kirche: Der Weg in die Anpassung* (Munich, Bertelsmann, 1993).

16 Cf. M. Fulbrook, 'The Limits of Totalitarianism: God, State and Society in the GDR', *Transactions of the Royal Historical Society*, 6th series: VII (1997), 25–52.

17 Jochen Černý, Dietmar Keller and Manfred Neuhaus (eds), *Ansichten zur Geschichte der DDR* (Eggersdorf, Verlag Matthias Kirchner, 1993–), V (1994), p. 7.

18 An exception has been Mary Fulbrook's *Anatomy of a Dictatorship: Inside the GDR 1949–89* (Oxford, Oxford University Press, 1995).

19 Cf. Klaus-Dietmar Henke (ed.), *Wann bricht schon mal ein Staat zusammen! Die Debatte über die Stasi-Akten auf dem 39. Historikertag 1992* (Munich, dtv, 1993).

2

Unite and rule: establishing
the GDR's political structures

First steps at war's end

Before examining the experience of Thuringia as a case study of the GDR's consolidation, we must briefly consider the broader framework which determined the region's postwar development. Though the Third Reich collapsed into apparent chaos in April and May 1945, many of the structures which would determine eastern Germany's development for the following forty-five years were quickly in place. The advancing Red Army had already occupied Germany's eastern territories and settled Polish populations in West Prussia, Silesia and eastern Pomerania, forcing the German citizens of these regions to flee westwards and creating enormous demographic upheaval. Germany's de facto loss of these lands was recognised in July 1945 at the Potsdam Conference of the three chief wartime allies: Great Britain, the Soviet Union and the USA. The conference also formalised the division of the remainder of Germany – west of the rivers Oder and Neisse – into zones of occupation. One allied power would hold supreme power in each. Berlin, as the capital of the Reich, was similarly divided into occupation sectors. Though not invited to Potsdam, France was shortly afterwards given equivalent status with the other allies – and both a western zone and a Berlin sector of occupation – so that Germany's fate henceforth depended on the agreement of all four allies. Though the allies proclaimed their intentions that Germany should remain a single economic unit and quickly re-emerge as a united state, the developing Cold War between the Soviet and American superpowers deepened and perpetuated Germany's division until the effective collapse of Soviet power in 1990.

The Soviet Union's postwar interests were twofold. First, the USSR was anxious to take hefty reparations from defeated Germany to rebuild its own greatly weakened infrastructure. Second – and for this book more significantly – Germany's capacity to threaten world peace generally and Soviet territory in particular was to be countered not only by demilitarisation and the removal from power of the leaders of Nazi society, but also by a restructuring of the economy along socialist lines. In the Soviet view, fascism represented the highest form of capitalism; thus a simple restoration of the Weimar Republic's political and economic order could not eliminate the possibility that Nazism would revive.

The Soviets' antifascist agenda did not imply an intention to bolshevise the whole of Germany, or even their own zone (the *Sowjetische Besatzungszone*, SBZ) in 1945. The expansion of Soviet power into the western zones of Germany could not have been achieved without a serious conflict with the USA, already in posses-sion of atomic weapons. This was beyond the weakened Soviet Union's capabilities. Rather, Stalin respected the zones of influence in eastern and western Europe which he had agreed with Britain and the USA. Nor did Stalin envisage Germany's long-term division into two ideologically opposed states. On the contrary, the Soviet Union hoped for a united, neutral Germany as a buffer state between the opposing Cold War blocks. This outcome would also have enabled the Soviet Union to con-tinue taking the reparations from Germany's western zones which had been agreed at Potsdam, but which were denied Stalin by the country's deepening division. However, the breakdown of trust between the superpowers after the defeat of their common enemy, Hitler, ensured that the structures created by the allies in each zone hardened by 1949 to form two separate states: the Federal Republic in the western zones and the GDR in the Soviet zone.

Within its zone, the Soviet Union moved quickly to establish an occupation regime which accorded with its own political and material interests. (In this it behaved no differently than the western powers in their zones, where populations also had to adopt the foundations of the social market economy and a western political system, whatever their personal preferences.) During the war, plans had been made in Moscow for Germany's occupation. Red Army commanders and exiled groups of German communists had been trained in their postwar tasks. As the war ended, three teams of German communists were dispatched by plane to different areas of the SBZ. The most important of these was the group led by Walter Ulbricht, a communist functionary of the Weimar Republic, which arrived in Berlin to rebuild the city administration and launch antifascist political life, and which tried (unsuccessfully) to lay permanent foundations throughout the city before the western allies could occupy their own sectors. With the support of the Red Army, the Ulbricht group sought out competent administrators and technicians to staff the city government and re-establish essential services. Ulbricht was careful to avoid the inevitably unpopular appearance of a communist take-over. The mayors appointed in the various boroughs were often locally respected figures, sometimes of no party affiliation. Social democrats were also given key positions. However, politically sensitive appointments were all shadowed by communist deputies, and communist nominees were given charge of policing and personnel departments, allowing them a broad spectrum of control. This blue-print for political control of the civil administration was adopted throughout the SBZ.

Meanwhile, efforts were made to re-establish a party system. In a decree issued as early as 10 June 1945, the Soviet military authority (SMAD or SMA) permitted political parties to form, providing they were antifascist in character. The SMAD reserved the right to intervene in the personnel composition of the party leader-ships. The first party to emerge was the Communist Party of Germany (KPD), which issued a manifesto on 11 June. The document had been approved by the Kremlin, but it cautiously stressed that it would be wrong to impose the Soviet system on Germany. The term 'socialism' was conspicuous by its absence. A few days later the Social Democratic Party (SPD) was reborn with a more radical programme. In the immediate aftermath of the war, with antifascist sentiment at its height, many socialists in both parties had hoped for the creation of a single workers' party. However, the KPD leadership feared that specifically communist policy elements would find no place in a united party. In reconstituting an autonomous KPD, Ulbricht hoped to establish a strong communist functionary and membership corps to carry KPD ideology into a united party at a later date.

By year's end, the KPD was forced to rethink its tactics. The party suffered from its association with the communist Red Army occupiers, at whose hands many women had suffered rape, and its strong presence in the organs of local and regional government at a time of great material hardship. The poor communist showing in the Austrian elections of November 1945 and the faster growth of the SPD made a heavy election defeat for the KPD seem inevitable in the promised SBZ elections. Though the enthusiasm of many social democrats for a united party had waned after several months of strained co-operation with the KPD in local government, the communists therefore launched a vigorous campaign for the two parties' merger. This, they claimed, was the inevitable consequence to be drawn from the socialists' failure to stand united against Hitler before 1933.

After a number of joint KPD/SPD conferences and negotiations, and a campaign for working-class political unity which appeared spontaneous but was largely orchestrated by the SMAD and the central and regional KPD leaderships, the Socialist Unity Party of Germany (SED) was created in April 1946 in the Soviet zone alone, effectively splitting the German party system between east and west. The SPD leader in the western zones, Kurt Schumacher, was vigorously anti-communist and refused to contemplate such a merger. This position left Otto Grotewohl, his SBZ counterpart, politically exposed, while dependent on the SMAD's support for his party's survival. In the SBZ provinces, too, regional SMAD commandants favoured social democrat leaders who supported a merger with the KPD and in some cases took steps to silence opponents. To many social democrats, the merger seemed to be a *Zwangsvereinigung*, a forced union. Others regarded the merger as a logical development in the fight against a rebirth of fascism and enthusiastically participated in the SED's transformation, by 1948, into a Leninist 'party of a new type', in which the parity of former social democrats and communists in leadership positions was abandoned. This development formed an integral part of Moscow's tightening of its grip in eastern Europe following the ideological breakaway of the Yugoslav party under Marshall Tito.

In the absence of an independent social democratic opposition – and with the support of the SMAD – the SED became the undisputed leading force in SBZ politics, and its functionaries filled the key roles in the emergent government structures. However, the party faced opposition from two non-socialist, so-called 'bourgeois' parties, which principally represented middle-class interests. These were the Christian Democratic Union (CDU) – an interdenominational party of traditional values which later spearheaded West Germany's capitalist economic miracle – and the Liberal Democratic Party (LDPD) – a merger of several earlier parties with a high proportion of small traders and craftsmen among its clientele. Both parties were legalised in 1945 as symbols of a political pluralism which was essential to the new system's democratic credibility as an alternative both to the Third Reich and the one-party Soviet Union. Jointly they usually matched (and sometimes outstripped) the SED vote in the first local and regional elections held in the SBZ.

Changing Soviet strategy as Germany's division deepened during the late 1940s – and the impending establishment of a socialist German state in the Soviet zone – required politics and societal structures to be brought under SED control. In a *Gleichschaltung* ('co-ordination') reminiscent of Hitler's subordination of Germany's political system to Nazi Party (NSDAP) domination, the SED and the SMAD sought to bring the two 'bourgeois' parties into line with SED policies and to diminish their potential to undermine SED rule.[1] This was attempted (and essentially achieved) by three principal methods. First, the SMAD intervened on occasion to intimidate and remove CDU and LDPD politicians who vigorously opposed socialist measures. Second, in June 1945 the KPD invited all the parties to co-operate in an 'antifascist-democratic bloc' (known as the Democratic Bloc), which would promote a united approach on important issues. As the unity of democrats was perceived to be essential to ward off any fascist threat, it was agreed that all decisions of the bloc should be unanimous. This allowed the KPD/SED to obstruct motions by the other parties it considered undesirable; when other parties adopted the same tactic against communist proposals, they were denounced in the KPD/SED press (which dominated the SBZ's media landscape) as undemocratic and risking a fascist revival. Third, the SED created two satellite parties in 1948 to compete with the CDU and LDPD for votes. These were the Democratic Farmers' Party (DBD) and the National Democratic Party (NDPD), the latter a political home for German nationalists and former nominal members of the Nazi party who now wished to help build the new Germany. Together with these new satellite parties, the SED held a majority in the Democratic Bloc. In conjunction with the Soviet occupation forces, the party worked hard to denounce and remove anti-socialist forces in the CDU and LDPD, while promoting leaders who wished to co-operate with the SED in building a socialist future. By 1952 the central and regional leaderships of the eastern CDU and LDPD had been brought into line and recognised the SED's leading role.

By this point – indeed ever since the GDR's creation in October 1949 – the electoral system had in any case been structured to guarantee SED hegemony. The CDU and LDPD were persuaded to join the SED, DBD, NDPD and various SED-controlled 'mass organisations' – including the FDJ, the Free German Trades Union League (*Freier Deutscher Gewerkschaftsbund*, FDGB) and similar institutions, each of which was the only permitted organisation for its respective target group – in placing its candidates on a single electoral list, under the umbrella of the

'National Front of Democratic Germany'. The number of places to be allocated to each party or organisation in the GDR parliament (the *Volkskammer*, 'People's Chamber') and the regional and local councils was decided in advance. The voter had only to vote 'Yes' or 'No' to the entire list. As the electorate was urged to vote publicly as a sign of commitment to the NF's manifesto of peace and unity, in practice few sought out the polling booths to vote 'No'.

Thus, by the early 1950s the GDR's formal political structures were firmly in SED hands, granting the party an omnipotent role in political patronage. This patronage extended into the economic sphere as increasing numbers of businesses were nationalised after 1945. The SBZ and later the GDR were also subject to rigorous economic planning by the central ministries and their SED placemen in Berlin after 1948. East German agriculture had also been drastically re-organised after 1945 in a land reform which redistributed the holdings of dispossessed rich landlords to farm workers and refugees from the lost eastern territories.

These developments set the parameters for the GDR's development over the following forty years. With these in mind, we now turn to the specific features of Thuringia.

The Thuringian background

As a political entity Thuringia emerged from centuries of dynastic divisions only in 1920, albeit without Erfurt and several other traditionally 'Thuringian' areas. These territories remained Prussian until the Soviet occupation authorities merged them into a new *Land Thüringen* (the Thuringian province or state) with territorial integrity in July 1945.

Thuringia's new boundaries were not entirely uncontroversial. The greatest difficulty was the Roman Catholic Eichsfeld region in northwest Thuringia, previously divided between two Prussian provinces. Once this largely insignificant provincial border became the demarcation line between two occupation zones – and then a mainly impassable Cold War frontier – the area, its families and economic ties were rent asunder, with the bulk of the Eichsfeld left in *Land Thüringen* but a third in the British zone. The Thuringian Eichsfeld also gave the SBZ/GDR its only majority Catholic community: 84 per cent of the Eichsfeld's population was Catholic, compared with only 12 per cent across the whole SBZ.[2] In Heiligenstadt the proportion of Catholics was higher still. The strength of Catholicism, which perceived itself as a community under threat and which prepared its defences accordingly, created significant problems for the essentially atheist SED's Thuringian organisation.

According to the first census of the Soviet occupation period, in 1946 some 16 per cent of the SBZ's population – 2,943,251 people – lived in the newly formed *Land Thüringen*, by area the SBZ's smallest *Land*. More than 17,000 other people resided in various transit, refugee/evacuee and POW camps on census day,[3] reflecting postwar upheavals. Erfurt alone sheltered 667,570 refugees and evacuees between April 1945 and 1949, and some two million such people passed through the town.[4] Many people arriving in Thuringia, as elsewhere in the Soviet zone, had been expelled from Germany's lost eastern territories and other areas of eastern Europe which Germany had occupied.

In economic terms, Thuringia – along with neighbouring Saxony-Anhalt and Saxony – belonged to the southern, more industrialised half of the Soviet zone; only Saxony had a greater proportion of industrial and craft workers, and Thuringia's industry had remained active throughout the war. However, alongside the textiles, optical and car-manufacturing industry of some towns, much of the region's productive economy was based on specialised, small-scale light industry, such as the toy manufacturers of southern Thuringia. Though wartime demands had somewhat altered the region's economic structure, a 1947 report noted that 'despite heavy industrialisation, Thuringia has a distinctly agricultural character'. Agriculture and forestry occupied more than a quarter of the workforce in 1946. In 1938 the Saxony-Anhalt/Thuringia region had been a net exporter of goods. However, as Thuringia was largely dependent on raw material imports, the deepening division of Germany inevitably brought economic problems.[5]

Politically, Thuringia is often described as having been 'red'.[6] Symbolically, it hosted three significant founding or programmatic conferences of German socialism in Eisenach (1869), Gotha (1875) and Erfurt (1891). Before 1914 Thuringia was 'a Socialist stronghold',[7] where the SPD gained 47 per cent of votes in 1912. This left-wing domination continued after the First World War, despite party-political fragmentation. The SPD and the breakaway independent social democrats (USPD) together garnered 57 per cent in the 1919 national elections and, despite progressively weakening after the 1918 revolution, the left-wing parties together still achieved 49.4 per cent of the vote in the 1920 elections to the Thuringian regional parliament (the *Landtag*).[8] However, the left's support fell below 40 per cent in 1924 following the socialist *Land* government's radical measures between 1921 and 1923. While still slightly higher than the left's vote elsewhere in Germany, this development consigned the Thuringian SPD to permanent opposition. Tracey observes that the 'almost even [division] between industrial workers and non-industrial economic groups ... meant a very close balance between the parties of the left and right, a situation made even more difficult by the absence of any moderating centre forces of consequence ... The consequences included an ... exaggerated importance for minority parties, and a high degree of political polarisation.'[9]

Tracey's reasoning accounts for the significantly higher level of voter support for extremist parties. KPD support in Thuringia was always between 2 and 5 per cent higher than the national average, even in 1933. Of greater long-term significance was the strong showing made by the various guises of the national socialist party, which was higher than average in Thuringia even in the early 1920s. This trend persisted as Hitler's party grew. By 1930 NSDAP support in Thuringia was so comparatively strong that the *Land* became a test-bed for NSDAP government participation. In 1932 the NSDAP formed the Thuringian government. Even in

Third Reich elections, the NSDAP usually recorded slightly more absolute support in Thuringia than elsewhere.

In summary, Thuringia was traditionally 'red' insofar as the SPD was consistently the region's largest single party until 1932, except during the USPD's separation. The KPD also found more support in Thuringia than in most regions. Yet despite the left's apparent strength, a right-wing government coalition outvoted the combined Thuringian left for much of the Weimar era, even without the NSDAP. As a whole, the region's most striking political feature, however, is its tendency to lean towards extremism and/or exaggerate national trends. This was true of SPD support in pre-republican days, of the unusually large USPD vote in 1918–19, of Nazism's swift rise,[10] and, especially in *Bezirk* Erfurt, of 1990s overwhelming CDU vote. Thus, although the region's immediate political past seemed inauspicious for launching a communist experiment in 1945, its tendency to conform to new political trends suggested that Thuringians might rally to a new cause.

At war's end, Thuringia faced problems typical across Germany. Although losses were generally less significant than in other German regions, the war cost some 90,000 Thuringian soldiers' lives and over 10,000 civilians were killed in bomb raids. The most devastating air raids were those on Nordhausen on 3 and 4 April 1945, when some 8,300 people (14 per cent of the population) were killed and 78.8 per cent of buildings were entirely or partly destroyed. Housing stock was also lost in the major towns and cities, and particularly in Nordhausen.[11] The social hardships exacerbated by such factors and harsh economic conditions are important in understanding many citizens' dissatisfaction with the GDR in the early years.

Thuringia between Third Reich and Soviet occupation

Although Thuringia was allotted to the Soviet Occupation Zone, military requirements meant that the region was initially conquered in April 1945 by the Americans. They remained until an agreed hand-over on 1 July 1945, the day on which the Soviets permitted the western allies to enter Berlin. Thus, the populations of Thuringia and other SBZ border areas were uniquely able to compare American and Soviet occupation.[12]

As clear central occupation policies were lacking, the Americans made varied impressions. Although mainly fearful and apprehensive, Germans were often surprised at the Americans' modern equipment and healthy and tidy appearance. In Saalfeld distrust diminished and was replaced with relief after the first days passed peacefully. Americans generally behaved correctly to Germans, though one observer disparagingly concluded: 'The Americans' attitude was essentially that of civilised victors over underdeveloped natives who had invited punishment of their own fault.'[13]

Some memoirs recall arrogance, especially among American officers, and an initial tendency to regard all Germans as 'Nazis', but reports of open attacks (verbal or physical) on Germans are scarce. Although many Germans suffered indignities and irritations at American hands, there were also reports of troops giving children chocolate.[14]

Beyond the most urgent denazification measures and attempts to secure public health, the Americans essentially conducted a holding operation, knowing they would not be in Thuringia long. The regular turnover of American personnel while the war continued also militated against much concerted action. Later, the generally non-interventionist nature of American rule contrasted sharply and favourably with the intrusive nature of politics under the SMAD and SED.

Support for Nazism at war's end is hard to gauge accurately, but it is clear that confidence in and acceptance of the Nazi regime had seriously declined during 1945. Once the war was over, the external symbols of Nazism were quickly discarded: Third Reich uniforms and busts of Hitler were deposited into the Eichsfeld's rivers,[15] and, prior to Saalfeld's surrender 'people had buried, burnt, thrown away or otherwise destroyed the flags, books and emblems, indeed anything which might have reminded them of their own involvement with national socialism. Probably there was no longer any attachment to national socialism left by the last war year, so it was easy to part with the external symbols of this system.'[16]

These were, of course, only outward signs, and many still retained an inner attachment to familiar political forms. Even days after American occupation, a Berkach vicar noted that popular opinion was 'unfathomable': 'They still expect a radical change and reversal of the war ... and still believe in the *Führer* ... '[17] Similarly, Ernst Thape, a social democrat held in Buchenwald, noted on 22 April that very few Weimar residents believed the Nazi system had collapsed; they feared the Nazis would return and take their revenge.[18]

Though NSDAP membership alone is no clear guide to inner beliefs, an October 1945 survey showed more than 187,000 registered ex-NSDAP members lived in Thuringia, some 6 per cent of the total population. There were 23,000 in Erfurt alone, almost 10 per cent of the city's inhabitants. Thuringia had a far higher than average percentage of NSDAP teachers (98 per cent) and local authority employees (96 per cent) than in the *Reich* overall (75 per cent).[19] While extremist incidents – such as the murder by Nazi sympathisers of a KPD member near Wehnde[20] – were exceptional, Nazi allegiances did not disappear overnight. The Americans reacted to this by organising visits for local residents to concentration camps. Initially, one thousand Weimar citizens were forced to visit nearby Buchenwald on 16 April 1945. Various sources note the deep impact of such visits as they were reported throughout the population.[21]

Although Thuringia was later portrayed as an important centre of antifascist resistance during 1944 and 1945,[22] little was practically achieved beyond local efforts to disrupt the war effort and alleviate the worst effects of war and Nazi terror on individual prisoners and other groups. The most effective wartime resistance came when local groups, some led by underground socialists, ignored Nazi orders to destroy facilities before the allies arrived.[23] Thuringia's communist leader, Theodor

Neubauer, perceptively wrote in late 1943: 'Unfortunately there is a widespread current in Germany's working class that expects all salvation from the "Red Army" and would like to look on passively until the "Russians come and liberate us".'[24]

Of greatest significance for Thuringia's later political development were the illegal political activities within Buchenwald concentration camp, as a large number of leading communists and social democrats were imprisoned there. Many key postwar Thuringian politicians were influenced by these experiences.

Alongside a non-party political International Camp Committee, which co-ordinated resistance work, Buchenwald had three principal political organisations: a complex communist network, some of whose members formed the first postwar Thuringian KPD leadership; a smaller, non-communist left-wing organisation, developed shortly before Buchenwald's dissolution and later the kernel of the Thuringian SPD; and the non-party, antifascist Popular Front (*Volksfront*) initiative, elements of which formed the antifascist Democratic Bloc in August 1945.[25]

Although resistance work contributed little to Nazism's overthrow, it had three important longer term consequences. First, the wartime groupings shared great solidarity and often became the nucleus of antifascist committees and party organisations after liberation. Their many underground meetings provided forums to discuss postwar possibilities and to spread anything known of the political line of the exiled KPD leadership. Communists arriving in Buchenwald transmitted news from the outside world to fellow inmates. Antifascists of other political persuasions who lacked this wartime experience usually reorganised themselves more slowly, allowing communist and social democratic groups to take the initiative. Second, where communists and social democrats collaborated in conspiratory wartime activities, foundations were laid for a united workers' party. This was forcefully reflected by August Frölich, a Thuringian SPD minister in the 1920s who became a regional SED elder statesman after the war. In August 1944 he was taken, chained to Theodor Neubauer, to a *Gestapo* (the secret police of the Third Reich) prison in Berlin. He later recalled his thoughts: 'Did we really have to be tied together like two desperate criminals by our deadly enemies …? Why didn't we, as social democrats and communists, combine in the united struggle before 1933 instead of fighting each other? The answer to this question became a personal vow: if you should survive the Nazi period, then you will start afresh and work to unite the two workers' parties.'[26]

Third, the (often exaggerated) record of dedicated antifascist wartime resistance by communists and social democrats, as presented in official SED histories, was exploited as far as possible and proved perhaps the largest element in the popular legitimation of SED hegemony, at least until autumn 1989. Although Frölich's private convictions were undoubtedly sincere – given his postwar active loyalty to the SED – publicly they could be used to strengthen such propaganda, giving rise to what some post-*Wende* (i.e. post-1989) commentators have controversially dubbed the 'antifascist myth'.[27]

The Americans' departure from Thuringia in early July 1945 greatly shocked many.[28] The allied agreements on zonal borders remained largely unknown to Thuringians. The Americans and Hermann Brill, the American-appointed social democrat Thuringian president, had in late June denied rumours of the feared Soviets' imminent arrival.[29]

As the Americans retreated, Soviet occupation forces advanced from Saxony. They met a mixed reaction. Communists in some towns held special ceremonies. The liberal mayor of Gera, Dr Rudolf Paul, also ensured that he was prominent in welcoming the Soviets.[30] Conversely, there was little welcome in Weimar: the Thuringian premier, Brill, refused to greet his new masters, and, as elsewhere, residents remained safely indoors, mindful of Nazi scaremongering about barbarians and bolshevists.[31]

The road to socialist unity[32]

As noted above, the postwar Thuringian KPD had its origins in the communist group in Buchenwald concentration camp, which assumed the regional leadership role and began to establish local party groups within days of the liberation. Other communist groups which formed spontaneously in Thuringia quickly recognised the Buchenwald group's leadership. By 1 July 1945, when the Red Army arrived, the KPD had established a functioning apparatus, despite considerable communications problems and the refusal of the American authorities formally to legalise party political activity. Within days of the Soviets' arrival in Thuringia, Walter Ulbricht, the KPD's effective leader, visited the Thuringian party and acquainted its leaders with the central political line and their first priorities. The Central Committee imposed a new leader, Georg Schneider, who was quickly replaced by a more competent functionary, Werner Eggerath. The still potent force of internal communist party discipline ensured there was no opposition to the Berlin leadership's domination of the regional party. Much of the following year was devoted to extending a functioning party organisation across Thuringia.[33]

Meanwhile, the Thuringian SPD's re-emergence was complicated by the views of Hermann Brill. Brill, the leading social democrat in Buchenwald, had visions of a new, united working-class party on the model of the British Labour Party and established a League of Democratic Socialists (BDS) during US occupation. Close analysis of Brill's programmatic publications reveals certain inconsistencies and an idealism which was wholly inappropriate in a country which had recently signed an unconditional surrender.[34] Nonetheless, Brill's appointment by the Americans in June 1945 as president of the German administration in Thuringia, the force of his personality and the absence of an alternative leader with such strong antifascist credentials ensured Brill's initial dominance of Thuringian social democracy. However, his position was undermined when the Soviets refused to license the BDS. By August Brill had to abandon the title 'BDS' in favour of 'SPD' and recognise that party's Berlin leadership. By December Brill left the SBZ for a post with the American military government. As an ardent anti-communist he had come under Soviet pressure to support the SPD's merger with the KPD. Brill was replaced as Thuringian SPD leader by Heinrich Hoffmann, a self-important social democrat who hoped for personal advantage from his good relations with the regional Soviet authorities, and was prepared to take the SPD into the proposed Socialist Unity Party (SED).

After Brill withdrew from Thuringian politics, institutional KPD/SPD unity came relatively smoothly, and essentially followed the pattern of the merger which took place in the rest of the SBZ. Local initiatives were emphasised to suggest the unity campaign had started at the grass-roots. Thus, following the key Berlin KPD/SPD conference of 20–21 December 1945, the *Kreis* (district) organisations of the two parties in Rudolstadt decided on 22 December to work jointly towards unity. The Gera and Greiz parties jointly adopted similar pro-unity resolutions in the following days. A meeting of the two Thuringian parties' leading regional functionaries on 6 January 1946 also produced a resolution which welcomed the Berlin agreement to increase co-operation, and pledged joint action in various spheres, including 'joint functionary meetings to discuss all local questions'. Both parties pledged that 'all obstacles in the path of this development towards a true working class unity must be pushed aside.'[35] This effectively pre-empted any alternative course and warned off any member of either party who disagreed.

From early January, the grass-roots unity campaign progressed as party organisations at all levels formed joint committees and adopted pro-unity resolutions. The details, publicised locally and regionally, themselves fuelled the movement. The 6 January meeting summoned a 'joint *Land* functionaries' conference' to Jena on 19 and 20 January, to be addressed by the parties' respective zonal leaders, the veteran communist Wilhelm Pieck, and Otto Grotewohl. Prior joint meetings in the districts resolved that delegates in Jena should call for immediate unification of the two parties. However, as the Berlin leaderships had themselves not yet finally agreed the merger, the Jena delegates merely agreed that membership meetings and party education programmes should be organised jointly henceforth. After this conference, local party groups went a stage further and independently announced their formal mergers. While communists clearly forced the pace of unity in many areas, there is also little evidence of local resistance by social democrats to the campaign, except where personal differences existed in small communities. Though the communists forced the movement, many members of both parties (such as the social democrat August Frölich) accepted the argument for working-class unity and were happy to merge at the grass-roots.[36]

The final phase began at a joint meeting of the two parties' regional executives on 5 February at which Hoffmann unexpectedly announced the Thuringian SPD's view that the merger should take place on 28 April. The parties settled on unity conferences on 6 and 7 April in Gotha. This decision apparently greatly surprised the central party leaderships in Berlin.[37] It possibly accelerated their agreement on 26 February to a zonal merger after negotiations broke down between the SPD in the Soviet zone and its sister party in the western zones. The Thuringian resolution of 5 February re-emphasised that opposition to unity would not be tolerated: 'The leaderships of both parties in Thuringia commit themselves to supporting all steps for the speedy creation of unity and declare the fiercest battle against all opponents of a united workers' party.'[38]

Thereafter the unity campaign geared up, culminating in district conferences of each party to elect delegates to the unity conference. The Thuringian KPD and SPD conferences of 6 April and the unity conference the following day were accompanied by celebrations throughout the region, repeated at zonal level on 21 and 22 April to mark the parties' official merger as the new Socialist Unity Party of Germany (SED) in the Soviet zone.

In the following years, the Thuringian SED leadership made concerted efforts under several leaders to establish an efficient party organisation. These were often frustrated by inefficient or uncommitted staff, as well as by shortages of fuel and other resources.[39] In Thuringia as throughout the Soviet zone, there were increasing efforts after 1948 to reduce social democratic influence in the party. These culminated in the checks on every party member held during 1950 and 1951 which uncovered many remnants of social democracy in the 'party of a new type' and revealed the presence of active oppositional communists such as members of the KPO (Communist Party Opposition).[40] The party took this opportunity to rid itself of the uncommitted, the opportunists and the opponents within its ranks but, as later chapters demonstrate, soon discovered that it had only scratched the surface.

Thus, socialist unity had been created, at least superficially. However, SED hegemony depended not only on uniting the political working class, but also on dominating and co-opting other political forces and the non-political social interest groups.

The 'bloc parties' and the mass organisations

The SED's stabilisation under communists loyal to Moscow could not alone guarantee the party's complete control of the SBZ/GDR's political landscape. Alongside the various categories of socialists, either united in the SED or banished from the zone's political life by intimidation, were those of other political persuasions and interest groups, as well as the uncommitted and apolitical. The SED aimed to win the acceptance, and preferably the loyalty, of all these people. The non-socialist masses had to be involved in building socialism, and those with divergent political interests had to be reconciled to the SED's cause or politically neutralised.

Local material demonstrates that these structures for co-opting and neutralising political opponents remained vital to SED hegemony for decades. However, although the 'bloc' parties were outwardly loyal allies of the SED, as judged by their national and regional leaders' public declarations, locally their memberships often remained highly critical, well into the 1960s. The SED nonetheless succeeded in politically neutralising and effectively co-opting its potential opponents through their membership of a political party with an apparent stake in the GDR's government. By these methods the SED dominated the political system. Equally, the SED-dominated mass organisations failed to convert the mass of the apolitical population, but by their very existence occupied the available space for societal activities and thus largely prevented the emergence of alternatives. Though the bloc party and mass organisation structures appeared secure, particularly at national level, at the grass roots they often rested on shaky foundations.

The SMAD's initial plans for a four-party system were implemented relatively easily in Thuringia because this arrangement had essentially developed autonomously during the American period. Alongside the KPD and SPD, non-socialist groupings emerged parallel to those established in Berlin.

Former Weimar members of the pre-1933 liberal German Democratic Party (DDP) formed a local group of the 'Democratic Party' on 23 April 1945, seven weeks before the Berlin LDPD was founded. Several other Thuringian groups existed by early July. The Thuringian 'Democratic Party' was legally established on 29 July and eventually recognised the Berlin leadership and adopted the name 'LDPD' in December 1945. Weber's assertion that the SMAD forced the LDPD's creation is untrue of Thuringia.[41]

As a non-denominational Christian party, the CDU was a new phenomenon in Germany, but perhaps naturally at home in Thuringia with its Protestant majority but sizeable Catholic population. Though a Christian party apparently formed spontaneously only in the Eichsfeld during US occupation, several leading members of the former Catholic Centre Party contributed to Thuringia's civil administration under American rule. Such activity encouraged the Thuringian CDU's formation on 22 July.[42] However, neither Christian democrats nor liberal democrats were as well organised or ideologically secure in mid-1945 as the two socialist parties. Consequently they took fewer political initiatives as the postwar framework settled into place.

The SMAD's initial party system complete, on 17 August 1945 a Thuringian 'Democratic Bloc' of the four parties was established as a regional equivalent of the central Soviet zone bloc in Berlin and with a programme of denazification, economic reconstruction and democratic rights. The bloc's standing orders stipulated weekly meetings and a chairmanship that rotated monthly between the parties. The requirement for unanimous decisions was not specifically included,[43] but the practice was soon established and exploited by the KPD/SED. Once the central Thuringian bloc was established, the parties also formed district and local blocs.

Meanwhile, would-be founders of other political movements (principally the antifascist committees which developed spontaneously after the war in many localities) had either to subordinate themselves to the permitted parties or suspend their activities. Thus on 3 August 1945 the Thuringian government prohibited the *Thüringer Volkspartei* ('Thuringian People's Party'), the intended successor to the pre-1933 liberal *Deutsche Volkspartei* ('German People's Party').[44] This set a precedent which prevented the spontaneous formation of political or social organisations until late 1989. Undeterred, some of the *Volkspartei*'s founders, including August Bach, later the party's national chairman, joined the CDU.

The CDU and LDPD gained considerable support in the early postwar period. By mid-1946 the Thuringian CDU had around 35,000 members and the Thuringian LDPD slightly more. Although the Thuringian SED's membership (approximately 270,000 by mid-1947) far outnumbered even their combined total,[45] the CDU and LDPD represented a significant electoral threat to the SED, which the population perceived as mainly responsible for their hardships.[46] In 1946 the CDU and LDPD jointly controlled forty-seven of the Thuringian parliament's hundred seats and eight of the twelve town or city councils. The SED was stronger in rural districts, with majorities in twelve of the twenty-two district councils (*Kreistage*). In a further six *Kreise* the SED depended on support from the allied farmers' co-operative movement (the Association for Mutual Farmers' Assistance, or VdgB). Of the two 'bourgeois' parties, the LDPD was stronger in urban areas, but the CDU was slightly more popular in rural districts, and enjoyed a clear majority in the Catholic Eichsfeld (67.3 per cent support).[47]

The relative success of the 'bourgeois' parties was achieved despite intervention by the Soviets who, for instance, disbanded the local CDU or LDPD groups in Rudolstadt before the 1946 elections, and prevented their candidates from standing in many constituencies.[48] The strength of the 'bourgeois' parties in 1946, their reluctance to co-operate with the SED during 1947, and the prospect of future elections encouraged a hardline approach to the bloc parties and sparked the party system's expansion.

The local CDU and LDPD leaders correctly perceived the creation of the nationalists' NDPD and farmers' DBD as competing parties in 1948 as an SED attempt to splinter the non-socialist camp.[49] The SED had feared that farmers were responsible for the CDU's relatively strong showing. In Catholic Heiligenstadt the party later considered that the new parties were highly instrumental in breaking the district CDU's power. To counter the threat, the CDU unsuccessfully attempted to create a local LDPD organisation as an ally.[50] The new DBD was a particularly important creation in Thuringia, where the *Landbund* ('Agricultural League') had been important in Weimar Republic politics. However, its creation underlined the KPD/SED's failure to attract farmers – ever wary of collectivisation – in its own right.

The SED entrusted the DBD and NDPD to leaders sympathetic to itself. Thus the Thuringian NDPD's founder was a pre-war KPD member who had joined the SED in 1946.[51] All *Land* and, as far as possible, *Kreis* NDPD executive members were approved by the Thuringian SED, which gave the new party a monthly subsidy of 10,000 Marks.[52] Thuringia's SED interior minister decreed that the NDPD should receive special protection, and requested the police not to arrest its leaders.[53] However, the two new creations initially attracted little spontaneous support. For instance, in Rudolstadt the DBD's inaugural meeting was called by the head of the district agricultural office, a 'fairly helpless' SED man. Of the

DBD's five-strong *Kreis* executive, three were SED members. Feeling among the farmers present was negative. The NDPD's creation also excited no public interest in the town. In Greiz district, most farmers responded passively to the DBD.[54]

Furthermore, despite being created as an SED tool, the DBD's new members were not always clear about the subordinate role intended for them and sometimes tried to establish an independent role. Thus the SED had to remind a DBD representative who called for strong DBD representation on an agricultural commission that the SED also represented farmers' interests. Similarly, two DBD district functionaries made veiled attacks on SED agricultural policy and functionaries at a party meeting in Weissensee.[55]

As most people remained wary of political parties after their experiences in the Third Reich, different organisations were required to win popular support for SED policies. The SMAD and the KPD/SED considered it essential that these 'mass organisations' should be clearly under KPD/SED control. Therefore only one, 'united' organisation was licensed for each societal interest group because, it was argued, the institutional divisions in the Weimar Republic had facilitated Nazism. The Buchenwald communists, who desired 'anti-Nazi mass organisations like unity trades unions for the workers', had already endorsed this policy in April 1945.[56] The comparatively well organised communists quickly took the initiative in founding such movements.

The Thuringian FDGB was founded illegally under American occupation mainly by two communists, Willy Albrecht (ex-Buchenwald) and Richard Eyermann. By May the principle of antifascist unity had brought the FDGB widespread support from social democratic and communist functionaries alike. Despite the general chaos, 6,000 Erfurt workers joined the FDGB by 18 June and were organised in a complex hierarchical structure, whose central secretariat was firmly under Albrecht's, and therefore the KPD's, control. Similar unified trades unions emerged independently elsewhere during the American period.[57] After the Soviets' arrival these various unions were brought within a Thuringian FDGB under Albrecht's leadership. This development removed the danger that independent factory committees might pursue alternative political lines.[58]

Communists also sponsored the other 'unity' mass organisations such as the FDJ, which was organised with limited success in Thuringia by December 1945 and steadily grew with SED support thereafter, and the *Gesellschaft für Deutsch–Sowjetische Freundschaft* ('Society for German–Soviet Friendship', DSF), which emerged in Thuringia from a 'German–Russian Club' founded at the initiative of the Thuringian SED leader, Werner Eggerath.[59] Over the following years the SED established other organisations for women, younger children, sport, charitable work and the rest of the social spectrum.

This plurality brought potential dangers as well as benefits for the SED. The 'bourgeois' parties were founded with political goals sharply opposed to Marxist socialism. Though spawned by the SED, the DBD and NDPD also assembled elements traditionally suspicious of or opposed to socialism. For instance, in at least one village (Bienstädt), the DBD became a new political home for ex-NSDAP members. The Bienstädt DBD recruited sixty members within weeks, including all the former local NSDAP functionaries, whereas the local SED had taken four years to attract only twenty-six members.[60] The local leaderships were often an unknown quantity. Once Soviet tactics required a 'people's democracy' under SED hegemony, it became crucial to limit this pluralism and ensure the loyalty of each party and organisation, particularly as legal provision existed for elections and the participation of each licensed party in parliaments and administrations. As the mass organisations, which were also allotted parliamentary seats, each had a monopoly of their own target audience, their existence was less dangerous, providing they remained firmly under SED control and did not develop any separatist tendencies or become alternative powerbases.

The SED's control over this institutional framework partly depended on the Democratic Bloc and the NF, both of which represented all the parties and mass organisations. The latter structure developed from the 'People's Congress Movement for Unity and a Just Peace' of 1947–49, the body which formally adopted and promulgated the GDR's constitution in October 1949. Once the state had been established, the NF not only presented the parties' and organisations' joint manifesto and candidate list at elections, but also attempted to involve every last citizen, whether organised in a party or not, in the GDR's political life and to rally the population behind Soviet and SED policy on the German question. The Thuringian SED noted on 25 May 1949: 'It is necessary that the entire population be addressed within this movement, and that it must be relieved of all party political differences.'[61] However, despite this officially non-partisan role, the true situation was that: 'The GDR's communists have never denied that the NF was established and developed under the SED's leadership. Its initiatives and activities fashioned the NF's political profile.'[62] Thus, the SED used the bloc and the NF to demonstrate the unanimous support apparently enjoyed by SED policies across society.

Enforcing loyalty: the transformation of the Thuringian bloc parties

Having permitted the establishment of 'bourgeois' parties, the SMAD and its SED allies attempted to co-opt them to support the USSR's policy on Germany, and to prevent them opposing key socialisation measures, such as the extensive land reform. Apart from hindering these parties' election campaigns in 1946,[63] the SMAD and SED achieved these ends principally by intimidating and/or removing CDU and LDPD leaders who pursued alternative policy avenues. Generally speaking, the SMAD expected that the bloc parties' members would follow the centrally adopted path and attempted to align them with the SED from top down. The machinations at central level in Berlin are well recorded, and include the SMAD's removal of the CDU's first leaders, Andreas Hermes and Walther Schreiber, in December 1945, and their successor, Jakob Kaiser, two years later.[64] The result of these moves was that leaders who supported strong coalition with the SED either

through conviction or pragmatism came to dominate the SBZ/GDR party leaderships by the early 1950s, and imposed this policy throughout their parties.

Pressure was also exerted where necessary to ensure the co-operation of the
Land leaderships. Between 1945 and 1950 a number of prominent CDU and LDPD
figures were either arrested or intimidated until they left the SBZ/GDR. These
developments are also fairly well recorded and require only sketching here.[65] The
Thuringian CDU received an early foretaste of later developments in November
1945 when one of its founder members, Max Kolter, Thuringia's first postwar director of agriculture and forestry, was charged with maladministration, failure to
implement denazification measures and resistance to the land reform. The Soviet
occupation authority for Thuringia (SMATh) decreed Kolter's removal on 5
November. The KPD initially accused Kolter of faking illness to excuse his departure, but he died on 22 December.[66] In the following years intimidation and force
removed from the CDU leadership those personalities who were not prepared to
subjugate their policies to the SED's. These included Georg Schneider, the
Thuringian party organiser, who had emphasised the clear difference between
Marxism and the CDU's idea of socialism. Schneider was removed from his post
and expelled from Thuringia by the SMATh shortly after Kaiser's removal in
Berlin. Fifteen Thuringian *Kreis* chairmen were also removed after Kaiser was
deposed.[67]

A further wave of party cleansing began in 1949–50 prior to the first GDR
unity list elections. The Thuringian CDU party chairman, Siegfried Trommsdorff,
was not re-appointed after his connections to West Berlin became known, but also
because he had protected the 'reactionary' CDU group in Erfurt despite instructions to expel its leader. Minister Georg Grosse also fled to the west after refusing
to accept the CDU's change of direction. Aloys Schaefer – himself sentenced to ten
years in a work camp for opposing Soviet policy when *Landrat* (senior district
administrator) in the Eichsfeld – lists eight Thuringian CDU functionaries who
were imprisoned and a further eleven senior figures, including four ministers and
three other *Landtag* members, who fled westwards to avoid similar fates. This list
does not include district functionaries outside the Eichsfeld, the members who fled
following a campaign to unmask an alleged financial conspiracy, or Walter Rücker,
the Thuringian trade minister, who was expelled from the party in 1950 for his
political differences with the SED and alleged involvement in the financial conspiracy.[68] Despite these explicit warnings to other members, the existence of opposition to the party leadership and links to the western CDU was great enough to
spark a series of trials in Erfurt and Gera in December 1952 and January 1953, at
which heavy sentences were imposed.[69] The arrest of the GDR's CDU foreign minister, Georg Dertinger, in January 1953 served as a further reminder to the party's
regional and local leaderships to toe the SED line. The Heiligenstadt district leadership, with which Dertinger had close contacts, responded by instituting a membership review. This decision was clearly a difficult one for the district chairman
who was so shocked by Dertinger's arrest that he could not work for two days,[70]

suggesting indecision between leaving the Eichsfeld to avoid a similar fate or remaining and actively acknowledging SED hegemony. In all, some 1,536 Thuringian CDU members fled to the west between 1948 and 1953.[71]

The LDPD suffered similar losses, including the well recorded case of its *Landtag* leader, Hermann Becker. Becker was arrested by the Soviet secret police (the NKVD, the KGB's forerunner) in July 1948, presumably in connection with his activities as editor of the LDPD's Thuringian newspaper.[72] This arrest frightened several other CDU and LDPD politicians into escape.[73] In the same month Alphons Gaertner, President of the Thuringian Credit Bank, fled to the west. Gaertner, the SMAD's favoured candidate to succeed the recently deceased Wilhelm Külz as the LDPD's zonal leader, had demanded, and been refused, the party's right to pursue liberal policies. Three years later Leonhard Moog, Thuringia's minister of finance, also resigned his post once safely in West Berlin. Moog had attempted to deny the SED's 'leading role'.[74] Thereafter the SED implicated Moog, Gaertner and other senior LDPD figures in a grave financial scandal,[75] having discussed how Moog's departure could best be used to discredit his Thuringian LDPD colleagues.[76] Obeying the Thuringian SED's decisions, workers assembled at LDPD offices around Thuringia demanding the party's condemnation of Moog and explanations for its failure to remove him.[77] In the following days, the LDPD was subjected to a campaign of embarrassment which targeted local party representatives believed to sympathise with Moog's independent line. Much was made in the SED's Arnstadt press of the district LDPD group's failure to criticise Moog without the prior approval of its *Land* executive, and in Gotha the SED's reports of further alleged LDPD financial improprieties punned with the term 'Moogelei'.[78]

Against this background, the CDU and LDPD leaders who remained could be in no doubt that their positions and personal safety depended on loyalty to the SED. However, many senior figures in these parties supported the SED's policies from genuine convictions that socialism represented the way ahead, born of the experience of Nazism and the Second World War.[79] The GDR's party system could not have functioned without them. Nonetheless, they could not have dominated their parties without the interventionist role played by the SMAD and SED in these early years.

Despite the installation of loyal bloc leaders by these methods at GDR and regional level, there remained much to be done to hinder opposition in the localities. Many district and local executives and members did not respect their regional and national leaders' loyalty to the SED. Apart from campaigns against individuals, the SED used the Democratic Bloc and the National Front to ensure the parties' local loyalties and if necessary to bypass them.

A united front: Democratic Bloc and National Front

Though originally created to achieve party consensus, the local blocs became as essential to the SED's attempts to neutralise the 'bourgeois' parties as its crusades against leading 'reactionary' politicians.[80] Initially, however, this was not immediately apparent since the blocs concentrated on practical issues. During 1945 the Thuringian bloc issued urgent appeals to support harvest and reconstruction work. The bloc's precise role quickly became unclear as conditions settled, and its quasi-governmental role superfluous once parliamentary life resumed in 1946. Its recommendations had always been non-binding and after 1946 the parties debated government policy in the *Landtag*, generally agreeing a common stance in preliminary party meetings. Meanwhile, other powers initially assumed by the bloc passed outside Thuringian control to the SBZ's German Economics Commission (DWK) and later the GDR government. By 1948 the bloc met on average only monthly (just fifty meetings were held in the first three years). The bloc's role had already largely shifted from co-ordinating views on government policy to ensuring unanimity of approach in internal party matters, such as the rights of former NSDAP members to join political parties. The bloc also reconciled inter-party divisions over the filling of key posts.

The SED increasingly used the bloc to demonstrate cross-party support for SED schemes via public resolutions, such as that welcoming the new SED-led government for East Berlin established in November 1948 amid the Berlin Blockade.[81] However, the SED avoided divisive discussions by not attempting to achieve unanimous bloc support for pro-SED resolutions on controversial matters such as the currency reform and the Berlin blockade if it feared the CDU and/or LDPD would disagree. In the late 1940s the principle of unanimous decisions allowed the CDU and LDPD, still not entirely *gleichgeschaltet* ('co-ordinated'), to hinder SED plans. However, the CDU and LDPD could avoid actively supporting a bloc motion without being accused of reactionary behaviour because resolutions passed unless they were actively opposed.[82]

Despite its decreasing importance, the bloc nonetheless represented a potential source of political power. As such, the SED was anxious to dominate it. As the SED was outnumbered in the bloc by the CDU and LDPD's combined forces, the SED integrated the emergent but already loyal mass organisations. The central Thuringian bloc devoted much time to the rights of the mass organisations (and after 1948 the DBD and NDPD) to participate in political life on an equal footing with the original post-1945 parties. The bloc was widened on 2 December 1946 to include the FDJ, FDGB, women's committee (later Democratic Women's League of Germany, DFD), Cultural League (KB) and VdgB. The DBD and NDPD joined immediately after their formation in 1948. The SED also agitated for its close ally, the Nazi victims' association (VVN) to be admitted. The LDPD vetoed this for some time, arguing that the political parties would be further weakened if the mass organisations were allowed still more representation.[83]

In the late 1940s, as Germany's division became more entrenched, the bloc was deployed to support the SED's battle to neutralise the CDU and LDPD leaderships. In February 1949 the Thuringian bloc passed an SED resolution demanding energetic action against anti-Soviet, nationalist, chauvinist and neo-fascist tendencies in the parties and organisations.[84] Though the minutes of this meeting are missing, it is clear that CDU and LDPD representatives could not have opposed the motion without exposing themselves to similar charges. Similarly, the LDPD bloc representatives condemned their own party colleagues in Brandenburg for 'reactionary' comments in January 1950.[85] In January 1953, shortly after the CDU foreign minister, Dertinger, was removed on conspiracy and spying charges, the bloc considered the question of 'democratic vigilance'. The discussion demonstrated the CDU and LDPD regional leaderships' loyalty when both parties assured the bloc that the right conclusions had been reached, and when the LDPD representative even asked those present to help his party exclude elements which did not belong in the LDPD.[86]

However, the Thuringian bloc reflected the CDU and LDPD regional leaderships' increased loyalty, rather than having been the instrument which principally achieved it. Even before the parties and organisations formally recognised the SED's leading role, by the early 1950s the *Gleichschaltung* of their regional leaderships meant the Thuringian SED no longer needed regional bloc meetings to coerce the other parties. By this point, at *Land* level – and later at *Bezirk* level – the only important remnant of the bloc's original role as a mediator between the parties was its function in formally agreeing election mechanisms. Thus it was in the bloc that the parties agreed to the unity list elections of 1950,[87] thereafter to each party's and organisation's share of candidates, and finally to their share of government posts. In November 1950, bloc discussions were still important enough to initiate some reorganisation of Thuringia's ministries.[88]

Beyond this the bloc remained the forum in which the political parties demonstrated to the general public both their apparent diversity and their official unity via resolutions which supported SED standpoints and the USSR, and condemned developments in the Federal Republic. The bloc's diminished importance was underlined in 1951 when its Thuringian secretariat was disbanded and its administration entrusted to the National Front.[89] Acquiescence to SED policies was clear from the new *Bezirk* bloc's November 1952 guidelines. In these the regional branches of the parties and mass organisations committed themselves, as their national leaders had done, to the 'building of socialism under the leadership of the working class', a task which 'corresponds to the interests of the entire German nation'. By way of double assurance, the guidelines committed the regional parties and organisations to follow the policies of the loyal central bloc and imposed these conditions on the subordinate district and local blocs.[90] Thus was party discipline extended to the bloc parties.

However, the district and local blocs generally took rather longer to comply than the *Land/Bezirk* bloc. Their records demonstrate the wide gulf between the politics pursued by the bloc parties' upper echelons, who were persuaded or even handpicked by the SMAD to support SED policies, and these same parties' local members. Even when genuine debate had given way to socialist unity at regional level, the class struggle was still being fought in the localities. Here the SED used bloc meetings to expose and depose local leaders who opposed the SED's 'progressive' line and thus achieve full compliance in the localities. The local blocs' SED representatives had the task of clarifying the SED's line to members in other parties who had not yet grasped the 'scientific' truth of Marxism-Leninism, and persuading the other parties to distance themselves from 'reactionary forces' in their midst.[91] Though the chairmanship of the blocs rotated monthly between the parties, by 1950 80 per cent of Thuringia's district bloc secretaries were SED members who could dictate agendas.[92]

The Heiligenstadt district bloc offers several examples of how SED intimidation operated in practice.[93] As a CDU stronghold, the Eichsfeld particularly concerned the SED. By late 1952, however, the SED optimistically felt it had 'broken the CDU's predominance by systematic work and the growth of our party'.[94] Much depended on the attitudes of individual CDU leaders. The SED was anxious to remove its opponents, and to intimidate the others into cautious loyalty. Particularly during 1949 and 1950 the SED used the bloc to contest the moral high ground over the CDU's supposed misdeeds. This entirely accorded with the zonal bloc's policy, adopted at the SED's insistence in June 1949 after numerous incidents of CDU and LDPD opposition during the May 1949 People's Congress election campaign, upon which the future GDR constitution depended. The CDU and LDPD's loyal central organs agreed that their parties would exclude 'reactionary elements' at all levels.[95] Thereafter the SED's campaign began in earnest.

In August 1949 the Heiligenstadt SED demanded a full inquiry into an article in the CDU's *Thüringer Tageblatt* newspaper which had accused SED officials of attempting to prevent a CDU mayor being elected in Heuthen. This attack foreshadowed various similar actions during 1950, mainly prior to the October elections. In February the bloc investigated the case of Opfermann, a prominent local CDU member and deputy *Landrat* accused of financial improprieties in the running of a cinema, possessing fascist literature and making ambiguous public statements about the NF. Though Opfermann gave a satisfactory explanation for his actions in February, the case was re-opened on 6 March. Matters came to a head in April when SED groups occupied the district council building and pushed Opfermann out of a window in the so-called 'Eichsfeld defenestration'. Opfermann, unhurt, and *Landrat* Braedel fled to the west thereafter.[96] Herr Schyma, a regular CDU bloc representative and local government official, also attracted the SED's wrath in February by refusing to support an SED resolution calling on all parties to co-operate in removing saboteurs. Schyma insisted the CDU needed 'no guardian angel'. In response the SED launched a full inquiry into ambiguous comments Schyma had allegedly made weeks earlier. (The district FDJ chairman, Tyra, had recently resigned his position in similar circumstances, but by contrast had not been expelled from the SED.) Though the case against Schyma was weak and disputed, it was referred (despite the CDU's objections) to the Thuringian central bloc. Ultimately Schyma also withdrew from public life.

In the same 6 March meeting the CDU's Otto Strecker, NF *Kreis* secretary, was attacked for withholding information about Opfermann. Despite being suspended, Strecker was able to return to public life and remained the CDU's district chairman in Worbis.[97] Similarly the CDU's Karl Jünemann, mayor of Heiligenstadt, was attacked in the bloc for apparently obstructing the FDJ's efforts to plaster the town with posters. The SED's newspaper reported his alleged remarks about the FDJ in a scurrilous article. He was again attacked in July for supposedly inappropriate wording in a poster he issued about Colorado beetles. Jünemann defended himself easily on both counts and remained mayor into the 1970s. The SED failed to remove Jünemann and Strecker, but demonstrated the precarious position of any bloc-party politician, even over trivial matters. To retain their positions Jünemann, Strecker and their colleagues knew they would have to display absolute loyalty, and did so in the following decades.[98]

The SED underscored this point with a final attack on König, a regular CDU bloc representative, chairman of the district council (*Kreistag*) and a politician who had done much to cement the CDU's alliance with the SED. This loyalty did not prevent his removal from the *Kreistag* and as a CDU bloc representative in August 1950 after he publicly criticised the GDR government for the late publication of certain agricultural directives. After this incident, the remaining CDU district leaders refrained from seriously opposing 'the development of socialism'. The next major attack in the district bloc, in 1951, concerned not personalities but the CDU newspaper's advertising methods.

The SED's success was evident in the Heiligenstadt bloc's agreement to the key issue of unity election lists (even though the local parties were still jockeying for position within the unity-list framework before the 1957 elections) and to numerous resolutions supporting GDR/USSR policies and condemning 'Anglo-American warmongers'. Though the SED noted the local CDU's failure to recognise the SED's leading role in October 1952, and felt the party often tried to regain its old predominance, the district bloc was essentially *gleichgeschaltet* by 1952. However, the SED recognised its limits and did not bring certain potentially divisive matters to the bloc. Thus, the Heiligenstadt bloc issued no resolution mourning the death of Stalin and did not discuss the closure of the nearby border to the west and the deportations of border populations during 1952 until after the uprisings throughout the GDR on and around 17 June 1953. Even then, the bloc parties remained essentially loyal to SED positions, though the discussion was slightly broader than usual. By 1954 the SED had begun to exercise its 'leading role' by using the bloc to give specific instructions to the other parties (as prior to the 1954 elections and the celebrations for 1 May 1955).

The Heiligenstadt *Kreis* bloc was fairly typical of Thuringia's other district blocs, where the SED also employed intimidation in the early 1950s. For instance, the Sondershausen *Kreis* bloc was used before the 1950 elections to launch a campaign against an LDPD teacher accused of making dubious comments.[99] In the same year similar investigations were conducted in Gotha, mainly into LDPD and CDU officials, but also into the DBD in Langenhain, which harboured many former LDPD members.[100]

The town and village blocs were more problematic. *Kreis* Heiligenstadt again provides examples of this. In many communities there was a serious lack of inter-party co-operation before the 1950 elections. That even local DBD groups caused the SED problems again suggests that its loyal national leaders were hardly representative of the wider membership. The lack of local co-operation meant most local bloc meetings held before the 1951 referendum to call for German unity were organised by district supervisors rather than local party groups. Often personal differences impeded village bloc work. Indeed, even by 1956 such work was often practically non-existent. However, where it did take place the bloc parties' representatives always accepted SED resolutions. When 'reactionary elements' seemed likely to create difficulties, the district SED pressurised the relevant party to remove those concerned. The principle of the next highest bloc checking local election candidates ensured that the more loyal *Kreis* bloc counteracted any 'reactionary' village tendencies. The still more reliable *Bezirk* level bloc in its turn corrected any irregularities in the district blocs.

Once the parties' and organisations' long-term alliance with the SED was firmly soldered, the blocs at all levels acquired a new, dual function. On the one hand, each member organisation reported the opinions of the part of the population for which it was particularly responsible. On the other, the SED used the meetings to co-ordinate the members' work in the overall framework of political campaigning, and to ensure the active participation of all parties and organisations. The SED's new Thuringian leader, Erich Mückenberger, insisted in 1950 that it was a 'priority to involve [the 'bourgeois' parties] in the strengthening of the GDR's antifascist-democratic order'.[101] In this way the 'bloc' parties might also attract public blame for continuing hardships. The SED's regional secretariat determined the content of bloc resolutions.[102] It was hoped that such resolutions would guide the political thought of the members in whose name they were issued. In the mid-1950s, when the loyalty of the bloc parties' rank and file was still not guaranteed, the SED stipulated that the bloc should 'influence the CDU's policy more strongly; the comrades must hold talks beforehand and then give the CDU specific tasks … which they must then report on. The progressive CDU members are to be obliged to argue more with the reactionary forces.'[103] The SED unambiguously set the bloc's agenda. As the SED's first secretary for *Bezirk* Erfurt, Alois Bräutigam, freely proclaimed on the regional bloc's twentieth anniversary: 'After every meeting of our Central Committee we conduct a joint discussion with the chairmen of the bloc parties, in which we explain the problems and conclusions for the *Bezirk* …'[104]

These meetings were always held after events such as SED party congresses to officially inform the other parties of the latest official line and secure their public welcome for it.[105] Other meetings concerned technical matters such as mobilising the workforce for the harvest. An SED official usually gave the keynote address, even when the topic was agriculture in a meeting formally called by the DBD.[106] There generally followed a brief discussion of potential problems in securing popular support for a measure, and finally a public resolution was issued in the name of all those present, symbolising the supposed unity of all sections of society. However, the *Bezirk* bloc's dwindling significance is reflected in the irregularity of its meetings by the mid-1950s.

The last trace of significant dissent between the parties in the Thuringian bloc came in meetings after the 1950 elections to agree nominations for new mayors and district executives. Although the CDU cited political and ideological reasons for claiming an extra post, the bloc's outward unity was maintained.[107] When candidates for the 1957 and 1958 elections were considered, the lengthy discussions were essentially of a technical nature.[108] Similarly, when the *Bezirk* Erfurt bloc discussed the political situation after the CPSU's Twentieth party congress – and again after the Hungarian and Polish crises of 1956 – it was essentially to consider the steps necessary to stabilise the GDR's socialist order, not to question the system itself. The LDPD did, however, advance carefully worded criticism of agricultural policy in April 1956.[109] Such criticisms as one member organisation made of another after the mid-1950s concerned inefficiencies in political campaigning for socialism rather than ideological differences. By the 1960s the *Bezirk* bloc had degenerated to become a public relations exercise in official unity,[110] a formality for the organisation of elections and the channelling of political campaigns, and retained no significant role.

Similarly, by the late 1950s district bloc records generally demonstrate the SED's hegemony and the subordinate positions which the other parties had adopted. Though, for example, the Heiligenstadt district bloc handled much more business and took more decisions than its *Land/Bezirk* counterpart in the 1950s, by the 1960s it had the same limited function. The discussions after SED speeches merely concerned practical problems of implementing the unanimously agreed policies.[111] In cases where problems did occur (mainly in the earlier 1950s), party discipline and 'democratic centralism' – the principle by which decisions made at a higher level were binding on subordinate bodies – were deployed to bring bloc-party members into line with SED policy. A *Kreis* Gotha SED representative made this clear in 1952 during a discussion about an LDPD representative's privately expressed political doubts. The SED man stated: 'We, the elected representatives of the parties and organisations, are duty bound to implement for the good of the people the policy decided by our friends in the central bloc and which we have recognised.'[112]

Thus, providing the SED ensured the loyalty of the bloc parties' national leaders, discipline within each party eventually ensured local loyalty. When, particularly in the earlier years, loyalty was lacking, the party hierarchy intervened. For instance, when LDPD members in Holzengel did not support their party's agreement to the Oder–Neisse border in 1950, the LDPD's *Kreis* Sondershausen executive removed the local chairman and installed more reliable bloc representatives.[113] But although the bloc parties' disciplinary measures overcame local difficulties, and prevented them from challenging the authority of the parties' national organisations, local members' enforced silence did not necessarily mean the argument had been won, as a *Kreis* Bad Langensalza report hinted: 'Our party's [SED] proposals in the bloc are accepted without contradiction and without statements by the individual bloc parties.'[114]

Even in 1959 the Nordhausen SED could specifically report only that the bloc parties' *Kreis* leaders recognised the SED's leading role. At a lower level: 'The bloc friends in Mackenrode are unclear about our party's leading role because they make this dependent on numerical strength.'[115]

Though the political battles of the early 1950s intimidated bloc-party officials into subservience, before 1961 some were clearly unhappy with the situation and exploited the open borders to escape their political cage. Between 1956 and 1958, three *Kreis* Gotha NF members (one CDU, one NDPD and one KB) 'fled the republic'.[116]

The district and local blocs perhaps had greater importance than their *Bezirk* counterparts – where the SED's most loyal allies were already in place – in securing the bloc parties' agreement to SED policies before local councils discussed them.[117] However, bloc work was often entirely lacking in some localities. Typically, local bloc work in *Kreis* Weimar was 'variable', with no co-operation at all between the parties in numerous localities.[118] The *Kreis* Heiligenstadt local blocs met ever less regularly by the late 1950s, and the *Kreis* Nordhausen bloc had not met 'for a long time' by 1955.[119] In most of *Kreis* Apolda the local blocs did not meet for months and the parties worked 'alongside rather than with one another'.[120] Although lethargy and a lack of political commitment – even in those responsible for maintaining the system – undoubtedly prevented the bloc from fulfilling a more significant role in the GDR's local politics, there were other reasons. These included the imposition of 'democratic centralism' in government but also, as noted above, the creation of the NF in early 1950.

The NF's responsibilities largely overlapped with the bloc's. Confusion developed about the two bodies' respective roles. In *Kreis* Nordhausen 'comrades are also unable to decide which tasks (and in which form) should be handled in the bloc and [which] in the local committee of the NF.'[121] This in turn provoked a reluctance to participate in either: 'After all, it is always the same faces, whether in the bloc or the local committee of the National Front, and not very much really comes out of the meetings.'[122]

The Thuringian SED made considerable efforts to ensure that the NF, like the blocs, worked within the party's framework. The NF's first Thuringian secretary, Paul Dahm, was an SED nominee who regularly received detailed instructions about his duties from the party, and under the principle of party discipline he was bound by them.[123] As at all layers of political and economic life, the SED also attempted to create party groups within each district's NF secretariat. These groups co-ordinated SED members' efforts within the NF according to the SED *Kreis* organisations' instructions. However, although the SED thereby gained a clear advantage over the other less-well co-ordinated parties, by 1952 these structures were still not functioning efficiently, reflecting the SED's own unsettled internal situation: 'The SED group in the Thuringian committee still does not exert the leading role.'[124]

Though the SED was anxious that 'the bourgeois parties must not be allowed to play second fiddle', the NF was, like the bloc, an attempt to further involve and implicate the other parties and mass organisations in SED policies ('how can we activate the movement in the towns, particularly the bourgeois forces?').[125] One of the Thuringian NF's first resolutions was designed to 'unmask and render harmless all reactionaries and two-faced [members]' in the parties and mass organisations.[126] Given the movement's broad, common-denominator aims, the SED could easily criticise members of other parties who failed to give active support to the NF, even when this involved propagating specifically SED policies.

Though the NF had its own structures, the bloc parties effectively headed its organisation. The NF increasingly duplicated and assumed the bloc's function of collating information about the opinions of the various sections of society. This enabled the NF to plan differentiated political campaigns. However, local NF committees, if formed at all, usually remained largely dormant unless activated by SED envoys during election campaigns.[127] The active committees were dominated by SED loyalists. The local CDU and LDPD organisations remained distanced from the movement, despite their central leaderships' policies. As only a small proportion of committee members were without party or organisational affiliation, the SED's control of the organisation was secure.

Despite repeated attempts to mobilise the population for numerous political campaigns, the level of public involvement in the NF remained relatively low during the early 1950s. This slowly taught the SED an important lesson. The masses would never be willing to fight actively for socialism, or any other political cause, particularly while there were other pressing practical concerns. In the 1950s these included poor food supplies and the accommodation of the many settlers from the lost eastern provinces. By sponsoring so many different organisations (the parties, the trades union and the other mass organisations, the NF, the various ban the bomb campaigns, etc.) and insisting that each organisation provided members to actively help each of the others, the SED achieved overkill. The apolitical majority merely contributed their signatures on petitions or attended occasional processions (particularly if these took place during working hours). Many realised that the NF's 'aim is communism' and avoided the movement.[128] Meanwhile the committed minority became overworked and unable to match the hectic demands of political life. The SED secretary (theoretically at the 'vanguard of the proletariat') and NF chairman in a border village of *Kreis* Heiligenstadt summed up many Thuringians' feelings in 1950: 'We have no instruction groups and no peace committees either. We've had enough, we're all in favour of peace, we don't need any other organisation.'[129]

However, the SED did not significantly drop the pace of its political campaigning via the NF, the parties and mass organisations until the 1960s, when it began to content itself with the active support of only a proportion of the population and the passive support or lack of opposition of the rest.

Though the SED's initial hopes of involving the entire population were doomed to fail, the NF did provide a useful forum for addressing a wide variety of sectors of the population in differentiated meetings. Many churchgoers and the intelligentsia, naturally suspicious of the SED, were nevertheless prepared to attend NF events. The tactic of appealing to such groups on an officially non-party political basis was already established by the 1958 election, and was further developed by 1961 in the form of specific working groups for Christians, intelligentsia, women, etc. However, some groups which were established on paper in accordance with central directives failed to function in practice.[130]

Despite its shortcomings from the SED's perspective, the NF was partially successful. It took the SED's message to hundreds of thousands of individuals across *Bezirk* Erfurt at each election campaign, and on numerous other political occasions, thus cementing the status quo in the popular consciousness. The NF provided a mechanism for involving thousands of citizens outside the mainstream of political life in signing petitions and even in writing letters of protest to deputies in the FRG's *Bundestag*. Though the NF's planned 'house and village communities' never involved the entire population – and though those which did exist did not match the SED's original aspirations – large numbers attended community meetings before each election or were approached by NF instructors. For instance, across *Bezirk* Erfurt some 1,350,685 participants participated in 84,771 NF election events during the 1963 campaign, most of them 'differentiated discussions'.[131] However, not every NF meeting achieved its goal: though a public meeting in Wehnde (*Kreis* Worbis) attracted a good turnout, no speaker mentioned the 'National Document', the meeting's purpose, but instead discussed border security installations, footpaths, new waterpipes and local roads.[132]

Despite such failings, we can conclude that the SED could not have achieved these levels of even outward conformity purely in its own right. The system of the bloc parties and mass organisations, the Democratic Bloc and the National Front – each body headed centrally by SED loyalists who could be relied upon to impose strict internal discipline through the administrative structure – created a facade of political unity and ensured that no legal framework existed for organised opposition. Consequently, the system held firm (for forty years), whatever the opinions of individual rank and file members, whose motivations for participation ranged from commitment to opportunism. It is against this political background that we can consider popular responses to the key events and changing circumstances of the GDR in the 1950s and 1960s.

Notes

1 This process is well recorded at SBZ/GDR level. See, e.g., H. Weber, *Parteiensystem zwischen Demokratie und Volksdemokratie* (Cologne, Verlag Wissenschaft und Politik, 1982).
2 *Elections and Political Parties in Germany* (Bad Godesberg, Office of the High

Commissioner for Germany, 1952), p. 12; *Statistische Praxis* 3:9 (September 1948), Beilage.

3 *Statistische Praxis* 1:3 (December 1946), Karteiblatt; *ibid.*, 1:3 (December 1946), 37; *ibid.*, 3:5 (May 1948), Beilage.

4 W. Gutsche, *Geschichte der Stadt Erfurt*, 2nd edn (Weimar, Hermann Böhlaus Nachfolger, 1989), p. 475.

5 *Statistische Praxis* 2:5 (May 1947), Karteiblatt; *ibid.*, 3:11 (November 1948), Beilage, p. 6; *ibid.*, 2:9 (September 1947), Karteiblatt; Gutsche, *Geschichte der Stadt Erfurt*, p. 472.

6 U. Feist and H.-J. Hoffmann, 'Die Landtagswahlen in der ehemaligen DDR am 14. Oktober 1990', *Zeitschrift für Parlamentsfragen*, 22 (1991), 5–34 (p. 10).

7 D. R. Tracey, 'Reform in the early Weimar Republic', *Journal of Modern History*, 44 (1972), p. 197.

8 On Thuringia between 1918 and 1933, see D. Heiden and G. Mai (eds), *Thüringen auf dem Weg ins »Dritte Reich«* (Erfurt, Landeszentrale für politische Bildung Thüringen, [no date]); election results taken from Ed. Heilfron, *Die deutsche Nationalversammlung im Jahre 1919 und ihre Arbeit für den Aufbau des neuen deutschen Volksstaates*, 9 vols (Berlin, Norddeutsche Buchdruckerei und Verlagsanstalt [no date], I, 209, and G. Dressel, *Wahlen und Abstimmungsergebnisse 1920–95*, Quellen zur Geschichte Thüringens, 4 (Erfurt, Landeszentrale für politische Bildung Thüringen, 1995).

9 D.R. Tracey, 'The Development of the National Socialist Party in Thuringia, 1924–30', *Central European History*, 8 (1975), pp. 23–4.

10 Franz Walter has, however, demonstrated that the NSDAP did not make inroads in Thuringian districts where a strong socialist milieu existed: F. Walter, 'Von der roten zur braunen Hochburg', in Heiden and Mai (eds), *Thüringen*, pp. 119–46.

11 F. Facius, 'Politische Geschichte von 1828 bis 1945', in H. Patze and W. Schlesinger (eds), *Geschichte Thüringens*, V, Part 2 (Cologne, Böhlau, 1978), pp. 549, 559; H. Hömig, 'Thüringen unter dem Nationalsozialismus', *Kultur und Geschichte Thüringens*, 8–9 (1988–89), p. 20.

12 On the American period, see, e.g., L. Elm, *et al.* (eds), *Vor 50 Jahren: Thüringen unterm Sternenbanner* (Jena, Schriften des Jenaer Forums für Bildung und Wissenschaft e.V., 1995); L. Fuchs, 'Die Besetzung Thüringens durch die amerikanischen Truppen', in H. Müller (ed.), *Beiträge zur Geschichte Thüringens 1968* (Erfurt, Museen der Stadt Erfurt, 1968), pp. 53–111.

13 H. Siebert, *Das Eichsfeld unter dem Sowjetstern* (Duderstadt, Mecke Druck und Verlag, 1992), p. 38; various reports in *Kultur und Geschichte Thüringens*, 8–9 (1988–89), especially H. Kreutzer, 'Die Besetzung Saalfelds durch die Amerikaner 1945: Kommunal- und Regionalverwaltung in der "Stunde Null"', pp. 39–40 (quote).

14 G. Albrecht, 'Nochmals Hildburghausen', *Kultur und Geschichte Thüringens*, 8–9 (1988–89), p. 117; Siebert, *Das Eichsfeld*, p. 40; K. Meyer-Weyrich, '… was wäre uns nicht alles erspart geblieben', *Kultur und Geschichte Thüringens*, 8–9 (1988–89), p. 138.

15 Siebert, *Das Eichsfeld*, p. 17.

16 Kreutzer, 'Die Besetzung Saalfelds', p. 40.

17 W. Meyer, 'Kriegsende im Hennebergischen', *Kultur und Geschichte Thüringens*, 8–9 (1988–89), p. 92.

18 F. Moraw, *Die Parole der »Einheit« und die Sozialdemokratie* (Bonn/Bad Godesberg, Verlag Neue Gesellschaft, 1973), p. 67.

19 Thüringisches Hauptstaatsarchiv, Weimar (hereafter ThHStAW), MdI/5, 18, 'Meldung der Einwohnerzahl…', 23 October 1945, fol. 42; Fuchs, 'Die Besetzung Thüringens', p. 57.

20 LPA, V/5/006, report by Ernst Egert, p. 4.

21 E.g., G. Günther and L. Wallraf, eds, *Geschichte der Stadt Weimar* (Weimar, Hermann

Böhlaus Nachfolger, 1975), p. 634; Kreutzer, 'Die Besetung Saalfelds', p. 41.

22 G. Benser, *Die KPD im Jahre der Befreiung* (Berlin, Dietz, 1985), p. 66.

23 E.g., Egert (note 20), p. 4, reports how his KPD cell saved a local potash works.

24 Cited in G. Glondajewski and H. Schumann, *Die Neubauer-Poser Gruppe* (Berlin, Dietz, 1957), p. 41.

25 On Buchenwald prisoners' political institutions, and the whole of this period, see V. Wahl, 'Der Beginn der antifaschistisch-demokratischen Umwälzung in Thüringen: Die Organisierung der gesellschaftlichen Kräfte und der Neuaufbau der Landesverwaltung 1945' (PhD thesis, Friedrich-Schiller-Universität Jena, 1976), here especially pp. 82–5, 92–3, 104, 113–14.

26 A. Frölich, 'Der Höhepunkt meines politischen Lebens', in F. Rosner, *et al.* (eds), *Vereint sind wir alles* (Berlin, Dietz, 1966), pp. 516–17.

27 Cf. A. Grunenberg, *Antifaschismus: ein deutscher Mythos* (Hamburg, Rowohlt, 1993), especially pp. 120–44.

28 Cf., e.g., Kreutzer, 'Die Besetzung', p. 45; R. Knabe, 'In der Stadtverwaltung von Hildburghausen', *Kultur und Geschichte Thüringens*, 8–9 (1988–89), p. 112.

29 LPA, V/6/6-16, H. Hoffmann, 'Vereinte Kraft Grosses schafft' (1968), p. 40.

30 I. Kolesnitschenko, *Im gemeinsamen Kampf für das neue antifaschistisch-demokratische Deutschland entwickelte und festigte sich unsere unverbrüchliche Freundschaft*, Beiträge zur Geschichte Thüringens (Erfurt, SED Bezirksleitung Erfurt/Bezirkskommission zur Erforschung der Geschichte der örtlichen Arbeiterbewegung, 1985), pp. 10–12.

31 ThHStAW, MdI 273, fol. 15, 'Bericht an die Bezirksleitung der K.P.D.', 15 July 1945; Hoffmann, 'Vereinte Kraft' (note 29), p. 41; R. Barthel, *Major M.B. Dsilichow, erster sowjetischer Kommandant des Kreises Eichsfeld 1945/46, Eichsfelder Heimathefte* (Worbis, Eichsfelder Heimathefte, 1984), pp. 28–9.

32 On the KPD, SPD and their merger in Thuringia, see principally: Wahl, 'Der Beginn'; S. Kachel, 'Das Wiedererwachen der Arbeiterbewegung und die thüringische Sozialdemokratie' (master's dissertation, Universität Leipzig, 1993). Also of interest are M. Overesch, *Hermann Brill in Thüringen 1895–1946: Ein Kämpfer gegen Hitler und Ulbricht* (Bonn, J.H.W. Dietz Nachf., 1992); M. Oversech, *Machtergreifung von links: Thüringen 1945–46* (Hildesheim, Georg Olms, 1993); various detailed references to Thuringia in H. Krisch, *German Politics Under Soviet Occupation* (New York, Columbia University Press, 1974); Ä. Anweiler, *Zur Geschichte der Vereinigung von KPD und SPD in Thüringen 1945–1946*, Beiträge zur Geschichte Thüringens (Erfurt, SED BL Erfurt/Bezirkskommission zur Erforschung der Geschichte der örtlichen Arbeiterbewegung, 1971); Kolesnitschenko, *Im gemeinsamen Kampf*, pp. 59–71.

33 Cf. records in the sequence LPA, I/1.

34 This is not the view of his main biographer, Overesch, in *Hermann Brill*.

35 Cited in Anweiler, *Zur Geschichte*, p. 108.

36 The controversy over the nature of the SED's founding as *Zwangsvereinigung* or voluntary union cannot be pursued in depth here. For typically opposing views, cf., e.g., B. Bouvier and H.-P. Schulz, *"…die SPD aber aufgehört hat zu existieren": Sozialdemokraten unter sowjetischer Besatzung* (Bonn, J.H.W. Dietz Nachf., 1991) and H.-J. Krusch, 'Arbeiterbewegung, gesellschaftspolitische Forderungen und Einheit der Arbeiterparteien 1945/46', in D. Keller, H. Modrow and H. Wolf (eds), *Ansichten zur Geschichte der DDR*, (Bonn, PDS/Linke Liste im Deutschen Bundestag, 1993–), I (1993), pp. 61–79. For a more balanced survey of the debates, see D. Staritz, *Was war: Historische Studien zu Geschichte und Politik der DDR* (Berlin, Metropol Verlag, 1994), pp. 105–36; *Einheitsdrang? Einheitszwang? Die Entstehung der SED. Betrachtung und Erinnerungen nach*

50 Jahren, Schriftenreihe des Jenaer Forums für Bildung und Wissenschaft e.V., Heft 24 (Jena, 1996).

37 W. Eggerath, *Die fröhliche Beichte* (Berlin, Dietz, 1975), pp. 357–8.

38 Cited in Anweiler, *Zur Geschichte*, p. 121.

39 Cf. LPA sequence IV/L/2-30-IV/L/2-37 (Thuringian SED secretariat records); G. Braun, '"Regierungsangelegenheiten" in Thüringen im Spannungsfeld von sowjetischer Deutschlandpolitik und SED-Kalkülen 1947', *Beiträge zur Geschichte der Arbeiterbewegung*, 34 (1992), 67–91.

40 LPA AIV/2/4-119, AIV/2/4-127, AIV/2/4-139.

41 R. Agsten, M. Bogisch and W. Orth, *LDPD 1945 bis 1961 im festen Bündnis mit der Arbeiterklasse und ihrer Partei* (Berlin, Sekretariat des Zentralvorstandes der LDPD im Buchverlag Der Morgen, 1985), pp. 43, 45; R. Agsten and M. Bogisch, *Bürgertum am Wendepunkt: Die Herausbildung der antifaschistisch-demokratischen und antiimperialistischen Grundhaltung bei den Mitgliedern der LDPD 1945/1946* (Berlin, Buchverlag Der Morgen, [1970]), pp. 23–4, 29–30; H. Weber, 'Einleitung: Zum Transformationsprozeß des Parteiensystems in der SBZ/DDR', in Weber, *Parteiensystem*, p. 29.

42 Siebert, *Das Eichsfeld*, pp. 108, 133–4.

43 *Dokumente und Materialien zur Geschichte der Arbeiterbewegung in Thüringen 1945–1950*, Harry Sieber, *et al.* (eds), Beiträge zur Geschichte Thüringens (Erfurt, SED Bezirksleitung Erfurt/Bezirkskommission zur Erforschung der Geschichte der örtlichen Arbeiterbewegung/Staatsarchiv Weimar, 1986), pp. 44–6; LPA, V/6/14-002, 'Geschäftsordnung für den Block antifaschistischer Parteien', undated.

44 ThHStAW, BdMP 660, July–August 1945 correspondence on the *Thüringer Volkspartei*, fols 63–71.

45 M. Broszat and H. Weber (eds), *SBZ-Handbuch* (Munich, R. Oldenbourg, 1990), pp. 510, 540, 570.

46 See Chapter 3.

47 Figures calculated from Dressel, *Wahlen*, pp. 154–65; E. Krippendorff, *Die Liberal-Demokratische Partei in der Sowjetischen Besatzungszone 1945/48: Entstehung, Struktur, Politik* (Düsseldorf, Droste Verlag, [1963?]), p. 96.

48 Krippendorff, *Die LDPD*, p. 19; S. Suckut, 'Zum Wandel von Rolle und Funktion der Christlich-Demokratischen Union Deutschlands (CDUD) im Parteiensystem der SBZ/DDR (1945–52)', in Weber, *Parteiensystem*, p. 146.

49 ThHStAW, MdI/5, 19, May–June 1948 SED reports, especially fols 230, 235, 238, 257, 262.

50 LPA, IV/4.06/144, Kreis Heiligenstadt bloc work report, undated [summer 1952?], p. 1.

51 D. Staritz, 'Die National-Demokratische Partei Deutschlands (NDPD)', in Weber, *Parteiensystem*, p. 217.

52 September 1949 document cited by B. Wernet, 'Zur Rolle und Funktion der Vereinigung der gegenseitigen Bauernhilfe (VdgB) und Demokratischen Bauernpartei Deutschlands (DBD) im Parteiensystem der SBZ/DDR (1945–52)', in Weber, *Parteiensystem*, p. 275.

53 ThHStAW, MdI 305, letter from Gebhardt (SED), 1 April 1949, fol. 5.

54 ThHStAW, MdI/5, 19, fol. 286, 'Zur Information Nr. 96', 30 June 1948, p. 2; *ibid.*, fol. 257, 'Zur Information Nr. 88', 11 June 1948, p. 2; *ibid.*, fol. 262, 'Zur Information Nr. 90', 14 June 1948, p. 1.

55 ThHStAW, MdI 263, fol. 86, Thuringian bloc minutes, 20 January 1949; *ibid.*, Afl 87, Weissensee DBD report, 20 December 1949.

56 LPA, V/6/19-002, KPD Buchenwald resolution, 22 April 1945.

57 LPA, V/1/78, W. Albrecht, 'Tätigkeitsbericht des vorbereitenden Gewerkschafts-

Ausschusses', 18 June 1945; *ibid.*, V/5/094, K. Kuron, 'Schaut wie stark wir sind: 20 Jahre FDGB', undated manuscript.

58 Wahl, 'Der Beginn', pp. 156–7. An independent body existed at Zeiss and Schott in Jena. Cf. an undated leaflet in LPA, V/6/14-003.

59 LPA, V/6/6-30, H. Hoffmann, 'Zur Entstehungsgeschichte der Gesellschaft für deutsch-sowjetische Freundschaft in Thüringen', 1968, p. 20.

60 ThHStAW, AfI 86, Gotha DBD report, 1 December 1949.

61 LPA, IV/L/2/3-036, SED Thuringia *Kleines Sekretariat* minutes, 25 May 1949.

62 H. Neef *et al.*, *Die Nationale Front der DDR: Geschichtlicher Überblick* (Berlin, Dietz, 1984), p. 46.

63 Cf. a CDU letter to the Soviet occupation authority for Thuringia, 26 August 1946, complaining at numerous obstacles, cited by Suckut, 'Zum Wandel', p. 145.

64 Cf., e.g., J.B. Gradl, *Anfang unter dem Sowjetstern: Die CDU 1945–1948 in der sowjetischen Besatzungszone Deutschlands* (Cologne, Verlag Wissenschaft und Politik, 1981); Krippendorff, *Die LDPD*, especially p. 9 on the methods of intimidation; J. Frölich (ed.), *»Bürgerliche« Parteien in der SBZ/DDR: Zur Geschichte von CDU, LDP(D), DBD und NDPD 1945 bis 1953* (Cologne, Verlag Wissenschaft und Politik, 1995); Suckut, 'Zum Wandel', pp. 119, 125.

65 V. Thiel records serious ideological conflicts in the CDU: *Christen Thüringens in der Bewährung*, Christlich-Demokratische Union Deutschlands: Beiträge zur Geschichte (Halle/Saale, Sekretariat des Hauptvorstandes der CDU, 1970).

66 Cf. *Thüringer Volkszeitung*, 14 November 1945, p. 2, and 22 November 1945, p. 2. Kolter died in Soviet imprisonment: cf. A. Schaefer, *Lebensbericht: Landrat im Eichsfeld, Zeuge der Besatzungszeit*, 2nd edn (Heiligenstadt, F.W. Cordier, 1994), p. 99.

67 Thiel, *Christen Thüringens*, p. 25; Schaefer, *Lebensbericht*, p. 101; Gradl, *Anfang*, p. 156.

68 Thiel, *Christen Thüringens*, pp. 38, 42, 56–9; Gradl, *Anfang*, p. 158; Schaefer, *Lebensbericht*, pp. 100–1.

69 M. Richter, *Die Ost-CDU 1948–1952: Zwischen Widerstand und Gleichschaltung*, Forschungen und Quellen zur Zeitgeschichte, 19, 2nd edn (Düsseldorf, Droste Verlag, 1991), pp. 285–6. Richter also details the other incidents of intimidation against the Thuringian CDU, passim.

70 LPA, IV/4.06/095, SED Heiligenstadt, 'Informationsnotiz 2/53', 22 January 1953.

71 Richter, *Die Ost-CDU*, p. 391.

72 K.W. Fricke, *Politik und Justiz in der DDR* (Cologne, Verlag Wissenschaft und Politik, 1979), pp. 61–2.

73 Gradl, *Anfang*, p. 155.

74 H. Weber, *Geschichte der DDR* (Munich, dtv, 1985), pp. 165–6, 204.

75 Cf. Werner Eggerath's speech to the *Landtag*, 24 February 1950, reproduced in *Dokumente und Materialien zur Geschichte der Arbeiterbewegung in Thüringen 1949–1952*, ed. by H. Sieber, G. Börnert and G. Michel-Triller, Beiträge zur Geschichte Thüringens (Erfurt, SED Bezirksleitung Erfurt/Bezirkskommission zur Erforschung der Geschichte der örtlichen Arbeiterbewegung, 1978), pp. 40–50.

76 LPA, IV/L/2/3-038, SED Thuringa *Kleines Sekretariat* minutes, 19 January 1950, pp. 4–8.

77 Cf., e.g., ThHStAW, AfI 87, Kreisrat Weißensee to MdI, 21 January 1950.

78 ThHStAW, AfI 86, 'Herr Meinhardt zeigt sein wahres Gesicht', 28 January 1950; 'Hält der Landesverband der LDP sein Wort?', *Thüringer Volk* (Arnstadt edition), 2 February 1950; 'Moogelei mit Protektion', *Thüringer Volk* (Gotha edition), 3 February 1950.

79 Cf. typical GDR biographies of loyal Thuringian bloc politicians, e.g., *Das Wirken Christlicher Demokraten im Bezirksverband Erfurt* ([Erfurt?], Bezirksverband Erfurt der

CDU, [1980?]), and *Wegbereiter unserer Partei*, Schriften der LDPD, 38 (Berlin, Sekretariat des Zentralvorstandes der Liberal-Demokratischen Partei Deutschlands im Buchverlag Der Morgen, 1986).

80 The general comments made about the Thuringian and Bezirk Erfurt bloc are drawn from the (incomplete) records in: ThHStAW, BdMP 658, 659, 666-673; LT 200-201; MdI 263, 274; Vs/St 701; S 542; NF 209, 210; LPA BIV/2/15-735.

81 ThHStAW, MdI 263, fol. 76, Thuringian bloc minutes, 15 December 1948.

82 E.g., the SED's proposal for an aid committee for Berlin was accepted without active CDU and LDPD support: *ibid.*, fol. 81, Thuringian bloc minutes, 20 January 1949.

83 *Ibid.*, fols 2–17, Thuringian bloc minutes, 2 October 1947, and fol. 35, 15 June 1948.

84 *Chronik zur Geschichte der Arbeiterbewegung in Thüringen 1945 bis 1952*, p. 121.

85 *Ibid.*, p. 141.

86 ThHStAW, Vs/St 701, fol. 94 ff., especially fol. 100, Bezirk Erfurt bloc minutes, 30 January 1953.

87 K.-H. Schöneburg (ed.), *Vom Werden unseres Staates: Eine Chronik*, 2 vols (Berlin, Staatsverlag der Deutschen Demokratischen Republik, 1966, 1968), II, 96.

88 ThHStAW, BdMP 666-673, fol. 116, Thuringian bloc minutes, 20 November 1950.

89 *Ibid.*, fols 172–3, Thuringian bloc minutes, 1 March 1951.

90 ThHStAW, Vs/St 707, fols 10–11, 'Richtlinien der Arbeit…' [3 November 1952].

91 LPA, IV/4.05/123, Gotha bloc minutes, 4 December 1952, p. 10; *ibid.*, IV/4.13/167, SED report on Worbis bloc, 17 June 1954, p. 2.

92 LPA, IV/L/2/3-043, SED Thuringia secretariat minutes, 8 June 1950; these posts, presumably superfluous by 1951, were later abolished to save money: *ibid.*, IV/L/2/3-051, SED Thuringia secretariat minutes, 1 February 1951, p. 17.

93 This section relies principally on the extensive records that exist for the Heiligenstadt district and local blocs in LPA, IV/4.06/144.

94 1952[?] report (note 50).

95 M. Koch, 'Der Demokratische Block', in Weber, *Parteiensystem*, pp. 291–2; Schöneburg, *Vom Werden*, I, pp. 292–3.

96 Cf. Richter, *Die Ost-CDU*, p. 231.

97 Thiel, *Christen Thüringens*, p. 67.

98 *Das Wirken christlicher Demokraten im Bezirksverband Erfurt*, pp. 17–19.

99 LPA, IV/4.11/263, Sondershausen bloc minutes.

100 LPA, IV/4.05/123, Gotha bloc minutes, especially 27 January, 1 March, 2 June and 4 July 1950.

101 LPA, IV/L/2/3-038, SED Thuringia secretariat minutes, 2 January 1950, p. 3.

102 1 February 1951 minutes (note 92).

103 LPA, IV/4.12/1-227, SED Weimar-Stadt report, 2 December 1953, p. 1.

104 LPA, BIV/2/15-735, untitled speech by Alois Bräutigam [1965].

105 E.g. ThHStAW, NF 209, fols 125–9, *Bezirk* Erfurt bloc minutes, 25 July 1958.

106 E.g. ThHStAW, NF 210, fol. 8ff, *Bezirk* Erfurt bloc minutes, 14 March 1962.

107 20 November 1950 minutes (note 88), especially fols 127, 137.

108 ThHStAW, NF 209, fols 57ff, 100ff, 152ff, 158, see especially *Bezirk* Erfurt bloc minutes of 8 April, 7 May, 23 and 27 September 1958.

109 *Ibid.*, fols 28–35, 47–52, 54–6, *Bezirk* Erfurt bloc minutes, 18 April, 29 October and 7 December 1956.

110 Surviving minutes for 1960s *Bezirksblock* meetings, ThHStAW, NF 210; LPA BIV/2/15-735.

111 E.g. LPA, IVA/4.06/140, minutes of some *Kreis* Heiligenstadt bloc meetings, 1963–67.

112   4 December 1952 minutes (note 91), p. 10.

113   LPA, IV/4.11/266, reports on 'Blockpolitik', undated [summer 1950?]) and May 1950.

114   LPA, IV/4.07/197, SED report on Langensalza bloc, 9 January 1956, p. 6.

115   LPA, IV/4.09/151, SED report on Nordhausen bloc, undated [1959?].

116   LPA, IV/4.05/122, SED report on Gotha NF, 7 May 1958, pp. 12, 25.

117   LPA, IV/4.13/167, SED report on Worbis bloc, 22 September 1958, p. 1; the
      Sondershausen *Kreisblock* agreed in 1950 that its decisions would be binding on the
      parties' local council groups. Nonetheless, the DSF and SED had to struggle before the
      CDU and LDPD accepted a bloc resolution on the renaming of a street in the council
      meeting: May 1950 report (note 113), pp. 3–4.

118   LPA, IV/4.12/206, SED report on Weimar-Land bloc, 10 January 1956, p. 4.

119   LPA, IV/4.13/167, SED Worbis, 'Bericht über den Stand der Blockarbeit…', 22
      September 1958, p. 2; LPA, BIV/2/15-001, SED report on bloc work, 6 January 1955, p. 2.

120   LPA, BIV/2/15-001, SED report on Apolda bloc, 25 February 1960, p. 4.

121   1959[?] report (note 115), p. 4.

122   22 September 1958 report (note 119), p. 3.

123   Cf., e.g., the SED's resolutions to Dahm on future NF activities: 1 February 1951 minutes
      (note 92).

124   ThHStAW, BdMP 674/1, 'Informationsbericht-Nr. 15/52', 15 February 1952 (quote); LPA,
      IV/L/2/3-057, SED Thuringia secretariat minutes, 12 July 1951, p. 15.

125   LPA, IV/L/2/3-036, SED Thuringia secretariat minutes, 6 July 1949 (point 5).

126   NF *Landessekretariat*, 'Arbeitsprogramm', 31 January 1950, cited in Richter, *Die Ost-CDU*,
      p. 230.

127   ThHStAW, BdMP 233, 'Bericht Nr. 641', 20 November 1950.

128   ThHStAW, BdMP 229, 'Bericht-Nr. 201', 13 July 1950.

129   *Ibid.*, 'Bericht-Nr. 200/50', 13 July 1950.

130   In *Kreis* Worbis, only one NF working group was active in mid-1963: ThHStAW, S 547,
      fol. 27, 'Information (Monat Juni bis 5.7.1963)'.

131   LPA, BIV/2/13-725, 'Entwurf! Analyse über die Vorbereitung und Durchführung der
      Volkswahlen…', undated [1963], pp. 53–4.

132   ThHStAW, S 547, fol. 48, 'Informationsbericht VII/62', 12 April 1962.

3

From postwar survival to June revolt

1945–49: Thuringians in the postwar framework

We saw in the previous chapter that an active minority quickly concerned itself with shaping the postwar political order. For most of the Thuringian population, however, such considerations must have appeared rather abstract and secondary in the first years after 1945. Most people's perception of life was dominated by the prevailing poor material conditions. This had important ramifications for the rate and degree of political stabilisation, as clear connections were made in the public mind between such difficulties and the actions of the Soviet military authorities and their German favourites, the KPD/SED. Often life-threatening conditions produced political apathy and resentment of Thuringia's new rulers, factors which were to undermine public confidence in SED rule throughout the GDR period.

The initial collapse of this popular trust occurred in the 1945–49 period. Though Hitler's war, rather than the KPD/SED and the SMAD, were principally responsible for the harsh conditions, public opinion almost inevitably blamed those currently in power for their hardships. Thuringians faced severe shortages of food, livestock, fuel and raw materials. As they had largely been spared such conditions during the war, the Soviet takeover must have seemed like a step backwards. The dismantling or sequestering of factories, railway lines and other installations for reparations diminished economic capacity. Thuringia had to supply other regions and the SMAD with significant amounts of its industrial and agricultural output. Meanwhile, urgently needed supplies from the western zones were usually inaccessible.[1]

Some two million refugees and POWs poured through Thuringia, placing extra demands on the overstretched infrastructure; 700,000 'resettlers' remained in Thuringia,[2] and had to be housed, fed, clothed, employed and integrated. Simultaneously the loss of the many thousands of enslaved foreign agricultural workers caused a labour shortage.

Inadequate food supplies, cramped accommodation and even soap shortages produced disease and epidemic. Typhoid, typhus, diphtheria and tuberculosis were prevalent, killing many and necessitating widespread immunisation campaigns well into the late 1940s. Infant mortality also rose sharply. The lack of medical supplies, caused by interzonal trade restrictions, hindered further improvements. Meanwhile, denazification removed many badly needed but politically unacceptable doctors.[3]

The early months and years saw desperate searches for firewood before winter. Electricity and gas were rationed, and soup kitchens opened; household equipment, shoes, textiles and money were collected for refugees. Even the KPD recognised that most Thuringians were living 'hand to mouth' in December 1945. Though calorie levels were higher than in some SBZ provinces, famine was reported in certain localities, and food supplies remained uncertain and inadequate in the following years. For instance, only children received meat rations in Gera during September 1946; Altenburg restaurant diners were required to supply their own potatoes.[4]

Despite wartime destruction, industrial output increased significantly after the Soviet takeover. By January 1946 90.8 per cent of Thuringian firms were operating, and productivity rose, despite setbacks during the harsh winter of 1946–47 and the SMAD's mismanagement. Many of the goods produced were initially exported (albeit for payment) to the USSR, rather than benefiting Thuringians.[5] Even when raw material and food supplies improved, conditions normalised only slowly. In 1948–49 wartime rubble still remained in parts of Erfurt and, despite Soviet decrees and municipal ordinances, in Weimar, where popular criticism grew. In March 1947 paper supplies became so short that even the SED's Thuringian newspaper was reduced to a single sheet.

Against the background of these harsh conditions, four strands of popular response crystallised: anti-Soviet feeling, anti-SED feeling, political apathy and resistance to the early socialisation policies.

First, the Red Army did much to shape public perceptions in these early years. GDR histories presented the Soviet liberators as anxious to rebuild the country, ensure food supplies and restore normality, and even post-1989 memoirs are not exclusively damning.[6] Nonetheless, the occupiers quickly made themselves unpopular. For instance, they requisitioned Weimar's one remaining hospital, leading to births on the streets and deaths.[7] Soviet soldiers also committed violent crimes, often when drunk. These included armed robbery, assault and, frequently, rape.[8] Individual soldiers regularly 'requisitioned' food supplies, despite their commandants' express orders. On occasion non-compliant Germans were killed or injured. Soviet demands sometimes jeopardised adequate supplies to the local population. Even German policemen were forced at gunpoint to surrender bicycles and motorcycles.[9] By April 1946 the Nordhausen district prosecutor's office alone had around 80 cases against Soviet soldiers outstanding from the previous few months. Although not every complaint against the occupying forces was upheld, the Soviets' plunder and rape convinced many Thuringians that allied policy was the destruction not merely of Nazism, but of Germany herself. Deep distrust grew in the very working-class circles upon which the future political course depended. One British officer reported: 'From every side I received evidence of their [Germans'] hatred for and fear of the Russians. They regard no woman as safe if living in a Russian area and repeated stories of assault and rape are circulated among them and believed wholeheartedly.'[10]

Rape and pillage were not even temporary features resulting from battle fatigue, as the Soviet troops who occupied Thuringia had been at peace for two months by July 1945. Rapes occurred even years later, and harassment of women was still apparent in late 1949.[11]

Unwarranted arrests by the SMAD and particularly the NKVD caused further unrest. The SED's Thuringian Interior Minister, Ernst Busse, complained to the SMAD's Major Ivan Kolesnitschenko about arbitrary NKVD actions in December 1945, but even in 1948 the Red Army could not reverse them. Gallingly, some Thuringians were imprisoned in Buchenwald alongside ex-Nazis and political prisoners for no apparent reason except general intimidation of the population. As Prime Minister (*Ministerpräsident*), Werner Eggerath complained in June 1947 that men working near the camp were threatened with arrest if they ventured too close. Some arrests resulted from Soviet mistakes or flimsy denunciations by Germans.[12]

In the first days of occupation, minor acts of resistance against Soviet troops could result in serious reprisals for an entire village. In Küllstedt local youths caused a disturbance on 9 July 1945 after Soviet soldiers tried to buy scarce food supplies. Thirty-two men were arrested, of whom seven were shot and nine transported to the USSR.[13] The NKVD compounded problems by intervening in numerous cases to protect both Russians who had committed crimes and corrupt German officials appointed by the SMAD. Consequently, confidence in the justice system collapsed.[14] Influenced by these arbitrary actions and earlier Nazi propaganda, many feared young people would be arrested and deported. The extraction of reparations led to much additional bitterness.

Unfavourable comparison with the Americans was quick; optimistic rumours quickly spread that the British would soon replace the Russians. Despite a Thuringian 'Law Against Rumour Mongering' of 20 December 1945 similar rumours persisted for years. This was one of many examples of wishful thinking: any positive rumour was seized on and exaggerated in the hope that deliverance from the arduous postwar situation was close. Even in late 1949, for instance, Meiningen farmers delayed their produce deliveries because of rumours that the Soviets would soon leave and take the harvest with them, before being replaced by the Americans.[15]

Although some Germans viewed Soviet occupation as a necessary consequence of defeat, rapes, thefts, reparations demands, economic mismanagement and Soviet soldiers' stupidity or arrogance were frequent enough to provoke caution or rejection of the Soviets in large sections of the population. Significantly, workers at the prestigious, though largely dismantled, Zeiss and Schott works in Jena staged a 'go slow' in protest at the production quotas imposed by the representatives of the supposed motherland of the international proletariat.[16] Even loyal trade unionist functionaries noted many workers' prejudices against the USSR.[17] Such attitudes militated against a revival of a popular socialist internationalist movement. Often ignorant of conditions elsewhere in Germany, Thuringians believed their treatment to be particularly harsh. A British observer noted: 'Despite the recent cuts in the

British Zone, people still believe that the ration scale in the Russian Zone is far less.' The Soviets enjoyed genuine widespread support only when they proposed that all occupying troops should leave Germany.[18]

By 1947, with the shock of the Nazi collapse receding, some Thuringians voiced the opinion that the 'Russian rabble' was exploiting Germans and should be thrown out. In this context, comments that 'we are already Russian' were hardly complimentary. Early reports about the DSF also reflect growing anti-Soviet opinion. Gotha officials felt that rising DSF membership figures were in sharp contrast to the prevailing lack of true friendship for the USSR. Rising DSF membership instead reflected the population's growing realisation of the societal and career advantages inherent in joining the mass organisations. While Gotha functionaries assumed Goebbels' propaganda was responsible for persistent anti-Soviet sentiment, Mühlhausen officials noted more credible reasons: 'The man in the street is saying "He [the Russian] should first give us more to eat, then there'll be friendship!"' Even SED members hesitated about DSF membership, citing relatives in Soviet internment or clashes with Russian soldiers in 1945–46.[19] Clearly, the occupation power's misdeeds had implications for popular acceptance of the emerging political order, often perceived as a punishment for losing the war. The KPD's reminders that Nazism, not communism, had caused Germany's catastrophe were mainly ineffective.

The second strand of popular response – anti-KPD/SED attitudes – existed both independently and as a product of anti-Soviet opinion. The party's high profile in government and close working links with the Soviet authorities ensured that the public quickly related grievances of all kinds to communist rule. Internally, the SED leadership realised that its poor standing during 1947 and 1948 resulted from anti-SED propaganda and, more crucially, the inadequate food supplies for which it was blamed. In Weimar the SED was called the 'Russian party' and its newspaper a 'communist paper' whose one-sided reports were disbelieved.[20]

As the group hit worst by the material difficulties and shortages, the working class in particular lacked confidence in the party which claimed to be their own. Price rises and low pay naturally hit their morale badly. Events such as the FDGB festival in Eisenach, where trade union functionaries feasted despite the scarcity of food supplies, caused indignation.[21] A comrade visiting from Berlin noted the ironic tragedy that 'we come from the working class ... and we are largely unpopular among the workers.'[22] Anti-SED feeling was such that activists at an Arnstadt conference in December 1948 were denounced as 'Russian lackeys' by their workmates and pelted with screws.[23] Many Erfurt firms lacked SED groups as workers refused to join a party which was blamed for all problems. The party's emphasis in the late 1940s on reinforcing its ideological homogeneity distracted its leaders from practical problems, with consequences for popular support. Even Eggerath concluded that the relatively poor 1949 election results reflected the party's ignorance of 'the questions which move the masses'.[24]

By the time the GDR was founded on 7 October 1949, support for the SED was severely lacking. Greiz observers noted that: 'The entire population disap-proved of the party's measures ... Among workers, the party's standing is only rising insofar as they are supplied with material goods.' The 'intelligentsia' were still sceptical, while the 'petit-bourgeoisie' 'hardly recognised the party's work' and in Schleiz viewed the SED as their class's 'gravedigger'. Farmers, the party's main target group in 1945, mainly judged the SED sceptically or with reserve. Poor living standards and incidences of corruption similarly influenced attitudes to the SED-dominated state administration.[25]

Third, alongside widespread rejection of the Red Army and the SED, was the ultimately more potent phenomenon of political apathy. Preoccupation with daily survival and natural political scepticism following the collapse of Nazism made gen-eral passivity understandable. However, the KPD/SED's aspirations required popu-lar enthusiasm and revolutionary spirit. The triumphal optimism of the Thuringian KPD newspaper during the merger of the communist and social democratic parties, and again during the 1946 election campaign, was greatly at odds with popular sen-timent, which cared little for politics and more for material issues and personal needs. Even at the culmination of the KPD/SPD merger, the Ilmenau public pros-ecutor's office noted complete disinterest amongst workers and all other groups. Ironically the Gotha office, the scene of the Thuringian merger, noted in the very same week that older people in particular 'are collapsing under the weight of their cares and can see no other escape from the current hardships than suicide'.[26]

People discussed food, coal and clothing rations rather than the political future. Though not all negative reactions were specifically political, the SED and SMAD were often heavily criticised. For instance, rumours spread in Jena that elec-tricity cuts in September 1946 were a punishment for the town's relatively low SED vote (36 per cent), and there were inevitably political dimensions to the frequent complaints about the favoured treatment for the 'intelligentsia'. An old trade unionist remarked bitterly: 'I've been in the union all my life and taken part in one strike after another against exploitation. Now we have a workers' government again, but all I get as thanks is to finish my retirement days starving.'[27]

Almost from the beginning of Soviet occupation and KPD/SED rule, the widespread non-politically motivated dissent existed alongside the fourth strand of popular reaction, active resistance. Despite little sign of active Nazism or belief in Nazi ideology, swastikas (quicker and easier to daub than the black–red–gold flag which had been appropriated by the SED) retained validity as a national symbol of opposition to foreign rule, whether by the Red Army or the 'Russian party'. They particularly surfaced to coincide with the new order's political rituals and celebra-tions, and were increasingly used to protest against a party which defined itself as 'antifascist', rather than to promote the restoration of national socialist rule. This is not to suggest that all Nazi symbols used in opposition to SED rule were ideo-logically value free. Clearly, some citizens still mourned the Third Reich, and did so into the 1950s and beyond, as the appearance in Gotha in 1949 of a large poster of Hitler bearing the motto 'Ein Volk, ein Reich, ein Führer' suggests.[28]

Opposition to SED rule often consisted of spontaneous responses to particular circumstances. Examples are the defacing, by workers, of pictures of SED leaders and the murdered KPD leader Ernst Thälmann, revered as a martyr by the party; or the disruption of an Apolda local council meeting by 100 workers angry at plans to rename *Viktoriastraße* (Victoria Street) 'Peace Street'. The widespread vandalising of SED materials before the 1946 elections clearly reflected the party's poor reputation at a time of food and fuel shortages. Physical attacks on SED members and the derision of pupils who had joined socialist youth groups often reflected individual frustrations or personal rivalries. However, other incidents suggest a more carefully orchestrated opposition to socialism itself. These included the bomb attack on the SED's Mühlhausen headquarters (not an isolated incident), allegedly the work of SED members; the distribution of the West Berlin *Telegraf* newspaper in Eisenach; and the politically explosive posters which appeared throughout Altenburg in 1946 comparing the FDJ to the Hitler Youth and attacking the FDGB.[29]

Finally, a further widespread form of popular opposition was *Zonen-* or *Republikflucht* ('fleeing the zone/republic'). Figures for this phenomenon between 1945 and 1949 would be difficult to compile, as large numbers passed through and left the SBZ legally in those years. However, the attempts at strong border security even in these early years, and reports of high placed officials and party members heading westwards,[30] suggest that many east Germans left for the western zones in the hope of better political and economic conditions.

Public opinion at the end of the 1945–49 period can be gauged by examining reactions to the foundation of the GDR on 7 October 1949. Opinion was split between the three groups which had clearly established themselves since 1945: supporters (the smallest group), opponents and (seemingly a majority) those who had no particular opinion.

Supporters of the new state included people with a personal or career stake in the state machinery or one of the political parties, and those who believed the SED's assurances that the new GDR would strengthen German unity, despite the existence of two competing German governments. There were hopes that the despised Russians would disappear and the economic situation would improve. Such opinions reflected wishful thinking in a difficult situation rather than a considered reaction. To encourage positive reactions, the government organised big parades in the major towns. Young people, in particular, were bussed to Berlin to participate in the 'national' events. Yet some contemporary reports noted disappointing attendances at local events, reflecting a 'wait and see' attitude.[31]

More common, however, was the view that a separate East German government would deepen the division, perhaps permanently. Many (perceptively) felt the GDR's creation was a Soviet measure and that Moscow controlled the government. Some even feared war.[32] A regular criticism was that no elections would be held for a further year, and that the government did not reflect current political opinion, implying that the SED had lost much ground since the 1946 elections.

The SED was widely accused of 'tactical behaviour'. Gotha students believed the SED could never win elections. Some citizens took a differentiated approach, emphasising their acceptance of the new state but their disapproval of the new government's policies and their insistence that the GDR should not be a Soviet puppet state. Others disapproved of the GDR on principle, but supported the government's much vaunted peace policies.

The bloc parties' grassroots were often sceptical or opposed to the new state. While CDU local meetings mainly avoided the issue, scepticism and a 'flood of negative discussions' characterised LDPD events, particularly after the SED's pronouncement that 'elections are not essential to democracy'. The GDR's creation highlighted the loyal LDPD leadership's distance from its more rebellious grassroots. However, some SED members were also confused. An Elxleben SED meeting on 11 1949 October seemingly failed to mention the birth of the GDR. More embarrassingly, various local celebrations of the GDR's birth were cancelled because bloc-party representatives and some SED members failed to appear.[33]

Some concrete opposition also emerged. Opponents generally concealed their opinions, but tried 'to influence the population or reflect general feelings with malicious comments and jokes'. An oft-repeated crack was that together Grotewohl, Pieck and Ulbricht (respectively the new state's prime minister, president and deputy prime minister) made 'GPU', the former initials of the Soviet secret police. In isolated instances, posters opposing the new state appeared, and the large torchlit procession to mark the GDR's birth in Gotha was marred by students' barracking, leading to one arrest.[34]

However, the most common reaction noted in the reports commissioned to depict popular opinions on the new state, apart from confusion, was indifference. The new state's birth was entirely overshadowed by the potato shortage. Even in January 1950, some Thuringians hardly realised that they now lived in the GDR. Those who did often saw no difference between the young GDR and the government in Bonn, or any previous governments. The political events of October 1949, though later presented as a watershed, mattered little to those still anxious to secure the next day's meals. Workers, described as 'incomprehensibly politically immature', typically commented: 'I don't care who's in charge up there as long as I get more to eat.' Conversely, those workers who did care about the government's composition were angered at the inclusion of 'bourgeois' bloc-party politicians. The prevailing atmosphere among workers was one of scepticism and rejection until the new government achieved concrete successes. Pensioners, those dependent on state benefits and refugees from the former German territories had even less confidence in the new government. Young people were more often prepared to involve themselves in the new state, but the many church adherents rejected the GDR government altogether, while private traders merely hoped (vainly) for better trading conditions.[35]

The 1945–49 period was, then, characterised by a pervasive 'feel bad' factor, caused essentially by extremely harsh material conditions but exacerbated by incompetence and errors by the SMAD and KPD/SED, which cost them much potential political support, particularly among workers, whose 'class consciousness' dwindled when confronted with the struggle to survive. On 7 October 1949, as the new era dawned, the Thuringian Information Office concluded: 'Political clarity among the masses is extremely bad, the "stomach question" controls everything.'[36]

1953: Act one – Stalin's death

By 1953 the contours of the GDR's political life were fairly clearly defined. An election in 1950 and a referendum the following year had secured the active participation of practically the entire population. The celebrations of events such as May Day and SED party congresses were becoming regular rituals, and the SED's Second Party Conference of 1952 had resolved 'the building of socialism in the GDR'. After the western allies had rejected Stalin's note proposing German unification in the same year, the GDR's future seemed more certain. The snapshot of 1953 provides an insight into how the GDR's population viewed this situation, and to what extent the GDR's political masters were in control of their state in a year which saw both the death of Stalin on 5 March, and a popular uprising on 17 June which suggested a total legitimacy deficit for the SED government.

The death of Stalin, the GDR's godfather, stood out from the constant succession of political events to which the party hierarchy expected appropriate popular responses. As Stalin was the leading symbol of world socialism, reactions to his death shed light on popular attitudes to socialism itself. The SED recognised this in commissioning special reports during the fortnight following Stalin's death.[37]

The official responses to Stalin's death were as grandiose as might be expected in a monarchy on the sovereign's death. Special newspapers were published, and flags flew at half mast. Ordinary citizens were encouraged to display flags on their homes. On the SED's instructions, the state organs, parties, firms, co-operative farms and prominent individuals made formal visits to the Soviet commandant's offices to present their written condolences, while party executives, local parliaments and blocs held mourning ceremonies. To mark Stalin's funeral, workers participated in mourning processions. Guards of honour were mounted at statues of Stalin, and wreaths were laid at Soviet war cemeteries.

Although most, but not all, official acts passed smoothly, the bloc parties' local organisations' loyalty was revealed as equivocal. Despite issuing clear protocol instructions, the SED indignantly noted that the CDU's regional executive did not visit the Soviet commandant until 7 March, and then only in a joint delegation following a special bloc meeting. The regional LDPD leadership, meanwhile, visited only once and presented no documents. In Erfurt's local bloc meeting, the LDPD made only a short statement about Stalin's death, while the CDU and DBD said nothing at all. The LDPD's local deputy chairman failed to attend the mourning procession, while a Bad Langensalza CDU court official commented that she would rather sweep the streets than join the DSF to mark Stalin's passing.

Throughout the *Bezirk* the bloc parties were 'very restrained' in their comments, though the SED was relieved at similar restraint from the churches, which generally refrained from openly rejoicing, perhaps sensitive of the palpable public shock. Although one sermon claimed that 'Jesus has chased off the highest devil', Heiligenstadt's two Catholic churches rang their bells to mark the funeral and offered an 'Our Father' for Stalin.

The SED was also disappointed at the relatively poor display of flags. Although many private shops were appropriately decorated, state-owned shops were not, despite the SED's specific instructions to comrades employed there. Most residential accommodation also lacked flags. In Weimar, the SED noted that 'the number of flags in the town suggests the SED has only five hundred, not five thousand, members.'

Nonetheless, participation in the special ceremonies and processions was generally high, even in small rural communities. In many towns large halls could not accommodate all who wished to attend the events, which attracted people who otherwise took no part in the GDR's frenetic mass political activity. Over 35 per cent of the population flocked to the marches held in the thirteen district centres, with sizeable turnouts even in the Catholic Eichsfeld. A further 25,200 marched in smaller communities. Some mourners took Stalin's death very much to heart: one housewife of no party affiliation commented she would rather have lost her father than Stalin. However, Soviet soldiers were absent from some processions, as in Nordhausen where they played football during the funeral.

Despite the public mourning, comparatively few pledges were made to increase production in the major factories 'relative to the strength of the party organisation and the workforce'. The number of new productivity pledges was drying up by 17 March, despite the brief revival encouraged by the death of the Czechoslovak president, Klement Gottwald, on 14 March. Most pledges were merely promises to study Stalin's works or find new members for the mass organisations. However, in the wake of Stalin's death, 1,066 applications to join the SED were received, though tellingly only 571 to join the DSF, despite the nature of the event.[38]

In the first days following Stalin's death, there were practically no disturbances and few recorded negative comments about the deceased, though high-school pupils 'lacked discipline' and talked during the processions. This initial 'unnatural reserve' gave way to isolated incidents of protest after about four days. Guards of honour were insulted and sometimes doused in water or earth from flowerpots by school children; typed anti-Stalin letters were circulated; an SED man's window was broken by a catapult, and a woman whose picture had appeared in the party's regional paper, *Das Volk*, alongside her eulogy to Stalin received a telephone threat. Children in particular, probably tactlessly repeating their parents' comments, welcomed Stalin's death and hoped Adenauer would bring peace and German unity.

Occasionally people commented openly that they were glad Stalin had 'croaked', repeated West German radio reports that he really died 'years ago', or discussed western radio features about Stalin's murder of Lenin's associates. More widespread, and significant, was the view that Stalin's death would bring policy changes and increase the risk of war, as his successors' peace policy might not be as successful. SED members and the general public alike expressed such opinions and speculated about Kremlin power struggles. These reactions suggested that Stalin's official portrayal as a progressive 'dove' had found widespread acceptance, but more significantly that 'these people do not recognise the great strength of the Communist Party of the Soviet Union'. Rumours also circulated widely that the GDR's president, Wilhelm Pieck, who had not attended the Moscow ceremonies, was seriously ill.

The public's attention found new focus within a fortnight of Stalin's death, notably the poor food supplies and West Germany's ratification of the Paris Treaties for a western European defence alliance, an easy target for SED propaganda. While there were hardly any hints of the later widespread rejection of Stalin and Stalinism (indeed quite the reverse), the public clearly perceived that Stalin's death had weakened the world communist movement and that no smooth transition had occurred to guarantee the continuation of his policies. Although most citizens conformed to the required loyal behaviour patterns, belief in the scientifically proven, inevitable progression to communism was clearly lacking, and hopes of possible German reunification were reawakened. Some farmers optimistically foresaw the return of capitalism in the USSR. This clear awareness of potential problems in the leadership of both the USSR and the GDR (Pieck) almost certainly, if subconsciously, encouraged a sense that active opposition to the SED's hardline attempts during 1952–53 to construct socialism at any cost might bear some fruit in a period when communist rule seemed less secure.

1953: Act two – June uprising

The background to the crisis which occurred just three months after Stalin's death is well known. Most commentators agree that its roots lay in particular in the implementation of the decisions of the SED's Second Party Conference (July 1952), which resolved to 'build socialism in the GDR',[39] though one can also see the uprising as the culmination of the frustrations born of poor living conditions. The attempt to build socialism was made at the cost of inadequate provision of consumer requirements. It brought an intensified 'class struggle' against real and supposed opponents of socialism; reduced social welfare payments; the swift establishment of co-operative farms (LPGs) and the associated food shortages when many farmers emigrated in protest; and ultimately the raising of work quotas, which effectively meant that the 'workers' government' cut workers' pay. The overall effect of these measures was the worsening of already low living standards and increasing popular resentment of the SED and of the Soviet Union which seemed intent on deepening Germany's division.

Though Thuringian records confirm this traditional view of the causes of unrest, local materials allow further insights into the class nature of the uprising, which has proved more controversial. While some historians have classified 17 June as principally a workers' uprising, others believe it was a general revolt which crossed class boundaries. In *Bezirk* Erfurt, this was generally not the case. The date has also been seen as marking both the beginning of the GDR's ultimate collapse and the date of the state's effective foundation.[40] I hope to demonstrate that neither of these views is accurate.

Despite deep political rancour and great material hardship, the GDR remained peaceful during 1952 and early 1953. On 9 June the Soviet government, aware of the mounting tensions in the GDR, forced the SED to implement a U-turn, known as the 'New Course'. This rescinded most of the hardline policies of the previous twelve months, though significantly not the increased work quotas, while the farmers, students and others who had left the GDR under the pressures of the campaign to build socialism were urged to return, their former status guaranteed. The New Course was initially generally welcomed, and in some quarters there was optimism that great changes were imminent, such as the return of the American occupiers and the disbanding of the LPGs. Some of the hope was fuelled by reports that Ulbricht, Grotewohl and President Pieck were dead or had fled the country. Such rumours perhaps revived memories of the end of the Third Reich and suggest at least an unconscious comparison of the two regimes in the public mind. There was an initial wave of thanks to the government and party for relieving the population of so many burdens. However, scepticism about whether the promises would be kept quickly emerged, and thoughts turned to the source of past mistakes. Negative opinions of the government and SED began to dominate. Even an SED group secretary was heard to say that 'great crimes have been committed' and that all those responsible, including both Pieck and the West German chancellor, should have to answer before the courts. Various Heiligenstadt comrades felt similarly. However, the public was more impressed by the lowering of the prices for jam and public transport than the political implications of the New Course.[41]

The general history of 17 June 1953 has been often and well sketched,[42] and requires only brief rehearsal here. At the heart of events were strikes in Berlin, begun on 16 June by building workers who objected to increased productivity quotas and then marched on the GDR's ministry buildings, joined by thousands of other workers as they went. Although the government rescinded the increased quotas, a general strike took place on 17 June in Berlin. During the accompanying demonstrations SED buildings were set on fire. Around lunchtime martial law was declared and Soviet troops intervened to crush the remnants of the uprising.

The *Bezirk* Erfurt materials show that events took a somewhat different course in the region than in Berlin. First, the unrest, mainly but not exclusively in the form of strikes, was not restricted to 17 June 1953, but extended for several days afterwards in some provincial towns. Second, however, the level of participation in *Bezirk* Erfurt was surprisingly low. Only a small minority actively demonstrated dissatisfaction with the regime, though this was undoubtedly at least partly due to the presence or rumoured presence of Soviet troops (the 'friends', in SED parlance). Many areas experienced no unusual disturbances at all. Third, the perception of 17 June 1953 as a major watershed in the GDR's history can, perhaps, be relativised given the surprising speed with which 'normal' life resumed. At least in the provinces, the legend which grew up around 17 June 1953 was far more substantial than the events of June 1953 themselves.

There were some forewarnings before 17 June of the unrest to come. *Bezirk* Erfurt had already experienced at least one strike over higher work quotas (in a Gotha factory on 11–12 June). On 16 June small groups in Martinfeld voiced opposition to SED policies and youths swore at two SED members and overturned a party car. However, such incidents were not particularly unusual. The main wave of strikes and demonstrations took its lead from the disturbances in Berlin on 16 June. The police noted the influence on local workers of the West Berlin radio station, Rias, which had broadcast details of the Berlin demonstrations and strikes.[43]

The main sources of unrest on 17 June itself were workers and private farmers, the latter group angered by collectivisation and higher taxation policies. However, strikes occurred at only seven factories in *Bezirk* Erfurt on 17 June, concentrated in just four towns (Erfurt, Weimar, Eisenach and Sömmerda). Building workers at Erfurt's Pathological Institute and an FDGB holiday home in Friedrichsroda also went on strike. The other disturbances consisted of demonstrations, mainly led by farmers and principally designed to release people imprisoned during the 'class struggle', although specific economic grievances were also raised. These gatherings, which succeeded in releasing some prisoners by force, occurred in four district centres and in two smaller towns, but farmers from some smaller villages marched to the local centres to swell the larger protests. The Mühlhausen demonstration was particularly well attended.[44] Although the farmers' activities were not so widespread as to require a re-evaluation of Diedrich's thesis that 17 June 1953 was essentially a workers' uprising, these events do qualify his view that farmers were unable to rise spontaneously and join forces with others. Equally, the interpretation of 17 June as a workers' uprising does not mean that most workers revolted: they did not.[45]

Although these strikes and demonstrations were unprecedented in the GDR's history, on 17 June they remained limited to relatively few centres. On 18 June there were seven strikes, and on 19 June six, but the movement did not spread beyond Nordhausen and Gotha before it abated. By 19 June, most of the strikes were centred on Erfurt. Thereafter, no more strikes or demonstrations were reported and an uneasy peace reigned, amid rumours that Russian soldiers had, for instance, killed eighty people with machine guns. The police reports may not be entirely comprehensive, as other sources report much smaller strikes involving just a few workers. However, I calculate that only about 32,000 workers struck in *Bezirk* Erfurt in the days surrounding 17 June 1953, some 4 per cent of the working population. A further 10,600 took part in disturbances large enough to be classified as demonstrations.[46]

Apart from minor incidents which coincided with the larger events but which were not otherwise unusual (such as a Heiligenstadt comrade who had a noose of material tightened around her neck for defending SED policies),[47] another problem area was schools. Although teachers worked normally through the crisis, schoolchildren in some districts were excited into copycat actions, frequently declaring their own 'strikes' or removing classroom pictures of Stalin and SED leaders. Presumably expressing their parents' feelings, pupils showed considerable resistance to Russian lessons. However, children were easily persuaded to revert to compliant behaviour. A Gispersleben Russian teacher responded to a strike call written on her blackboard by keeping her class in after school. 'The children went pale from fear and agitation and promised never to repeat such foolishness.' Similarly, school girls who threatened to leave the Young Pioneers – the children's wing of the FDJ – were told they could no longer participate in school sports. The girls remained in the association. However, although teachers kept order in occasionally riotous situations, many adopted the same 'wait and see' approach as much of the rest of the population.[48]

Overall, only a very small part of the population was directly involved in strikes or demonstrations, despite the visible concentrations in centres such as Sömmerda and Erfurt. Some of the factories which struck had been suffering particular difficulties for some time. The Sömmerda firm 'Rheinmetall', for instance, had laid off thousands of workers after losing major orders under the state plan, causing much local discontent which boiled over once the Berlin workers had given the lead.[49]

However, the statistics of successful strikes and demonstrations should not obscure the many other unsuccessful attempts. These failures, and the speed with which the strikes which did break out were brought under control, are testimony to the efficacy of the SED's emergency measures. Although the party had clearly been weak in allowing several entire workforces to strike, practically all state and party functionaries worked normally during the crisis. Their quick responses prevented more strikes breaking out.[50]

More importantly still, the party could rely on the loyalty of the police force and the state security service to restore order where necessary.[51] The integrated nature of the state's response demonstrated a high degree of administrative efficiency. Police actions in particular were carefully co-ordinated with the state security apparatus, the SED offices and the Soviet commandants who declared martial law throughout the *Bezirk* by early on 18 June. The Soviets also co-ordinated with the SED. In Weimar, for instance, the commandant followed the party's advice about shortening the curfew on 24 June.[52]

On 18 June the *Bezirk* police president ordered all provocateurs to be publicly shot without trial.[53] This order was reiterated on 19 June, along with instructions to shoot anyone resisting arrest during the curfew period. No police officers objected to this order, although in practice they fulfilled their duties without shooting anyone. Indeed, police officers obeyed all orders. The only criticism of the force (on 25 June) was that some policemen's haircuts appeared sloppy. Attention to such mundane detail itself reflects returning order.

The police and Soviet forces maintained order by two principal methods. First, loyal SED members and police occupied telephone exchanges, and police and Soviet tanks appeared at gates of striking factories to prevent workers leaving. This ensured strikers could not contact workers elsewhere to request support. Thus, as strikes developed in Erfurt on 19 June, two factories were 'secured by three lorries of friends' and it was decided to send in tanks unless calm was quickly restored. Similarly, when striking miners from the Mansfeld region in *Kreis* Halle (outside Thuringia) returned to their Eichsfeld homes, great efforts were made to prevent them inciting the local population to similar action. In Apolda, Soviet troops dispersed a crowd which had gathered to welcome home striking workers from the nearby Zeiss works in Jena. The local authorities were organised enough to move the bus stop where the Jena workers were expected to arrive away from the district SED headquarters. Where necessary, GDR police and/or Soviet soldiers occupied entire areas. In Weimar, Soviet forces secured all public buildings, and on 21 June the police occupied all Thuringia's important train stations to avoid a rumoured railway strike. Heavy patrols were mounted to intimidate the general population. In Erfurt every main street and important junction was manned, and every vehicle and pedestrian was checked. Soviet troops managed to disperse a crowd of three thousand in Mühlhausen which hoped to force the release of prisoners and had already compelled armed German police to retreat. Thus, at least in *Bezirk* Erfurt, the actions of Soviet troops were not quite as described by Arnulf Baring: rather than intervening once a strike or demonstration was over, they were essentially used to disperse workforces or crowds.

The second significant method was to remove the main ringleaders behind the strikes and demonstrations. Plain clothes police and state security officials mixed with demonstrators at strike meetings to identify those concerned. However, arrests were mainly made at night time to avoid launching major offensives in front of the ringleaders' colleagues, who only noticed their absence the following day. This strategy prevented the strike movement from forming any coherent leadership as an alternative to the SED and FDGB.

The lack of clear leadership severely weakened the strike movement. Where strike committees existed, they emerged fairly spontaneously, were unequal to police and state security tactics and arrests, and collapsed as quickly as they had formed. Another weakness was workers' and farmers' failure to unite in opposition to SED rule, just as they had not united to establish it in the mid-1940s. Thus, *Bezirk* Erfurt materials do not corroborate Manfred Hagen's view that general political demands proliferated because a solidarity developed between the different classes which overcame grievances specific to each.[54]

Most of those who participated in the strikes, spoke at meetings or joined strike committees were ordinary workers. However, they included a certain number of SED members. Thus it was an SED man who tore down the red flag at the SED headquarters in Apolda during a demonstration on 17 June.[55] Elsewhere some SED functionaries and rank and file members were influential in causing strikes or were elected to strike committees, as in various Erfurt plants where five members emerged as 'provocateurs'. Similarly, SED members had been among those trying (unsuccessfully) to incite strikes in *Kreis* Sondershausen. In all, eighty-nine members were expelled from the party by November 1953 as a result of their actions in mid-June. A further 163 members emigrated illegally in the three months after 17 June.[56] However, as this represented merely around 0.3 per cent of the SED's membership in *Bezirk* Erfurt, the importance of these figures should not be overstated.

However, there were larger numbers of SED members who had not displayed outward opposition, but who had also not rallied to the party in its hour of need. Thus, of the twenty-two 'most trustworthy and aware' comrades asked to protect buildings in central Erfurt on 21 June, only seventeen appeared, and five of these wore no party badge. One SED member employed in the city administration who refused this task said he felt 'not in the least connected with the party and the working class'.[57]

By the autumn an investigation was underway into members' actions during the June crisis. By this point it was clear that local party organisations were protecting their own disloyal members. Thus the party organisation in Erfurt's 'Optima' plant had still not uncovered the 'agents and saboteurs' behind the strike and launched only one disciplinary hearing. Fewer than half the group's members attended this meeting, and not all of these voted to expel the member concerned. The company also failed to sack the man. The inspection commission concluded: 'The party leaderships are shying away, there are strong tendencies of retreat and appeasement, a characteristic of social democracy ... '[58]

The 17 June therefore unmasked the serious ideological deficiencies within the SED rank and file which had partly accounted for the party's loss of control in some areas. There were individual cases of resignations from the party in response to the government's admission of mistakes, and at least one instance where party members commented that the SED should 'build a German communism which had nothing in common with Russian communism'. It is unlikely that the party investigators discovered all the cases where party groups failed to act against members harbouring doubts about the leadership's political line. Alongside the many committed socialists there were clearly many others who used their party membership for personal advantage. Most of these did not unmask themselves during the crisis, or at most left their party badges at home while awaiting the outcome. As 17 June effectively changed nothing, these less committed members were able to continue as though nothing had happened. However, there were at least enough loyal SED members, from whatever motivation, to ensure that the party organisation and the SED-dominated state structures did not disintegrate.

Comments in a Weimar report support these conclusions. The district party investigation commission noted that comrades had mainly supported the party and actively guarded 'our achievements' in the localities. 'However, there are also some comrades who are wavering or have capitulated ... It is evident that none of these comrades has ever acted as a comrade, and that they are only comrades because of their position. [Nonetheless,] it must be said that the comrades in the MTS [farm equipment stations] and the state apparatus have conducted themselves well as comrades, even if passively in some cases.'[59]

In defining the June crisis, the slogans used during the strikes and demonstrations are also instructive.[60] Initially, economic demands predominated, but these were quickly linked to and replaced by political points. On 17 June itself, most slogans concerned economic hardships or local grievances and included calls to reduce work quotas to 1952 levels, reinstate sacked and imprisoned workers and farmers, raise pensions and reduce the levels of produce farmers were expected to deliver to the state. However, a smaller number of political slogans also appeared on 17 June, including calls to remove the government and hold free elections throughout Germany, and for the Soviet Union to release all prisoners of war. Political slogans were more in evidence on the following day, encouraged particularly by the arrests of 17 June and the deaths of sixteen workers during the unrest in Berlin. By 19 June, political demands were clearly dominant. However, with the exception of calls for free, pan-German elections, the political demands were far vaguer than the economic grievances.

No group emerged with a specific action plan, and no-one doubted that Germany's political future still depended on the four allies. As the west had conspicuously failed to intervene, as the SED and its Soviet supporters had clearly succeeded in restoring order, and as the GDR's political system provided no outlet for calls for radical change, there was no direction for the population's political demands to take after 20 June when the strike movement was broken. Although these political demands were undoubtedly shared by a large proportion of Thuringians, only a minority of the population had positively stated them, even given the opportunity of 17 June granted by the demonstrators in Berlin. The dominant apolitical nature of public opinion persisted even through this crisis, and increasingly resumed once order had clearly been restored.

Nonetheless, the peace was uneasy as normality returned. The rural population was reported to be extremely reserved. Many wanted to see the concrete results of the government's promises. In public meetings, few volunteered to discuss the official interpretation of the recent unrest as a western imperialist plot to overthrow the GDR, and party and state propagandists found few interlocutors in the factories they visited.

In isolated cases, workforces were still making economic and political demands and threatening strikes in July. This was notably the case in the Jena Zeiss works (*Bezirk* Gera), where a union meeting of 7 July called for everything from better quality shoes to free elections and German unity. Public calls for the government to resign also continued into July. Sometimes they came from minor functionaries such as parish-council chairmen. More generally, the population used public meetings to complain about concrete material problems rather than abstract political issues. Thus, discussions concerned continuing shortages, specific local power abuses and the restrictions on travel into the border areas. The population report-edly expressed its mistrust of the government and hoped to retain this new freedom to discuss and criticise.[61]

Simultaneously, however, the population also resumed the compliant patterns of normal life. The National Front's house and village community elections con-tinued apace and local groups elaborated plans to improve local amenities and to 'increase vigilance' against any new 'putsch attempts'. Within a week of their strike, workers at the Sömmerda 'Rheinmetall' plant were persuaded to issue a statement welcoming the SED Central Committee's latest decisions. Similarly, 20,000 people gathered in Erfurt on 13 August to hear the SED Interior Minister, Willi Stoph, and unanimously endorsed a resolution calling on the allies to conclude a peace treaty with Germany. By mid-August, the bulk of discussion again centred on material problems, such as fuel and electricity shortages and issues such as the wage differ-entials between private firms and the better paid nationalised industries. By the fol-lowing year, when some 96 per cent of *Bezirk* Erfurt's population again voted for the National Front candidates in the *Volkskammer* elections (i.e. the GDR parlia-ment elections), clearly most people were as prepared to conform to the political behaviour expected of them as before 17 June.[62]

What conclusions can be drawn from the June 1953 crisis? Clearly, East Ger-mans were interested in political change, even if this interest was actively expressed by only a minority. However, it took a crisis of material welfare to unleash even this relatively minor level of public disruption. The speed with which normality resumed suggests that the unrest of mid-June was merely an interruption of an underlying preparedness at least to tolerate the status quo in the absence of any viable alternatives. That there were no viable alternatives had been proven by the success of German authorities (the police and/or the SED) in preventing the expression of a potentially far greater degree of open opposition, and by the effec-tiveness of Soviet troops in dispersing the crowds and forcing the strikers to resume work. Although numerous SED members demonstrated loyalty to the workers they believed they should be representing rather than to the national leadership, and although many others behaved cautiously while waiting to see which side would gain the upper hand, with few, parochial exceptions the party and state apparatus at no time seemed in danger of disintegrating. Clearly, the party did tem-porarily lose control of public order and require Soviet assistance to restore its hege-mony in some districts. However, the effectiveness of the GDR police and state security services bear testimony to the degree of control achieved by German authorities under the SED's direction within eight years of the end of the war. In this sense, 17 June 1953 did not mark the GDR's 'true founding': the state was already functioning relatively securely.[63]

Although 17 June clearly gave the SED leadership a fright, prompting the party to tighten control and ensure that basic living standards were maintained, and although that date was often referred to in subsequent years as a symbol of the pop-ulation's potential power, its historiographical status as a watershed in GDR history

seems overstated when viewed from a regional perspective. Thuringians did not initiate significant unrest before events began in Berlin, and most Thuringians did not
directly experience conflict with the authorities even during the crisis. Although
trust in the SED was further undermined,[64] for most people it was the photographic images of repression in Berlin rather than any personal experience which
remained potent as disproof of the regime's avowed humanitarian aims. In this
sense, those workers who raised the spectre of 17 June when disgruntled in later
years, particularly in 1956, were merely seizing a symbol. But their threats of a
repeat performance were bluster. The 17 June had been more of a failure for the
population than for the government, and all the structures of power remained
intact.

The authorities' response to 17 June merely confirmed a truth which had been
apparent since the end of the war: Germany was under foreign occupation, and
there were no alternatives. As anti-Soviet attitudes had been prevalent since before
1945, 17 June changed little. Since the disturbances had merely proved what was
already obvious, and as the authorities seemed keen to resume the normal round of
everyday life while making efforts to provide better living standards, most people
regarded a return to an apolitical life of making the best of things as the most
favourable option, at least until such time as the opportunity for change again
seemed to be within reach. However, in later years the population was not so quick
as in 1953 to take a lead from events elsewhere. This became particularly apparent
when the GDR remained mainly peaceful in 1956, despite the opportunity to
mimic the uprising in Hungary.

Notes

1 Public Record Office (hereafter PRO), FO 1050/105, report by Albu, undated; FO
  1014/40, 'Report on the situation in Thuringia', 29 October 1945; *Berichte der Landes- und
  Provinzialverwaltungen zur antifaschistisch-demokratischen Umwälzung 1945/46* (Berlin,
  Akademie Verlag, 1989), pp. 107–8.
2 W. Gutsche, *Geschichte der Stadt Erfurt*, 2nd edn (Weimar, Hermann Böhlaus Nachfolger,
  1989), p. 475; J. John, R. Jonscher and A. Stelzner, *Geschichte in Daten: Thüringen*
  (Munich, Koehler & Amelang, 1995), p. 272.
3 PRO, FO 1050/433, 'Consolidated Report No. 8', 28 February 1946, para. 32, and
  'Consolidated Report No. 9', 30 April 1946, p. 8; H. Löser, 'Zur Durchsetzung einer
  neuen, fortschrittlichen Gesundheitspolitk nach 1945 in der Stadt Erfurt und im Land
  Thüringen', in Horst Müller (ed.), *Beiträge zur Geschichte Thüringens* (Erfurt, Museen der
  Stadt), II (1970), p. 86; H. Domeinski, 'Der Aufbau eines demokratischen
  Gesundheitswesens in Thüringen von 1945 bis zur Gründung der Deutschen
  Demokratischen Republik', in H. Sieber, *et al.* (eds), *Beiträge zur Geschichte Thüringens*
  (Erfurt, SED Bezirksleitung Erfurt *et al.*), IV (1984), pp. 42, 62; PRO, FO 1005/1633,
  'Consolidated Report No. 12', 15 August 1946, Part B.
4 G. Günther and L. Wallraf (eds), *Geschichte der Stadt Weimar* (Weimar, Hermann Böhlaus
  Nachfolger, 1975), pp. 680, 686–7; E. Hartwig and V. Wahl, *Weimar auf dem Weg zum
  Sozialismus: Erster Teil, April 1945 bis April 1946*, Weimarer Schriften zur Heimatgeschichte

und Naturkunde 28 (Weimar, Stadtmuseum Weimar, 1976), p. 22; *Thüringer Volkszeitung*, 13 October 1945, pp. 4, 5; W. Eggerath, *Der fröhliche Beichte* (Berlin, Dietz, 1975), p. 298; PRO, FO 1050/433, 'Consolidated Report No. 11', 5 July 1946, p. 2; FO 1014/40, 'Report on the situation in Thuringia', 26 October 1945; FO 1005/1633, 'Consolidated Report No. 14', 15 November 1946, para. 30; ThHStAW, ObLW 12, Altenburg report, 15 April 1946.

5 W. Mühlfriedel, 'Thüringens Industrie im ersten Jahr der antifaschistisch-demokratischen Umwälzung', *Jahrbuch für Regionalgeschichte*, 9 (1982), p. 36; Gutsche, *Geschichte*, pp. 493–4; 30 April 1946 report (note 3), Part II, p. 1; PRO, FO 1050/433, 'Consolidated Report No. 8', 28 February 1946, Part II and Part VII, para. 293.

6 Local examples are, e.g., B. Fischer, 'Die Befreiung der Stadt Erfurt vom Faschismus 1945', *Aus der Vergangenheit der Stadt Erfurt*, n.s. 1 (1985), p. 16; K. Schmölling, 'Artern 1945: Als die Russen kamen', *Aratora*, 2 (1992), 85–8.

7 ThHStAW, MdI 273, fol. 15, 'Bericht an die Bezirksleitung der KPD … ', 15 July 1945.

8 ThHStAW, MdI/5, 386, fol. 84, Eichsfeld police, 'Lage- und Tätigkeitsbericht', 30 November 1945; *ibid.*, Eichsfeld police, 'Übergriffe russischer Soldaten', 22 October 1946; cf. N. Naimark, *The Russians in Germany* (Cambridge, MA, Belknap Press of Harvard University Press, 1995), Chapter 2.

9 ThHStAW, Landrat Worbis 96, untitled police report signed 'Schröder, Obwm', September 1946[?], and 'Übergriffe russischer Soldaten', 7 October 1946; MdI 203, fol. 3, 'Heutige Rücksprache … ', 24 July 1945; MdI/5, 18, fols 376, 381, notes of December 1945.

10 ThHStAW, ObLW 12 and 13, especially ObLW 13, fol. 21, Nordhausen report, 17 April 1946; MdI 203, fol. 18, 'Heutige Rücksprache … ', 31 August 1945; 15 July 1945 report (note 7); PRO, FO 1049/75, report by J.F. Christie, 4 August 1945, p. 2; FO 1049/68, report by J.R. Little, 3 July 1945, p. 2.

11 ThHStAW, MdI 69, fol. 76, 'Wochenbericht', 26 November 1949.

12 ThHStAW, BdMP 645, fol. 325, Busse to the Soviet occupation authority for Thuringia, 11 December 1945; BdMP 513, fol. 252, 'Aktenvermerk', 19 June 1948; BdMP 647, fol. 226; Naimark, *The Russians*, pp. 25–6; B. Ritscher, *Speziallager Nr. 2 Buchenwald* (Weimar, [n.pub.], 1993), especially pp. 35, 40–2; M. Klonovsky and J. von Flocken, *Stalins Lager in Deutschland* (Munich, dtv, 1993), p. 26.

13 H. Siebert, *Das Eichsfeld Unter dem Sowjetstern* (Duderstadt, Mecke Druck and Verlag, 1992), pp. 87–9.

14 ThHStAW, ObLW 12, fol. 112, Oberstaatsanwalt Meiningen, 'Politischer Stimmungsbericht', 16 January 1946.

15 ThHStAW, MdI/5, 19, fol. 40, 'Dienstbesprechung … ', 27 July 1946; MdI 273, fol. 20, 'Was sagt die Bevölkerung … ?', [undated, mid-1945?]; AfI 87, Kreisrat Meiningen, 'Informationsbericht … ', 3 September 1949 and similar Nordhausen reports.

16 ThHStAW, ObLW 12, Oberstaatsanwalt (Ilmenau), 'Politische Stimmungsberichte', p. 1, 23 April 1946; MdI/5, 386, fol. 61, Eichsfeld police, 'Lage = Tätigkeitsbericht', 6 November 1945; MdI 69, fol. 7, 'Bericht Nr. 2', 12 August 1949; 28 February 1946 report (note 5), para. 99.

17 W. Gienger, 'Die Jugend hungerte nach Brot und Wissen', in E. Lehmann, *et al.* (eds), *Aufbruch in unsere Zeit* (Berlin, Tribüne Verlag, 1975), pp. 80–1.

18 30 April 1946 report (note 3), p. 9; ThHStAW, MdI/5, 19, fol. 256, SED, 'Zur Information Nr. 88', 11 June 1948.

19 ThHStAW, BdMP 271/34, fol. 31, SED Erfurt, 'Stimmungs-Bericht', 2 October 1947; *ibid.*, fol. 235, 'Bericht eines Besuches …', 23 September 1947; AfI 86, RdS Gotha, 'Politik', 28 November 1949; AfI 87, RdS Mühlhausen, 'Deutsch-sowjetische Freundschaft', 7 October 1949.

20 ThHStAW, MdI/5, 19, fols 232, 265, SED reports, 28 May and 15 June 1948.

21 ThHStAW, BdMP 271/34, fol. 22, Berka police, 'Stimmungsbericht … ', 24 October 1947; *ibid.*, fol. 24, 'Vertrauliche Information' [undated, late 1947?].

22 ThHStAW, MdI/5, 19, fols 178, 185, 'Protokoll über die Polizeileitertagung in Tabarz am 11. und 12.10.1947'.

23 K. Kästner, '"Für eine bessere Zukunft": Erste Aktivistenkonferenz im Kreis Arnstadt im Dezember 1948', *Beiträge zur Heimatgeschichte: Stadt und Kreis Arnstadt*, 3 (1984), p. 10.

24 ThHStAW, MdI/5, 19, fol. 254, SED LV, 'Zur Information Nr. 87', 11 June 1948, p. 3; BdMP 674, fol. 107, 'Stellungnahme zum Wahlergebnis', 20 May 1949.

25 LPA, BIV/2/4-56, LPKK (*Landesparteikontrollkommission*, Regional Party Control Commission), 'Überblick über den Zustand und die Lage der Partei … ', 8 August 1949, section V.

26 ThHStAW, ObLW 12, Oberstaatsanwalt reports, 1945/46, especially Ilmenau, 9 April 1946, and Gotha, 8 April 1946.

27 *Ibid.*, Oberstaatsanwalt Rudolstadt, 'Politischer Stimmungsbericht', 8 April 1946; ThHStAW, MdI 100, fol. 25, 'Gas- und Stromversorgung der Stadt Jena', 30 September 1946; MdI 69, fol. 54, 'Wochenbericht', 22 October 1949; 15 June 1948 report (note 20), fol. 268.

28 ThHStAW, MdI/5, 386, fol. 287, Worbis police report, 21 January 1948, and fol. 61, Eichsfeld police, 'Lage = Tätigkeitsbericht', 6 November 1945; AfI 86, Informationsstelle Gotha report, 21 December 1949.

29 ThHStAW, MdI/5, 386, fol. 287, Worbis police report, 21 January 1948; MdI 69, fols 50, 57, 61, 'Wochenbericht', 1 and 29 October, 12 November 1949; MdI/5, 19, fol. 55, 'Dienstbesprechung … ', 7 September 1946; BdMP 674/1, SED, 'Faschistische Provokationen … ', 28 December 1949; ObLW 12, fol. 122, Oberstaatsanwalt Meiningen, 'Politischer Stimmungsbericht', 24 January 1946; MdI/5, 18, fol. 164, Altenburg police report, 4 May 1946; AfI 87, RdS Mühlhausen, 'Anschlag auf das SED Parteihaus', 30 September 1949; 20 May 1949 report (note 24), fol. 111.

30 E.g., ThHStAW, MdI 69, fols 49–50, 53, 'Wochenbericht', 1 and 22 October 1949.

31 ThHStAW, BdMP 674/1, untitled SED report, 25 November 1949; SED, 'Stimmen zur provisorischen Regierung', 14 October 1949, pp. 2–3; AfI 86, RdS Gotha, 'Politik', 8 October 1949; AfI 87, Kreisrat Nordhausen, 'Berichterstattung', 19 November 1949; M. Diller, '"Diesen Tag vergesse ich nie": Erinnerungen an den historischen Fackelzug der FDJ vor 35 Jahren', *Beiträge zur Heimatgeschichte: Stadt und Kreis Arnstadt* 3 (1984), 4–6; H. Günther, 'Erfurt zur Zeit der Gründung der Deutschen Demokratischen Republik', *Museen der Stadt Erfurt: Veröffentlichungen zur Stadtgeschichte und Volkskunde*, 1 (1984), 86–95.

32 8 and 14 October 1949 reports (note 31); ThHStAW, MdI 69, fol. 77, 'Wochenbericht', 26 November 1949.

33 ThHStAW, AfI 87, 'Bericht des Kreisrats Romrig, Werner, LDP', 7 November 1949; BdMP 674/1, SED, 'Die neue Situation und die CDU', 23 November 1949, and SED, 'Die LDP in der neuen Situation', both 23 November 1949; AfI 86, Kreisrat Arnstadt, 'Eine lebhafte Wahlversammlung … ', 11 October 1949; MdI 69, fols 58, 82, 'Wochenbericht', 29 October 1949 and 9 December 1949; 14 October 1949 report (note 31).

34 14 October and 25 November 1949 reports (note 31); ThHStAW, AfI 86, RdS Gotha, 'Politik', 13 October 1949.

35 ThHStAW, MdI 69, fols 53, 57–8, 'Wochenbericht', 22 and 29 October 1949; AfI 87, Abt. Information, Mühlhausen, 'Die Bevölkerung und die Deutsche Demokratische

Republik', 25 January 1950.

36 ThHStAW, AfI 87, 'Deutsch–Sowjetische Freundschaft', 7 October 1949.

37 The following paragraphs are principally based on reports in LPA, BIV/2/23-13.

38 LPA, IV/5.01/137, SED Erfurt, 'Monatsbericht', 28 March 1953; IV/4.06/095, SED Heiligenstadt, 'Informationsbericht Nr. 1053', 21 March 1953.

39 Cf. H. Weber, *Geschichte der DDR* (Munich, dtv, 1985), p. 232; T. Diedrich, *Der 17. Juni 1953 in der DDR* (Berlin, Dietz, 1991), p. 8.

40 For a summary of these interpretations, cf. A. Mitter, 'Der »Tag X« und die »Innere Staatsgründung der DDR«', in I.-S. Kowalczuk, A. Mitter and S. Wolle (eds), *Der Tag X – 17. Juni 1953*, Forschungen zur DDR-Geschichte, 3 (Berlin, C. Links, 1995), pp. 9–30 (especially pp. 12–13); for the view that 17 June 1953 marked the beginning of the GDR's end, cf. A. Mitter and S. Wolle, *Untergang auf Raten* (Munich, Bertelsmann, 1993), especially p. 551.

41 ThHStAW, MdI/20, 66, police reports, 11–13 June 1953; LPA, IV/4.06/095, 'Informationsbericht', 12 June 1953.

42 See especially A. Baring, *Uprising in East Germany: June 17, 1953* (New York, Cornell University Press, 1972).

43 LPA, BIV/2/4-48, SED Gotha, 'Situationsbericht', 24[?] June 1953; *ibid.*, KPKK Heiligenstadt, 'Gegenwärtige Lage … ', 19 June 1953; ThHStAW, MdI/20, 66, fol. 198, [BdVP], 'Telefonische Durchsage am 16.6.1953'; *ibid.*, fol. 543, 'Auswertung der Ereignisse … ', 29 June 1953.

44 ThHStAW, MdI/20, 66, fols 204–5, BdVP, 'Blitz-Fernschreiben', 17 June 1953; 24[?] and 29 June 1953 reports (note 43).

45 Diedrich, *Der 17. Juni 1953*, pp. 142, 148.

46 ThHStAW, MdI/20, 66, fols 269, 273, 306–9, police reports, 21 and 26 June 1953; LPA, BIV/2/4-48, KPKK Erfurt-Stadt report (untitled), 24 June 1953.

47 ThHStAW, MdI/20, 66, fol. 225, BdVP, 'Blitz-Fernschreiben', 18 June 1953.

48 LPA, BIV/2/9.02-011, 'Situation an den Schulen … ', 20 June 1953; FDGB letter, 18 June 1953; FDJ, 'Informationen … ', 18 June 1953; untitled report [September 1953?], p. 4; BIV/2/4-48, untitled, undated report.

49 29 June 1953 report (note 43), fols 541–2.

50 ThHStAW, OI 108, various reports; LPA, BIV/2/4-48, SED Sondershausen, 'Analyse über die Ereignisse … ', undated [November 1953?].

51 Cf. Diedrich, *Der 17. Juni 1953*, pp. 177–8.

52 29 June 1953 report (note 43), fols 559, 563–4; ThHStAW, MdI/20, 66, fol. 137, BdVP, 'SSD-Fernschreiben', 17 June 1953; OI 109, fol. 39, Weimar-Land report, 24 June 1953.

53 On police methods, see 29 June 1953 report (note 43), passim; ThHStAW, MdI/20, 66, fol. 118, BdVP, 'Einsatzbefehl', 19 June 1953; *ibid.*, fol. 140, 'SSD-BdVP Erfurt Nr. 442', 18 June 153; *ibid.*, fol. 126, KVP Erfurt, 'Standortbefehl Nr. 15/1953', 25 June 1953; fol. 236, BdVP, 'Lagebericht', 19 June 1953.

54 M. Hagen, *DDR – Juni '53* (Stuttgart, Franz Steiner Verlag, 1992), p. 200.

55 29 June 1953 report (note 43), fol. 549.

56 LPA, BIV/2/4-48, SED Erfurt-West, 'Zwischenbericht … ', 22 June 1953; BIV/2/5-066, 'Auswertung des Organisationsberichtes … ', 4 November 1953, p. 6a; November 1953[?] report (note 50).

57 LPA, BIV/2/4-48, SED Erfurt-Mitte, 'Situationsbericht der Parteikontrollkommission Mitte', 23 June 1953.

58 *Ibid.*, SED Erfurt-West, 'Analyse über die Ereignisse … ', 27 October 1953.

59 *Ibid.*, various reports, including KPKK Mühlhausen, 'Auswertung der

Wahlberichtsversammlung', 1 March 1954; SED Weimar-Land, 'Bericht über das Verhalten einiger Genossen … ', 23 June 1953.

60 On this topic see various police reports in ThHStAW, MdI/20, 66.

61 ThHStAW, OI 109, fol. 59, 'Bericht über die Durchführung der Ministerratsbeschlüsse', 15 July 1953; S 547, fols 235-6, NF, 'Informationsbericht Nr. 15/53', 9 July 1953.

62 *Ibid.*, fols 239–43, NF, 'Informationsbericht Nr. 18/53', 31 July 1953; H. Sieber and G. Kubik (eds), *Chronik zur Geschichte der Arbeiterbewegung im Bezirk Erfurt 1952 bis 1961*, Beiträge zur Geschichte Thüringens (Erfurt: SED Bezirksleitung Erfurt/ Bezirkskommission zur Erforschung der Geschichte der örtlichen Arbeiterbewegung, 1979), pp. 37, 43, 84; ThHStAW, S 547, fols 252–4, NF, 'Informationsbericht Nr. 19/53', 15 August 1953.

63 Cf. the title of Mitter's article (note 40).

64 Cf. Hagen, p. 204.

4

Before the Wall

1956: Destalinisation and the Hungarian example

While 1953 clearly marked a serious challenge for the SED, it was one which the party overcame. Life returned to normal fairly quickly, that is, to a combination of generally poor living standards which increasingly fell behind those achieved in West Germany, and outwardly conformist behaviour. Within this context, 1956 merits attention as a year of significant international and ideological tensions. Hesitant destalinisation by the Communist Party of the Soviet Union (CPSU), and the more pragmatic ideological approach introduced at its Twentieth Party Congress in February, created confusion within the SED and encouraged political scepticism and rejection in the population. The prospect that Poland and Hungary might overthrow socialism that autumn, culminating in civil war in Hungary in late October and the Soviet invasion of that country on 4 November, threatened to provoke copycat reactions in the GDR and to undermine SED rule. The party's inability to provide a cogent Marxist analysis of events acutely undermined its claim to ideological leadership. The differing popular reactions to the events of 1956 illustrate how the SED overcame these dangers.

Political attitudes in 1956 were often unsophisticated. The population remained divided into three groups: passionate adherents of the SED; passionate opponents of communism, further embittered by Germany's division; and those, probably a majority, who were concerned principally with their own material welfare. The continuing absence of guaranteed adequate living standards was crucial in determining the year's political outcome.

Even before the CPSU congress began, the SED invited general opposition by creating a National People's Army (NVA).[1] Reactions to this move indicate the degree of political stability the SED had achieved by early 1956. Although loyalists considered the move a justified reaction to West German militarism and NATO's expansion, it was reported that 'in the factories, tractor stations and state farms there are uncertainties and also a striking number of negative and directly dissenting discussions among workers, young people, white-collar workers and in some cases even among members of our party'. Even the NVA's supporters often emphasised the traditional empathies for military training rather than the ideological necessity of defending socialism. The issue revealed true feelings about the GDR: 'In many conversations, lacking faith in the working class's strength [and] insufficient attachment to our workers' and peasants' state were clearly apparent.' This 'insufficient attachment' signified continuing strong desires for German unification. Young people feared having to shoot western relatives, and many foresaw civil war, rather than a war between a socialist and a capitalist state. Pacifism was much in evidence. The NVA's creation quickly shattered the moral strength of the SED's formerly strong anti-militarism, particularly in comparisons which undermined the SED's antifascist legitimacy. For some, it was 'just like Hitler: there'll be conscription and then war'.[2] Many believed: 'The NVA's creation is incompatible with the peaceful unification of our fatherland. There is a contradiction here between the words and deeds of our government.'[3]

Many noted that the new NVA uniforms resembled those of the *Wehrmacht*, Hitler's wartime army, and some feared the reactions from countries which had experienced Nazi occupation. Furthermore, the official claim that NVA uniforms incorporated old German traditions encouraged the oppositional, if logical, response that the old national anthem, the imperialistic *Deutschlandlied*, should also be sung again. The population clearly identified SED coercion when they derided press reports that the NVA was founded to meet the demands of workers, farmers and the intelligentsia.

Young people, the group principally affected, were most vehement in their reaction. Despite their ideological preparation, the SED noted that 'only a small proportion of our youth' was enthusiastic, while most were cautious. Many youths vowed never to enlist voluntarily, and some to emigrate if conscription were introduced. Ex-soldiers' stories of rigorous army discipline dissuaded youngsters still further, as did fears that NVA soldiers might be posted to hotspots where socialist nations seemed threatened. Women, meanwhile, feared they would lose a new generation of menfolk in war.

More practically, given the food shortages, the rural population feared the new army would aggravate the shortage of agricultural workers. Others believed that diverting workers into regiments would reduce supplies of essential goods. The new army's finances dominated many discussions, and a direct link was made to price rises for furniture.

The depth of opposition to this new militarism, similar to that in West Germany against the new Federal Army (*Bundeswehr*), undoubtedly explains why conscription was not introduced until 1962 and suggests domestic limitations to SED hegemony, underlining the party's political and ideological insecurity eleven years after war's end. The SED forfeited much goodwill by allowing the political concerns which provoked the NVA's creation to outweigh antifascist idealism.

However, developments of greater ideological significance quickly overshadowed the issue. After the uneventful SED district delegate conferences in January 1956, where little attention was paid to Marxist theory, the party's ideological strength was tested by the CPSU's Twentieth Party Congress, at which Soviet leaders suggested a more pragmatic line on socialist expansion, emphasised peaceful coexistence with the capitalist world, and publicly distanced themselves from Stalin and the personality cult. Finally Khrushchev, who had emerged as the new paramount Soviet leader, denounced Stalin's methods in a 'secret speech'. After publishing the public details, the SED hesitantly began revising its own Stalinist outlook.

Reflecting the genuine shock at Stalin's death in 1953, many SED comrades were unwilling to denounce him. Many comrades felt that 'Comrade Stalin has not deserved such criticism'. Older members in particular warned they would distance themselves from the party if Stalin were belittled. Some members (and non-members) took Stalin's fall more pragmatically. Having already removed pictures of the Kaiser and Hitler, they enquired whether they should now remove Stalin's pictures and burn his books. More critically, others asked why such problems were not addressed during Stalin's lifetime. Some members drew wider consequences, noting that the whole Central Committee had supported Stalin, and that Ulbricht, too, had made mistakes. Such widespread comments, though dangerous to the SED hierarchy now, at least reflected the success of past party education and older members' genuine political enthusiasm. However, local party leaderships could not embrace the new line or answer members' questions about why the CPSU was only criticising Stalin very generally when other party members were subjected to detailed criticism.[4]

More seriously still, Khrushchev's assertion that there were various ways to socialism, and that a peaceful progression was possible in certain circumstances, was seen by many workers and SED members as legitimation of social democratic viewpoints. Many former social democrats in the SED concluded: 'There we have it, our theory ... was right. Now, after so many years, this path will be possible.'[5] In some areas, SED members discussed little else. These were dangerous signals for communist predominance within the SED, a party within which the fault line between the two founding ideologies (KPD and SPD) was clearly still present. Some, perhaps thinking of Germany, asked which countries could take Khrushchev's suggested parliamentary route to socialism.[6]

Confusion existed among the SED's rank and file and members in key positions alike. For instance, teachers – essential to young people's ideological development – were unclear about the personality cult, the GDR's class structure and whether 'antagonistic contradictions' existed in the GDR.[7] Such confusion was not created, merely exposed and aggravated by the Twentieth Party Congress.[8] The SED had already concluded in early February that despite some teachers' ideological progress, many frequently avoided 'aggressive debates' on political convictions, lacked faith in Germany's 'democratic forces' (the SED and its allies) and did not recognise the 'party's leading role in education questions'.[9] This message was reinforced in June 1956: 'A large proportion of comrade teachers is also encumbered with bourgeois thought ... Many older colleagues have a very hesitant attitude towards our state which is partly expressed in oppositional comments.'[10]

A significant change to communist ideology, the denunciation of Stalin or the admission that social democracy was legitimate were each bound to cause confusion within the SED's ranks and encourage opposition. For all three of these developments to have occurred simultaneously seriously undermined the party, even before the upheavals of November 1956.

During the late spring and summer 1956, by which point the 'secret speech' was well known, criticism and ideological uncertainty grew within the party. Increasingly criticism shifted to the SED's own leadership. Party groups in a Weimar factory were not alone in noting that 'the personality cult expresses itself here [in the GDR] in the emphasis placed on personalities such as Comrade Walter Ulbricht.' 'When will our Central Committee draw the necessary conclusions?', many comrades asked.[11] The contradiction between many members' rejection of Khrushchev's destalinisation and their simultaneous criticism of the SED hierarchy's own hardline approach went unnoticed.

The political and economic problems of 1956 caused the SED problems in expanding its membership. Whereas joining the party seemed advantageous in the initial postwar phase, now some workers felt that 'if a war comes, membership of our party would be disadvantageous', or commented: 'I'd be happy to join the party, but supposing things change? They've imprisoned the communists in West Germany.' Peer pressure also dissuaded some workers from joining the party.[12] Opportunistic reluctance to join the SED grew as the Hungarian crisis deepened in late October and November. Many potential candidates delayed their formal application to await the outcome.[13] Nonetheless, the *Bezirk* Erfurt party gained 5,716 new candidates during 1956, 2,241 of them in the last quarter.[14]

Despite their serious indictments of party practice, most SED members felt restrained by ingrained party discipline and the absence of political alternatives. The witch hunts of the early 1950s inhibited any thought of re-establishing a separate SPD. Paradoxically, members' concentration on pressing economic problems partially benefited the party: given the 'wealth of uncertainties about ideological questions in many of our party's basic organisations',[15] economic discussions were preferable to ideological debates which might have rent the party asunder following the CPSU's Twentieth Party Congress. Party work in the localities continued normally, and organisational rather than ideological problems dominated functionaries' agendas by May 1956.

In the wider population, too, attention was diverted from the communist movement's internal difficulties by more pressing concerns. Margarine, meat, marmalade and many other essentials were in very short supply and dominated discussions. Others wondered how a seven-hour day could be introduced when sausages were so expensive, or focused on housing difficulties and higher prices for work clothes. Price cuts in June further distracted attention from high politics. Although these were generally welcomed, many feared they would be short lived and demanded that the cuts be extended to food prices. Cynicism was widespread. Workers in particular demanded that their (workers') government should 'concentrate more on everyday items'.[16]

Other discussions centred on local matters, often to the exclusion of wider political issues. The key topic in Heiligenstadt schools by June 1956 was the

Catholic church's role, while village meetings discussed road-building and similar local improvements rather than the NVA and Khrushchev. Interest in ideological problems was also overshadowed when West Germany introduced conscription in May 1956, a more tangible issue which attracted general condemnation.[17]

Thus, ongoing concern about material conditions, combined with ideological insecurity and some criticism of the SED hierarchy over the NVA and Khrushchev's innovations, were the backdrop for reactions to the events in Poland and Hungary. The first major development – the Poznan uprising of 28 June – essentially resulted from Poles' frustration at inadequate wages and food supplies.[18] Immediate comparisons with 17 June 1953 were drawn in the GDR. There was widespread acceptance that Poles should protest at their poverty, and no credence for official explanations of imperialist provocations. However the subtext was that Thuringians considered themselves rather better off than 'backward' Poland. Thus there was no attempt at a copycat revolt which would have suggested Germans were no better than Poles. There are few indications that the population drew conclusions for the GDR at this juncture. Only farmers, often the first to wish the GDR's downfall, were reported as seeing the possible consequences for the GDR. Some drank to the Polish disturbances, and one commented: 'Now things are simmering everywhere and soon an end will be put to socialism.'[19]

Not until late October, when Władysław Gomułka was reinstalled as Polish party leader, did public opinion seriously concern itself with Poland and Hungary again.[20] On 22 October the SED expected reactions to an article on Poland in the previous day's *Neues Deutschland* (*ND*), the workers' party's official mouthpiece. However, reactions were slow: embarrassingly, it appeared that '*ND* is read very little among workers.'[21] Instead, western radio reports, wild rumours and speculation quickly spread from 23 October onwards. Warsaw was apparently occupied by Russian tanks; there had been disturbances in two GDR cities, Magdeburg and Halle; Poland would break with the USSR; thousands of Hungarian students had left the party to form their own organisation.[22] The Hungarian uprising, the subsequent withdrawal of Soviet troops from Hungary, rioting in that country and the ensuing Soviet invasion understandably fuelled these discussions. To what extent did East Germans question SED rule, the GDR as a separate state and socialism itself? In other words, to what extent did popular reactions to events in Poland and Hungary threaten SED rule, and why did this threat not cause the system to collapse in 1956?

Initial reactions were confused. Speculation centred on the causes of the Polish upheavals and was based on western radio reports rather than the unread *ND* article. In many factories 'workers are clear that the consequences of the personality cult can't be removed with a Central Committee resolution.' Some concluded that the problems resulted from the expulsion of Germans from Poland in 1945, and hoped that the old German-Polish border might be reinstated. However, on 22 October many still paid greater attention to the sugar shortage, and few political consequences were drawn from the Polish developments. One reporter depressingly concluded: 'In general we can say that apart from the continual discussions and disputes about production questions, material difficulties, housing problems and supply questions, the situation in the factories is normal.'[23]

Nonetheless, as tension mounted in Poland and particularly Hungary, political themes acquired greater currency. The SED's ideological authority was quickly challenged from two directions in late October. Some SED members could not comprehend that the Polish party leader, Gomułka, had been rehabilitated despite being removed from his posts and imprisoned in Stalin's last years, but other workers welcomed Poland's resistance to Soviet dictates and concluded 'it's time the same happened here'.[24]

Despite these ideological inconsistencies, a significant number of workers and many SED members quickly realised the potential dangers to socialism and rallied round, offering armed support if necessary. Although some acknowledged previous mistakes, or criticised the SED's portrayal of socialist construction as a 'pure victory march', they insisted workers did not want a return to capitalism. Some retained their idealism and hoped to reform socialism, as seemed to be happening in Hungary. Thus, eleven years after Hitler's defeat there remained many committed socialists who refused to abandon their achievements and risk merging with the monopoly capitalist, neo-fascist system they perceived to exist in West Germany. The danger that Hungarian fascism might return if communism there were overthrown strengthened the perception of general danger.[25]

Those who held the levers of power also took concrete steps to preserve the system. From 19 October the Erfurt police radio room was constantly staffed; rapid reaction forces were on permanent standby in all districts after 26 October.[26] Preparations were made to alert the working-class militias, the so-called *Kampfgruppen*, and supply them with guns, even though some groups lacked adequate training. Some *Kampfgruppen* commanders seemed only too eager to prepare for real action. Despite private doubts among many CDU members and the party's Heiligenstadt leadership, and 'negative tendencies' among LDPD members,[27] publicly the bloc parties also demonstrated their loyalty to the SED.[28]

However, ideological confusion within the SED itself quickly grew.[29] Some comrades could not understand that the Hungarian People's Army had supported the demonstrators in apparent defiance of the Marxist laws of history. Some comrades' belief that Poland was taking a 'special road to socialism' threatened the SED's insistence on subservience to the CPSU line rather than formulating a 'German road'. By late October some members reportedly believed the leadership was not building socialism correctly, and expected the Central Committee to be replaced by a group around Wilhelm Zaisser and Rudolf Herrnstadt, Ulbricht's principal internal opponents in 1953. Even various local party secretaries openly called for Ulbricht's removal.

The political troubles in Poland and Hungary focused complaints about the GDR's poor living standards. With socialism under attack in both those countries for failing to guarantee reasonable conditions, East Germans felt entitled to join in.

According to one report: 'In connection with the developments in Poland and Hungary there are still exhaustive discussions about supply and wage questions here in the GDR ... ' A Weimar shop assistant remarked: 'In socialism it is worse than capitalism, at least we could buy things then. Today there's no eggs, butter, milk and so on.'

By early November panic buying was underway. Goods were hoarded and savings accounts emptied as the international situation worsened. In some areas, customers provocatively asked for unavailable goods in order to complain. Many ordinary people warned that the Hungarian uprising would be repeated in the GDR if things did not improve. As the crisis deepened, some perceived a relationship between high food prices and the cost of the 'bloated administration' run by the parties, mass organisations and state. Many also feared that the likely imminent abolition of ration cards would mean shortages and price rises.

Linked to concerns about living standards were frequent comparisons between the Polish crisis (where work quotas had partly inflamed the masses) and the GDR's situation before 17 June 1953. In part they represented a warning that an uprising had already occurred once in the GDR and could happen again. The vocabulary of 1953 was intoned, as in Bad Langensalza where students began predicting a 'new course in the whole socialist camp', though with no conception of what this might mean. Many openly wondered why no lessons had been learned from 17 June. Conversely, 1953 was also cited by many rank and file comrades who believed the official explanations of capitalist provocations and again perceived a need to defend socialism. Equally, popular memories of the suppression undoubtedly militated against serious rebellion.

Beyond general unrest, there were many examples of oppositional activity during the crisis period, including isolated calls for strikes like those in Hungary and Poland, and a campaign of disruption in the Jena Zeiss works. Threats against SED members and functionaries proliferated and were encouraged in late October and early November by highly exaggerated reports that many Hungarian communist officials had been murdered. Thus the party secretary of an Arnstadt retail outlet, on refusing to buy a second round of drinks after work, was told: 'Just wait, you bigwigs, you'll soon get the same treatment as them in Hungary.' Elsewhere workers were heard discussing who would be hanged from which tree, or threatening that all SED members would be killed. Some threats came from known former Nazi activists, one of whom commented: 'We haven't forgotten what you did to us in 1945. Soon our time will come.' In Weimar, a window in the SED headquarters was broken, and in December an explosion was reported in the party newspaper's Heiligenstadt office. There were many other minor incidents, but a comparison of daily police reports of November and December 1956 with the comparable period in 1955 shows that they were not significantly more numerous or more serious.[30]

Understandably many SED functionaries were worried by the threats against them. Some were said to be 'helpless', and many, worried by reports from Hungary, asked: 'Is there no help for the working-class functionaries, must they all be slaughtered like that?' Some complained both that Soviet troops were withdrawn from Hungary before the situation stabilised, and that the GDR's media had reported a restoration of order when the opposite was true. Many SED members doubted Hungary's survival as a people's democracy and refused to answer critics of the GDR's government, adopting 'wait and see' attitudes. This tendency reflected either fear of reprisals if SED rule collapsed or a serious lack of faith in socialism. Others, no doubt desperate to preserve their positions, called for Soviet intervention in Hungary to maintain the status quo. These comrades criticised the eventual Soviet invasion of Hungary on 4 November only for coming so late.

The Red Army's actions in Hungary were decisive in shaping GDR opinion and raised the question of intervention by one socialist country in another's affairs. Even before the invasion there were complaints at Soviet interference. Thus a Heiligenstadt student asked why the Russians were intervening in Hungary, and added: 'The Russians should leave the GDR as well.' The situation became more acute after Britain and France attempted to defend the Suez Canal on 31 October. The SED's attempts to distinguish imperialist intervention in Egypt from fraternal assistance to defend socialism in Hungary predictably undermined the party's ideological position still further. Similarly, some noted the contradiction between official support for the Algerian 'uprising' and condemnation of the Hungarian 'putsch'.

Reactions to the eventual invasion were mixed. Some, convinced that socialism and their own positions must be protected, welcomed the move. Most, however, felt it was at best an unnecessary overreaction, at worst an illegal act. In isolated incidents, young people responded by leaving the German-Soviet Friendship Society or, as in Weimar, demanding the dismantling of the Stalin memorial. Workers in one factory agreed that the USSR had 'raped' Hungary. Elsewhere workers believed that 'the Russians can only keep and suppress these countries by force.'

Though the invasion ended the immediate Hungarian problem, it did not resolve the ideological uncertainty felt by many SED members; instead, serious weaknesses within the party came to light. When the mayor of Heuthen asked if members supported their party as much as in 1951–52, they unanimously replied 'No!', and complained 'the party does not represent working-class interests'. Many reports noted a 'certain confusion [Wirrwarr] among many comrades'. In Worbis district, party educators (theoretically the most loyal comrades) often admitted to doubts caused by western broadcasts they should not have heard. Members' meetings produced 'many debates about ideological uncertainties, misconceptions, etc. … the western broadcasters' arguments sometimes stick and comrades do not always adopt an appropriate class-based standpoint.' Added sources of confusion were the strong French Communist Party's failure to prevent French intervention over Suez, and the role of Hungary's prime minister János Kádár, presented as the Hungarian Communist Party's grave-digger and saviour within one week.

Many comrades attempted to mask uncertainties about Hungary by instead condemning Britain, France and Israel for invading Egypt, a less controversial issue. Attendance at membership meetings rose, dramatically in some cases, presumably because SED members perceived a need to achieve clarity in ideological issues or an opportunity to protest while the leadership was weakened. Although pre-1933 KPD members remained particularly loyal, they were by now a minority within the party, and their loyalty was offset by the fact that 'a large number of the party organisations are riven by personal disagreements and disunity amongst the comrades … In a few cases there are still comrades who belonged to the SPD before 1933 and retain a negative attitude to comrades who formerly belonged to the KPD.'[31]

Nor did the Soviet invasion of Hungary bring an end to threats of violence in the GDR. One comrade had never been so afraid, 'not even on 17 June', and Gebesee school children threatened to 'throw the mayor out of the window if things don't change'. Some SED members remained worried that Soviet troops might yet withdraw from the GDR, exposing them to the same retaliation their Hungarian comrades had suffered.

Apart from exposing the SED's fragility as a mass party, the crisis revealed signs that passive acceptance of the GDR system was completely breaking down in some quarters. Farmers were, as ever, prominent in this trend, taking the opportunity to call again for a free economy and an end to the detailed cultivation plans imposed on individual farms. Co-operative farmers, many of whom wished to re-establish their private smallholdings, felt they could be less conscientious in their work by 29 October because the Hungarian situation would spread to the GDR. On 1 November Ballstedt farmers decided to withhold food deliveries 'because the regime here can't last much longer'. By 3 November, various Worbis farmers refused to deliver food and advised each other not to sign new contracts with the state-sponsored Machine Tractor Stations until the international situation was clearer. When some farmers deliberately neglected the potato harvest, the effects were quickly felt in the shops. Although the Hungarian uprising was crushed, farmers remained militant weeks after 4 November, and refused to adopt cultivation plans in many villages (forty in Nordhausen district alone). Many remained confident that 'things will soon change'.

The potential long-term effects of the crisis were also visible in schools and colleges. Teachers, on whom the party depended to transmit ideological certainty to younger generations, particularly concerned the SED. The 'ideological-political situation' at schools, and particularly high schools, was 'very weak' in mid-1956. Teachers shared the same doubts and uncertainties as the rest of the population, and also relied principally on western radio for information, even to prepare current affairs classes.[32] The Worbis party executive quickly concluded that teachers and lecturers lacked the 'ideological strength to cope with the discussions'. Other districts reached similar conclusions after the Hungarian invasion. Even staff in the Sondershausen education department and the head of the town's high school, a long-standing SED member, harboured uncertainties and 'failed to support their staff'.[33] Though the specific problems of 1956 are not cited in official reports as reasons, *Republikflucht* ('fleeing the republic') was a serious problem in education. Two hundred and three *Bezirk* Erfurt teachers left the GDR between 1 January 1956 and 31 January 1957.[34] Clearly, education was not yet in reliable hands, despite the SED's strenuous attempts to recruit and train loyal teachers.

Pupils and students also demanded the party's special attention.[35] As early as 1 November, medical students voted 120 to 7 to demand an end to compulsory Russian classes. School children around the region also rejected Russian lessons. After all, some argued, 'in Hungary the Russian books were burned as well.' Parents demanded that English should replace Russian, and Russian teachers reported discipline problems. Of greater concern to the authorities were demands for an independent students' organisation to break the official FDJ's monopoly, and such isolated incidents as a sixth form's demands that flags be flown at half mast to mark the October revolution's anniversary. Young people displayed particular resistance to making donations for Hungary, while one teacher who made 'positive comments' about Hungary was pelted with gym shoes. Elsewhere children commented that SED meant 'So endet Deutschland' ('That's the end of Germany'). Clearly young people were prepared to embarrass or protest against the state and party, and represented a vent for the opinions their parents expressed in the privacy of their homes and/or the opinions of the western radio commentaries they heard there. For instance, some young people's open opposition could easily be traced to parents with fascist pasts. The SED considered that farmers and young people were the groups of greatest concern for longest after the crisis subsided.

Despite all the SED's anxieties, normality quickly resumed, SED rule was not seriously challenged and the system did not collapse. Though everyday problems remained, they were not greatly aggravated by the year's crises. The thousands who continued to 'flee the republic' did so principally for personal or economic reasons. The authorities did not record that Hungary and Poland or dissatisfaction over the NVA or destalinisation were particular causes; the total of those who left the GDR between January and August 1956 was, in fact, lower than in the equivalent period in 1955.[36] Nor were specific links made between these problems and the expulsion of 2,007 SED members from the party during 1956, considerably fewer than in 1955 and mainly not for ideological differences. More than half had already left the GDR, while many others had committed crimes or indulged in 'immoral behaviour'.[37] Even preparations for the *Jugendweihe* – the socialist coming-of-age ceremony (discussed in Chapter 5) – seemed undisturbed by the wider crisis during November 1956, with participation rates significantly higher than in 1955.[38] Normal life continued despite the unusually disruptive international framework.

Why was the crisis not far more damaging to SED rule? First, the party's inability to present a waterproof ideological explanation for the events of October and November 1956, though much discussed, was of secondary importance to the population's everyday concerns. Many workers were more interested in discussing their own factory's problems than arcane ideological disputes, and believed short-

comings could be overcome if functionaries acted on workers' complaints and suggestions. Essentially, these complaints were no worse in 1956 than in previous years
and, with the exception of some farmers, most people realised only greater effort
would resolve practical problems. Thus, the Hungarian crisis was not the sole topic
of discussion. Though these external problems were discussed at the meetings coin-
cidentally held during this period to elect new local union executives, the fourteen-
page SED report on these meetings mentions discussions of Hungary and Poland
only once, briefly. Workers used these occasions primarily to discuss factory issues
and grievances.[39] Within days of the invasion, discussion predominantly returned
to the severe winter food shortages. In some areas, the SED had trouble engaging
its members in any political discussions.[40]

Second, the Soviet invasion of Hungary was largely offset by the Suez Crisis,
an issue on which the population identified with the SED's standpoint and which
attracted general condemnation. The widespread fear that world war would begin
over Hungary and/or the Suez Crisis also (perhaps subconsciously) discouraged
further destabilising behaviour. By late November there was a 'depressed atmosphere among large parts of the population due to the overall political situation' and
a 'certain tension' linked to the fear of war. Some wondered if Christmas, only a
month away, would be spent at peace.[41]

Third, most ordinary people were very guarded in their public comments and
awaited the outcome of events before committing themselves. This attitude was
understandable given the experience of 17 June 1953 and its reinforcement by the
Soviet invasion of Hungary after 4 November 1956, though reports rarely record
such thoughts being expressed so directly. The Soviet presence in the GDR was still
very evident, the MfS's efficiency and profile was higher than in 1953, and the state's
administrative structures were much stronger. All these factors militated against all
but isolated attempts at serious resistance and made the emergence of opposition
leaders practically impossible. The few recorded strike calls or specific demands (for
an end to communism, Russian departure, new government, higher living standards, a united, free Germany) were found on placards posted on walls, not proclaimed at public meetings.[42]

Although peace prevailed, there were some serious consequences. The GDR's
media were highly discredited, for they had carried contradictory reports, suggested
that Hungary was quiet at the height of the revolutionary unrest, and been consistently behind with the news. Suspicions grew that Moscow censored the GDR's
news. Practically everyone, including SED members, listened to West German
radio or the 'neutral' Austrian and Swiss stations. From the 'secret speech' to the
Soviet occupation of Budapest, 1956 established the western media as essential
information sources in a crisis. Television, which was to fuel the 1989 revolution,
was barely available in 1956, so that West German pictures of the Hungarian riots
and bloodshed were not widely seen, although when there were they excited discussions, and complaints that GDR television had broadcast nothing comparable.[43]

The year 1956 also seriously undermined much of the optimism and faith in socialism. For many – whether party members or not – the lasting perception was that 'the events in Poland and Hungary prove there's something wrong in the socialist system.'[44] After the Hungarian rebellion was crushed, the SED dispatched its loyal supporters, often those with strong antifascist credentials and not necessarily party members, to shame doubters in the most oppositional factories and offices into submission. One reporter noted: 'This mass appearance of class-conscious workers found a very good reception in the whole factory, so that the negative elements crawled into their mouseholes.'[45] However, these 'negative elements' remained within the 'mouseholes' of society to argue their case another day. The SED had not won the argument, merely temporarily silenced it.

1960: 'Socialist springtime in agriculture'

The events of 1956 demonstrated how the GDR's population reacted to a period of major international and ideological crisis. The year 1960 brought upheavals of a similar significance in domestic policy with the final phase of agricultural collectivisation, forced through in March–April 1960. Popular reactions to this development illustrate patterns of conformity and opposition to SED rule, as collectivisation was an issue which directly affected most of the rural population. This was essentially a matter of direct local and personal significance, rather than a reaction to events in distant Berlin, Moscow or Budapest.

The overwhelming resistance of farmers and rural workers to socialism, their general refusal to join the KPD and fears of losing their land under communism in the late 1940s, and their withholding of food deliveries in October–November 1956, largely explain the SED's wish to neutralise the political disruption of this essential group of workers. The collectivisation of agriculture through the creation of co-operative farms was, therefore, one of a series of attempts to consolidate and stabilise SED rule.[46]

The first agricultural co-operatives (LPGs) were founded after the SED's Second Party Conference in 1952, but the movement developed relatively slowly during the 1950s. Only 37 per cent of the GDR's agricultural land was collectively farmed by December 1958, and 43.5 per cent by November 1959. *Bezirk* Erfurt, where independent farmers dominated, was significantly below average with comparable figures of only 17.7 and 33.4 per cent respectively.[47] That month the SED's Central Committee resolved to socialise agriculture quickly. Simultaneously the first entirely 'collective *Kreis*' was created and a campaign began to emulate this example around the country.

The Central Committee directed that all forces should be mobilised and collectivisation completed by almost any means. At *Bezirk* level, the SED, the DBD, Democratic Bloc, NF, CDU, FDGB, regional council and regional parliament all met to discuss ways of supporting the campaign, though at *Kreis* level the issue was sometimes dismissed as an 'SED matter', particularly by the CDU and local councils.[48] By 3 April 1960 the *Bezirk* was declared *vollgenossenschaftlich* ('entirely collectivised'), although a few farmers still tenaciously defended their independence. On paper at least, the speedy increase from 33.4 per cent to 85 per cent of agricultural land under collectivisation represented an enormous achievement.[49] But what obstacles had been overcome, and what real success was achieved in the following months?

The low figures achieved before 1960 clearly demonstrated that unusual measures were necessary to introduce socialism to the countryside. Simply sending 'leading comrades' from the *Bezirk* level to key localities did not achieve a 'break-through' in 1957 or in the following two years.[50] This was partly because the issue had not been tackled earlier. Full collectivisation would have been extremely unpopular in 1945, and was not attempted for numerous reasons (not least the Soviets' initial reluctance to endanger German unity), but it might have been accepted had it been presented as a political measure engendered by wartime defeat, alongside deindustrialisation and asset stripping. By the late 1950s, however, the population was less willing to accept such measures as the price of Nazism in a state which boasted full sovereignty. More importantly, many 'new farmers', former farm workers or settlers from the lost eastern provinces who had been given farms during the land reform of 1945–46, were now well established and insisted 'we … have no intention of being farm hands again'. Even 'new farmers' in the SED were 'developing into strong medium size farmers and resisting entering LPGs or forming new ones'.[51]

The SED's regional executive often received little practical support from the district party organisations, who sometimes only began campaigning for collectivisation once *Bezirk* staff arrived, or from the local party groups, which often lacked a 'common viewpoint' about socialising agriculture. Even 'agitators' for socialist agriculture dispatched from regional party headquarters were not wholly reliable, and some resisted duties in 'unfavourable' areas such as Catholic Heiligenstadt. Where the teams did appear, they often met resistance. Sometimes, farmers' relatives arrived from miles around to help resist collectivisation propaganda. Elsewhere, children insulted and hit LPG farmers' children, and farmers considering forming a new LPG were warned they would be 'pointed at',[52] a serious threat of ostracism in small communities. Elsewhere, farmers simply refused to talk to functionaries because they were 'allegedly too involved in agricultural work'.[53] Furthermore, many ordinary workers failed to support the SED as they often held small parcels of land which they were unwilling to surrender. Some workers supported independent farmers by helping them in their free time. Even the communal machine and tractor hire stations (MTS), designed as key SED supports in the countryside, lacked the requisite 'fighting spirit', and their functionaries could see no 'personal perspective'.[54]

The SED's problems were acute in the Eichsfeld districts, where pre-1960 plans foresaw a much slower development. In Heiligenstadt district, LPGs farmed only 10.5 per cent of agricultural land in January 1958. This figure was expected to rise to only 40 per cent by 1960. In practice, despite progress during 1958, LPGs controlled only 23.8 per cent of the district's land by July 1959. Where LPGs did exist, they often lacked SED members, so that the party was unable to exert the 'leading role'. Instead, 'the LPGs consist mainly of members of petty bourgeois parties'.[55]

The SED's weakness in the rural Eichsfeld was not confined to the LPGs. SED inspectors visiting Mühlhausen district in late 1959 concluded that 'the party organisations are not yet up to their tasks' and that in many areas 'the party's leading role is not secured'. Equally, many local blocs had not met for years and in practice many of the Associations for Mutual Farmers' Assistance (VdgB) – which existed mainly to encourage collectivisation – consistently opposed such further socialisation. Local state structures were also heavily criticised, not least Mühlhausen district council for its poor personnel policies. Some local council staff were 'neither able nor willing to implement the party's and government's decisions'. As an example of the unfavourable rural conditions just six months before collectivisation was completed, the brigade noted that in Großengottern the VdgB chairman was an ex-SS member who had served in Buchenwald, the CDU mayor was an NSDAP member from 1933 to 1945 and had served in Hitler's notorious *Waffen-SS*, and a leading local SED member had also been an NSDAP member and worked in the mayor's office under the Third Reich. The methods of local SED functionaries in their attempts to encourage LPG expansion often encouraged resistance. In Zella, for instance, the mayor threatened to sack the local kindergarten teacher unless her brother, the village CDU leader, joined the LPG. Corrupt comrades in some local administrations further complicated the situation.[56]

A similar situation existed in Heiligenstadt district, where local forces opposing collectivisation were so strong that even the SED instructors from the *Bezirk* level could not 'isolate and completely unmask' opponents in some villages. The campaign clearly demonstrated the district party's weaknesses. For instance, the 'strengthening brigades' sent to help new LPGs made little impact. However, as the district secretary reminded his *Bezirk* superiors, the entire SED organisation in Heiligenstadt district had fewer members than the party group in a single car plant in Eisenach. The *Bezirk* brigades met with similarly 'strong rudiments of bourgeois consciousness' in Worbis district and achieved little during January 1960. Clearly, significantly greater efforts were required.[57]

Farmers' reactions to the LPG campaign were quickly established during January 1960 once the major collectivisation drive began, and the same arguments were repeated throughout the campaign.[58] Typically, financially secure independent farmers resisted collectivisation because they feared they would earn less and have to work harder in LPGs. Many insisted they would never join voluntarily. In some cases farmers determined to resist for as long as possible, as 'things might change'. Their optimism lay in the continuing belief that socialism and the GDR might quickly collapse. Such thoughts were fuelled by speculation about the forthcoming Paris summit meeting in May. If this ended the division of Germany, or even if the Soviets swapped parts of Thuringia for West Berlin – as many farmers speculated – collectivisation could be avoided. Sometimes farmers openly doubted the wisdom of socialist economics in comments such as: 'The capitalist states have achieved world standards without co-operatives and without large field cultivation.'

Some farmers tried blackmail by making entry into an LPG dependent on their family retaining three acres for personal use, or receiving high guaranteed wages and full compensation for their land and livestock. Others had personal reasons for refusing to comply with measures perceived as imported from or imposed by the Soviet Union, such as a Großwelsbach farmer who remembered that the 'Russians had taken everything from him in 1945 and were not his friends', or the Oettern VdgB chairman whose wife had been taken by the Russians. There were more isolated examples of open opposition, such as the anonymous letter threatening the Apolda district council chairman with hanging if he co-operated with collectivisation, a warning reminiscent of the tactics of 1956.

As January brought relatively little progress, propaganda work increased during February. For instance, loudspeaker cars supported by teams of agitators toured the Erfurt area spreading propaganda and broadcasting individual farmers' opinions. In Nordhausen district alone, 1,317 agitators were operating by 7 February. However, many independent farmers, including some SED members, simply locked their doors and refused to discuss LPGs with the activist brigades, who were often denied accommodation in their target villages. Farmers avoided public meetings and those who did attend mainly did not join in discussion. In some villages, even parish councillors refused to attend meetings where the socialisation of agriculture appeared on the agenda. Some threatened to resign or commented that 'the GDR can go down the plughole, but I'm not joining the LPG,' reinforcing the view that SED control over local state structures was still far from total. Similarly, a Trebra parish councillor said he had been elected to prevent collectivisation, and the Jützenbach DBD chairman disloyally told farmers to throw agricultural commissions off their land 'because your land is your private property'.[59]

Anti-LPG sentiment among the most resistant seemed to increase proportionally to the SED's persuasion tactics. Thus a Mülverstedt farmer declared: 'Better to be carried out dead from the farm than join the LPG. Things may change. We're simply being forced into the LPGs, they're just trapping us.' However, by provoking such sharp reactions the SED's brigades were able to 'unmask' apparently reactionary forces, isolate them from the rest of their community, and thereby create moral pressure to join an LPG as a sign of good faith.

Despite activists' increasing efforts between January and mid-March, success remained elusive. For instance, though six hundred comrades and industrial workers were spread around fifty-seven communities in Weimar district, they recruited only forty-nine new LPG members by 8 February; only 1 per cent of agricultural land was collectivised in Mühlhausen district between 1 January and 20 February 1960. On 19 March only 39.8 per cent of the *Bezirk*'s agricultural land was under LPG control, an increase of just 1 per cent since 1 March. While Bad Langensalza district (57.2 per cent) was particularly successful, Heiligenstadt, Eisenach and Worbis districts languished at 27.5, 19.3 and 17.8 per cent respectively.[60]

The SED now initiated perhaps the most intensive campaign ever mounted outside election and referendum periods. On 21 March, 3,818 functionaries and workers were enrolled in the *Bezirk*'s agitation brigades; by 25 March there were 5,398, and the figure peaked the following day at 9,724, before receding to 1,729 on 2 April. By this point the collectivisation programme was essentially complete, and these staff were busy training the new LPG chairmen and treasurers. There was a clear correlation between the size of the brigades employed and the number of hectares collectivised, with 16.9 per cent of the *Bezirk*'s agricultural land collectivised between 26 and 28 March alone. At the height of the campaign, staff were drawn from various regional council departments, firms, authorities, the SED, the mass organisations and the other parties.[61]

From mid-March these brigades no longer took 'no' for an answer, despite many farmers' insistence that they wanted to harvest independently once more before joining a collective, an attempt to play for time in case the international situation changed. Some farmers admitted defeat once the large activist brigades arrived in mid-March. Many were persuaded of the severe financial disincentives of remaining independent in talks over the farmhouse kitchen table. In other cases coercion and force were necessary. Though specific mentions of this are rare, occasional references suggest this was a significant factor in achieving full collectivisation by 1 April. Thus, one farmer who refused to join an LPG was given a six months' suspended sentence, and the *Stasi* became involved when a Buttstädt farmer issued a fifteen-point plan, including mainly economic demands. The *Stasi* forced the local farmers to reject this plan, and also intervened in cases where farmers insulted brigade members.

Particular efforts were required in the Eichsfeld and especially the border zones, whither strengthened teams were dispatched in late March. As late as 28 March the frustrated Heiligenstadt district SED chairman could merely report that discussions were underway, and that Eichsfeld farmers were asking questions which had been resolved elsewhere years earlier: 'They're asking questions which we cleared up in Weimar district in 1953 in connection with 17 June. They're bringing up questions about democracy linked to the Hungarian events of 1956 and similar rubbish. It's as though we'd never discussed these questions with them or explained them to them.'[62] On 31 March all district council chairmen in the region were told to drop all other work and leave for Heiligenstadt district with 'two of their best comrades', to ensure the *Bezirk* was fully collectivised by the following morning.[63]

Although the *Bezirk* was proclaimed 'fully collectivised' on 1 April in time for a prearranged celebratory 'popular festival' on 2–3 April,[64] problems with individual farmers were still reported on 6 April. In some areas LPGs were founded on paper, even though they would not begin collective farming until the autumn. No 'hostile activity' was reported in the first days following the campaign's completion, but isolated oppositional incidents were noted, as in Struth where the new collective farmers ironically suggested their LPG be named 'Freedom' or '1st April'.[65]

Many problems remained even after the campaign was completed on paper. A special regional council meeting addressed the new LPGs' weakness on 13 April and concluded that all state functionaries, in all departments, should acquire a minimum knowledge of agriculture to support the co-operatives. Officials from older LPGs and state farms were co-opted to the new co-operatives.[66] However, co-operation between the various parties and organisations remained 'inadequate' in the localities.[67]

By the autumn, difficulties were still very apparent in the LPGs. Many co-operative farmers had not yet accepted their new status, resisted the calls to merge LPGs and disregard old farm and field boundaries, and hoped sabotage might yet reverse events. They told one another: 'Don't work so fast, the LPGs will collapse anyway.' Many felt bitter that the co-operatives had been forced upon them. In some LPGs, co-operative work did not begin, as in Herda where farmers simply ignored the LPG chairman's instructions. In some cases, LPG farmers withdrew from the co-operatives during the autumn and the following spring and summer. Various comrades in rural SED groups also still doubted the potential of socialist agriculture.[68]

More than a year after the LPGs were founded, the situation remained unstable. Slightly fewer than half the LPGs had SED groups to uphold the party line (and not all of these were necessarily reliable),[69] and there were still reports of LPG chairmen resigning and of members threatening to resign. In the Herda LPG alone, twenty-seven members threatened to withdraw during June 1961, though all but one was persuaded to stay. The problems often resulted from dictatorial management, but managers were also under pressure. The seven resigning LPG chairmen in Worbis district all blamed overwork, but the SED noted that in three of these LPGs there was no 'normal co-operative work'. Similar problems existed in the market gardening co-operatives (GPGs) in the Erfurt city area, where thirty-eight members issued withdrawal declarations during late June 1961. The local SED felt this reflected 'a lack of political certainty about the issue of a peace treaty with Germany and the prospects of the GPGs'.[70]

In some areas there were still signs of deliberate attempts to break up the LPGs during early 1961, particularly among farmers with close contacts to the Catholic church. There was evidence, for example, of sabotage in the Dingelstädt MTS station. The *Stasi* reviewed the situation closely,[71] and also tried to take the initiative by suggesting 'public trials' against politically vulnerable LPG farmers who had allegedly sabotaged co-operative work. The subject of one such trial was a farmer who, as an SS member, had killed Jews during the Warsaw Ghetto uprising, had attempted to 'flee the republic' and maintained links to the west. Such an individual was not surprisingly opposed to SED policies. The *Stasi* stated the political aims of the proposed public trial: 'the proof should be given that former fascist elements, influenced by West German broadcasters and revanchist organisations, are trying to hinder the development of the GDR's cattle industry ...'[72]

In other words, anyone who opposed collectivisation could be branded a fascist. In a similar fashion to 1956, the SED had not won the argument, but merely forced through its policies against massive popular opposition. In 1960, the success in agriculture was administrative, not political. Though farmers grew used to LPGs after the Berlin Wall was built, attempts to further socialise agriculture within the LPG framework met with continued resistance during the 1960s.

Collectivisation in the countryside was as important to rural communities as the Hungarian crisis of 1956 or the Berlin Wall's construction in 1961 were for the wider population. Yet neither agricultural collectivisation nor the Wall brought an immediate change in popular attitudes. In the longer term, there was a surprising degree of continuity in popular responses to SED rule in town and country alike. These issues are the focus of Chapter 6.

Notes

1 These paragraphs are based on reports in LPA, BIV/2/5-025.
2 *Ibid.*, 'Kurzinformation Nr. 2/56', 20 January 1956, pp. 1–3.
3 *Ibid.*, 'Kurzinformation Nr. 6/56', 8 February, p. 4.
4 *Ibid.*, 'Kurzinformation' reports, February–March 1956.
5 *Ibid.*, 23 February report, p. 2.
6 *Ibid.*, 18 February 1956 report, pp. 3–4.
7 ThHStAW, V 34, fol. 49, 'Informationsbericht … ', 3 March 1956, p. 1.
8 Many ideological problems of 1956 were apparent in 1955: cf. ThHStAW, Vs/St 656, fols 87–96v, 'Einschätzung der Lage in der Partei … ', undated [mid-1955].
9 LPA, BIV/2/5-025, 'Die Lage in der Intelligenz', 3 February 1956, p. 7.
10 LPA, BIV/2/5-026, 'Informatorischer Bericht über die Lage an den Hoch-, Ober- und Fachschulen … ', 16 June 1956.
11 *Ibid.*, 'Informationsnotizen', 3 August 1956, pp. 3–4.
12 *Ibid.*, 'Stand der Realisierung des Beschlusses … ', undated, pp. 5–6.
13 LPA, BIV/2/5-027, 'Bericht über die Durchführung des Beschlusses des ZK [Zentralkomitee] … ', 28 November 1956, p. 7.
14 LPA, BIV/2/5-066, 'Analyse über die Mitgliederbewegung im Jahre 1956', undated, p. 3.
15 LPA, BIV/2/5-026, 'Wie entwickelt sich die schöpferische Aktivität … ?', 24 September 1956, pp. 6–7.
16 LPA, BIV/2/5-050, 'Bericht über die Stimmung … ', 29 March 1956, p. 3; BIV/2/5-026, 'Kurzinformation Nr. 27/56', 5 June 1956; 3 August report (note 11), p. 5.
17 LPA, IV/4.06/131, SED Heiligenstadt, 'Einschätzung der Lage an der Oberschule', 12 June 1956; BIV/2/5-026, 'Kurzinformation Nr. 30/56', 9 July 1956.
18 T.V. Atkins, *The Dynamics of a Popular Revolt* (Ann Arbor, MI, Xerox University Microfilms, 1978), Chapter 4.
19 LPA, BIV/2/5-026, 'Kurzinformation Nr. 29/56', 29 June 1956; 'Informationsnotizen', 18 July 1956, p. 6.
20 On events in Hungary and Poland during 1956, cf. R.J. Crampton, *Eastern Europe in the Twentieth Century* (London, Routledge, 1994); B. Lomax, *Hungary 1956* (London, Villiers Publications, 1976).
21 LPA, BIV/2/5-026, 'Durchsage KL Mühlhausen', 22 October 1956, p. 2.
22 *Ibid.*, SED district reports, 23 October 1956. The SED suppressed reports of strikes in Magdeburg. Cf. M. Fulbrook, *Anatomy of a Dictatorship* (Oxford, Oxford University Press, 1995), p. 189.

23 LPA, BIV/2/5-026, Heiligenstadt and Eisenach reports, 22 October 1956.

24 *Ibid.*, Weimar-Stadt report, 22 October 1956.

25 *Ibid.*, 'Kurzinformation', 27 and 29 October 1956.

26 ThHStAW, MdI/20, 73, fols 3, 4, 21.

27 LPA, BIV/2/5-026 and BIV/2/5-027, SED reports, October–November 1956.

28 See, e.g., ThHStAW, NF 209, fols 47–52, Bezirk bloc minutes, 29 October 1956; district bloc minutes in LPA, IV/4.10/108, IV/4.07/197 and IV/4.06/144.

29 The following paragraphs are based on SED reports of October–November 1956 in LPA, BIV/2/5-026 and -027, and on police reports in ThHStAW, Vs/St 534.

30 Compare the daily police reports for these periods in ThHStAW, Vs/St 534 (1956) and Vs/St 545 (1955).

31 LPA, BIV/2/5-027, 'Informatorischer Bericht Nr. 49/56', 14 November 1956, pp. 1–2, 4.

32 ThHStAW, V 36, fol. 233, 'Informationen … ', 8 December 1956; LPA, IV/4.12/1-228, Weimar bloc minutes, 27 November 1956, p. 7.

33 LPA, BIV/2/5-027, Worbis and Sondershausen SED reports, 9 November 1956.

34 LPA, BIV/2/10-008, 'Republikflucht der Lehrer … ', 13 February 1957.

35 These comments are based on LPA, BIV/2/5-027 (SED reports), and ThHStAW, Vs/St 534 (police reports).

36 E.g., none of these reasons is cited in LPA, BIV/2/10-008, 'Republikflucht', 23 October 1956, or IV/4.06/162, Heiligenstadt KPKK, 'Fälle von Republikflucht … ', 19 September 1956.

37 Cf. undated report (note 14), pp. 3–4; LPA, IV/4.06/162, SED Heiligenstadt, 'Politische Einschätzung zur Durchführung von Parteiverfahren', 12 December 1956.

38 LPA, BIV/2/9.02-021, 'Informatorischer Bericht … ', 15 November 1956.

39 LPA, BIV/2/5-027, 'Situationsbericht', 6 November 1956.

40 *Ibid.*, 'Informationsbericht Nr. 51/56', 20 November 1956, pp. 5–7.

41 *Ibid.*, 'Informationen über bestimmte Erscheinungen … ', 23 November 1956, p. 1.

42 E.g., ThHStAW, Vs/St 534, fol. 160, BdVP, 'Lagebericht Nr. 55/56', 27 October 1956.

43 LPA, BIV/2/5-027, SED reports, November 1956.

44 LPA, BIV/2/5-026, Medizinische Akademie Erfurt, 'Über die politische Lage … ', 30 October 1956, p. 1.

45 20 November report (note 40), p. 3.

46 For the pre-1960 background of agricultural policy, see A. Bauerkämper, 'Von der Bodenreform zur Kollektivierung', in H. Kaelbe, J. Kocka and H. Zwahr (eds), *Sozialgeschichte der DDR* (Stuttgart, Klett Cotta, 1994), pp. 119–43.

47 Weber, *Geschichte*, p. 317; *Statistisches Jahrbuch 1966: Bezirk Erfurt* (Erfurt, Staatliche Zentralverwaltung für Statistik, Bezirksstelle Erfurt, 1966), p. 14.

48 ThHStAW, OI 271, fol.80, RdK Worbis, 'Informationsbericht … ', 19 January 1960.

49 *Statistisches Jahrbuch 1966: Bezirk Erfurt*, p. 14. The remaining land belonged to state farms or consisted of tiny plots owned by individuals.

50 LPA, BIV/2/7-24, 'Einsatz von leitenden Genossen … ', 5 November 1957.

51 *Ibid.*, 'Auswertung der Ergebnisse des Einsatzes leitender Funktionäre … ', 28 January 1958, pp. 3–4.

52 *Ibid.*, p. 3.

53 ThHStAW, S 515, fol. 82, '11./1959 Informationsbericht', 27 June 1959.

54 ThHStAW, OI 271 district reports, January 1960.

55 LPA, IV/4.06/120, SED Heiligenstadt, 'Etappenweise Entwicklung der sozialistischen Landwirtschaft … ', p. 1, and 'Die Arbeit der Kreisparteiorganisation … ', 11 August 1959, p. 1; *ibid.*, 'Bildung von LPG', 29 July 1958, p. 1.

56 LPA, BIV/2/7-24, 'Stellungnahme der Brigade ... ', 14 October 1959.

57 *Ibid.*, 'Abschlußbericht ... ', 3 February 1960; 19 January 1960 report (note 48), fol. 80.

58 The following paragraphs are based on reports in ThHStAW, OI 271, 272, 273, and Vs/St 335.

59 LPA, IV/2/3-323, SED BL, 'Kurzinfomation Nr. 20/60', 24 March 1960, p. 4.

60 Collectivisation statistics in ThHStAW, Vs/St 335.

61 ThHStAW, OI 274, fol. 2, '5./1960 Informationsbericht', 28 March 1960.

62 LPA, IV/2/1-076, SED BL, 'Protokoll der 12. Bezirksleitungssitzung am 28.3.1960 ... ', p. 70.

63 ThHStAW, Vs/St 335, fol. 66, 'Telefonische Durchsage', 31 March 1960.

64 H. Sieber, *et al.* (eds), *Chronik zur Geschichte der Arbeiterbewegung im Bezirk Erfurt 1952 bis 1961* (Erfurt, SED Bezirksleitung Erfurt, 1979), pp. 270–1.

65 ThHStAW, Vs/St 335, fols 75–6, 'Informationsberichte der Beauftragten der Räte der Kreise vom 6.4.1960'; *ibid.*, fol. 96, 'Anlage zur Meldung vom 26.3.1960'.

66 ThHStAW, Vs/St 336, fols 11–55, especially fols 18–19, 22, 'Sonderratssitzung am 13.4.1960'.

67 LPA, BIV/2/17-006, 'Bericht über die Verbesserung der massenpolitischen Arbeit ... ', 15 July 1960, p. 2.

68 LPA, BIV/2/5-039, 'Kurzinformation', 21 September and 27 October 1960; ThHStAW, Vs/St 571, police reports, 6 and 16 February 1961; MdI/20.1, 139, fol. 45, police report, 25 July 1961.

69 Calculated from LPA, BIV/2/7-6, *Kreis* reports [April 1961?].

70 LPA, BIV/2/5-041, 'Kurzinformation Nr. 26/61', 3 July 1961.

71 LPA, IV/4.13/192, KPKK Worbis, 'Bericht über legale Verzüge ... ', 17 April 1961, pp. 4–5.

72 ThHStAW, Vs/St 596, fols 12–15, MfS Bezirksverwaltung, 'Vorschlag zur Durchführung eines öffentlichen Prozesses', 21 November 1960.

5

The churches' basis challenged

This chapter departs from the chronological approach of the rest of the book to pay special attention to the difficulties the SED experienced in winning the support of the Christian population and in neutralising the influence of the churches throughout the 1945–68 period. The churches merit particular attention as a far older, alternative faith structure to that being constructed by the SED around the ideology of Marxist-Leninist socialism, and at times around the demigods Stalin and Ulbricht. In this sense, the new demands being made by the SED for popular loyalty were in competition with those made by the various churches. Conflict was made almost inevitable by the basic incompatibility of Marxism and Christianity.[1] However, the conflict was complicated for the SED by the fact that this avowedly antifascist party was politically bound to respect the religious practices of the mainly Christian population which it ruled, if it were not to undermine its legitimacy as the only viable alternative to the totalitarian aspirations of Nazism. Thus, the SED had to desensitise the Christian population to its anti-church policies by trying to prove that socialism and religion were compatible, while simultaneously attempting to undermine the churches' position in society.

The denominational character of *Bezirk* Erfurt was rather more complicated than in much of the rest of the GDR, where a single Protestant church dominated most regions. The regional SED had to cope not only with an overwhelming Roman Catholic majority in the Eichsfeld districts along the border to West Germany (the only strong Catholic concentration in the country), but also with two Protestant churches. Two thirds of the *Bezirk*'s Protestant churchgoers belonged to the Thuringian Church, based in Eisenach, while the formerly Prussian territories (Erfurt, the Eichsfeld and some smaller areas) fell under the jurisdiction of the Evangelical Church of the Church Province of Saxony, based in Magdeburg.[2] Though both churches belonged to the umbrella association of evangelical churches in Germany (EKD), they could each determine their own policies, and were divided theologically. While the Eisenach church followed the Lutheran tradition, which generally respected secular authority as the source of worldly order and gradually led its bishop, Moritz Mitzenheim, to a position of relative loyalty towards the socialist GDR, the Magdeburg church belonged to the 'reformed' movement, which believed that the state, like the churches, should be a 'good and holy institution appointed by God himself', and that the GDR under SED rule did not match this definition.[3] Magdeburg and Eisenach regularly disagreed on the most appropriate stance to take towards a state whose socialism both instinctively rejected.

Although most Thuringians claimed membership of one church or another, statistics of the number of believers alone do not reveal the extent of religious life. The Eichsfeld's Catholic community was (and remains) exceptionally devout, perhaps due to its position as an island in a Protestant see. Immediately after the war, all the churches played an important role, particularly for the many settlers from the east (mostly Catholics). During the early 1950s faith was still so widespread and deep that the first concerted attacks on the churches caused great resentment. Bishop Mitzenheim toured his diocese to denounce such moves and call for a united response from believers, often speaking to large congregations. The churches often criticised the great moral dilemmas Christians faced when confronted with a choice between obedience to the state or their faith.

Although religious influence was generally stronger in rural areas, there were exceptions: in the rural Erfurt-Land district, church attendance was reportedly extremely poor. One farmer felt the church was a 'necessary evil', and another said villagers paid no attention to sermons but liked to uphold traditions.[4] This lack of theological interest was potentially a great weakness for the churches.

A full discussion of the SED's relations with the church hierarchies, its attempts to win their loyalty or acceptance, and to avert or neutralise their resistance to socialist policies, would be beyond the scope of this book. Instead, in common with the rest of this work, the sections below principally concentrate on the response of the population and of local clergy to the party's attempts to render religious affiliations obsolete.

The state and the clergy

Given the SED's considerable difficulties in winning the sympathies, let alone support, of church leaders, great efforts were made to influence local clergy. Often these attempts involved the SED and the state authorities trying to prevent individual clerics from criticising SED policy in their sermons. Observers were regularly sent into the churches to report what was said. Bishop Mitzenheim complained in 1950 that some churches were being watched by undercover members of the SED's offshoot, the FDJ. 'It is more than alarming ... ', the bishop wrote, 'that our youth is being systematically misled into spying activities and provocative machinations just as during the era of the Hitler regime.'[5] In response the churches took precautionary measures, sometimes posting 'guards' at entrances. When vicars criticised state and party policies from the pulpit, the *Stasi* was informed and other measures taken. Dissenting clergy were often called in for discussions with SED and/or NF agitators. In at least one case an Erfurt vicar had to answer to the Thuringian Prime Minister, Werner Eggerath, after being overheard condemning the 1951 referendum which called for a 'just peace treaty' and the withdrawal of all occupation forces from Germany.[6]

State and party files contain many reports of 'hostile' sermons from the early 1950s. Thus the vicar of Pappenhaim borrowed SED terminology just before the Second Party Conference in 1952 to declare that there was only one 'party badge for the Christian', namely 'Jesus Christ ... At the end of world history there will be two opposing parties, the Christians' party and the murderers' party. Victory will belong to the Christians' party.'[7] Similarly, the vicar of Schernberg was reported for expressing the apparently treacherous view that the 'present times are characterised by insecurity, need and poverty'.[8] However, given the large number of sermons delivered every week, the number of these reports is relatively small. The SED's paranoia about the churches was mostly unnecessary. Although the party recorded as suspicious even sermons about God's omnipotence (presumably perceived as casting doubt on the party's leading role), 'most clergy address only religious themes in their sermons'.[9]

Nevertheless, well into the 1950s politically minded clergy were not intimidated by SED observers. Thus the government had to expect an increase in oppositional sermons on occasions such as the evacuations along the border to West Germany, election days, and prior to 17 June 1953. Clergy of the Magdeburg church in particular sometimes used the pulpit for political resistance, exercising their constitutional right to speak on issues affecting the people. Thus, in 1951 many clergy read a pastoral letter attacking the SED's collectivist agricultural policies. The letter made common cause with farmers by identifying both church and agriculture as institutions under threat.[10] Occasionally SED functionaries' enthusiasm caused farcical incidents in the early period, as during the 1951 referendum when the party's Eisenach district secretary refused to turn off the town's public-address system during church services. In response, the church choir sang ever louder, while the loudspeakers were repeatedly turned up in renewed competition. The SED man remarked afterwards: 'We showed the church who's stronger!'[11]

The GDR only occasionally imprisoned clerics. A rare example was on 17 June 1953 when Edgar Mitzenheim – the vicar of Eckolstädt and brother of Bishop Mitzenheim – and Gerhard Sammler – the superintendent in Bad Tennstedt – called for an uprising against the government and the SED. (The clergy were otherwise 'conspicuously restrained' on this day.) Other exceptions were a Heiligenstadt catechist sentenced to three months' imprisonment in 1958 for distributing a West German article criticising the controversial border with Poland, and the arrest of a Protestant youth vicar in Weimar, Giersch, who removed posters and other publicity before the 1957 elections. Bishop Mitzenheim readily distanced himself from Giersch's activities to preserve harmonious church–state relations, emphasising that this was an isolated incident.[12] Apart from such occasional cases of clergy imprisoned to make an example, the SED and the state authorities behaved cautiously, perhaps wishing to refute claims that they were engaged in a battle with the churches.[13] The churches also frequently made concessions. Thus, a Klettbach priest who insulted the CDU and the socialist development was not charged under

Article 6 of the constitution but suspended by the church and removed from the parish.[14] Such settlements protected the state's reputation.

The SED's contacts with parish clergy sometimes constituted attempts to influence the church leaderships. Signs of improving relations with some Magdeburg church clergy led the party to recommend more contacts with them, in the hope of similarly co-opting the church leadership. Equally, as relations with Catholic leaders were 'tense or unbending', the National Front, the CDU and respected personalities were required to approach Catholics individually, and the NF's 'Christian population' working group invited important Catholics for discussions. The aim was to break Catholics' centrally ordained resistance by the 'divide and rule' method. Priests who publicly supported election campaigns and other SED policies could expect practical assistance, while every priest who attacked the state in sermons or broke the law would be summoned to the district council and 'instructed' as required.[15] By making examples of 'good' and 'bad' behaviour in this schoolmasterly way, the SED hoped clergy at all levels would take note.

Elections posed a particular challenge to the SED. The clergy had to be persuaded to vote for the SED-sponsored candidates of the National Front and, as they were perceived to have significant influence over churchgoers (still a large proportion of the population in the 1950s) as leading national, diocesan or parish personalities, they were encouraged to declare their support openly. Where clergy failed to vote or even criticised the candidates and their policies, the SED feared they might spark wider opposition. Thus, the SED, CDU and National Front used all possible means to encourage the clergy's active support before elections. In urging priests to use their pulpits to call upon their flocks to vote on election days (Sundays), they tacitly recognised the churches' continuing influence. The clergy's voting behaviour is one yardstick for gauging the success of the SED's church policies.

The churches' influence was already clear during the 'ban the bomb' petition of May 1950, when the poorest results in the Eichsfeld were in villages where the priest had not signed. Despite the SED's best efforts, difficulties were still apparent before the first elections to the *Volkskammer* (the GDR parliament). By July 1950 the churches' anti-state and anti-election comments filled a ten-page report. Only six of the eighty personally invited clergy attended a meeting with the Thuringian prime minister on 2 October 1950, demonstrating the churches' reluctance to involve themselves in politics. Some clergy claimed they could not attend without their superiors' official approval.[16]

The SED's major operation to persuade the clergy to support the elections openly and encourage their congregations to vote produced few positive results. A party functionary recorded: 'A large number of the clergy was won over. Four comrades have visited hundreds of clergy, over thirty clergy have declared themselves in writing for the aims of the National Front and for the election on 15 Oct.' However, that only thirty Thuringian vicars or priests welcomed the elections could hardly be counted as satisfactory. The party admitted the serious problems the churches and their supporters had caused: 'The most active on election Sunday were the church and the sects. Half of the comments written on voting slips were of a religious nature. Political opponents [wrote] different comments and fewer of them.'[17]

It is unclear how many Catholic clergy voted in the 1950 election or the 1951 referendum. Eichsfeld reports claimed that most voted openly, unlike the Magdeburg church's local vicars, and that the Catholic priest of Faulungen made positive references to the elections during his service. Though Catholic leaders remained generally aloof, most Catholics felt beholden to respect secular authority (via elections) on biblical grounds and saw no conflict with their stiff resistance to specific measures such as the secularisation of education. Nonetheless, most people in the Eichsfeld voted only after the morning service, ignoring the SED's entreaties to vote early as a clear rejection of the western 'don't vote' campaign.[18]

Catholics' early positive response to GDR elections set a trend which continued for decades, despite the papacy's bitter opposition to communism. The pressure to conform to the state's demands was particularly keenly felt in the Eichsfeld after the expulsions from the border areas in 1952 and 1961. The desire to avoid resettlement may well explain Catholics' generally good voting record in this area.[19] A 1951 report noted how the Catholic church set great store by 'not placing itself in a position of open contradiction to the state'.[20] Only one Catholic priest refused to vote in Heiligenstadt district in 1954. At the 1961 election the SED believed that the Catholic clergy's high turnout reflected an 'extremely clever tactical change of course by the Catholic leadership' designed to avoid a deterioration of church–state relations. These had recently been harmed when the newly appointed Catholic bishop of (Greater) Berlin, Bengsch, discovered a bug which had been placed in his flat by the *Stasi*. However some clergy were exceptions: before the 1958 elections the priest of Steinbach, who did not vote, told officials that he had nothing against the state but objected to atheist propaganda.[21] Meanwhile, some clergy cleverly exploited the SED's exhortations to vote. Probably the most expensive vote cast was that of the Catholic dean, Lerch, in Siemerode, hard on the border to the west. Lerch promised the District Peace Council that he would call on his congregation to vote, but added that his dearest wish was to see a steeple built on his new church. The Peace Council ensured that he received 15,000 Marks before election day. This outlay was rewarded when the dean and the parish nuns all voted openly and publicly thanked the state.[22]

Meanwhile, without forming a united block, the Protestant clergy took a 'more negative stance' to elections and referenda than their Catholic counterparts. The Magdeburg church regarded elections as an opportunity to demonstrate sharp opposition to the state. In 1951, for example, it refused co-operation in the referendum because of the GDR's defamation campaign against the west, and complained against official calls to vote openly and the mistrustful treatment of those who voted secretly. Whereas by the mid-1950s the Eisenach church allowed its clergy to decide for themselves whether or not to vote, in 1957 the Magdeburg church planned a pastoral letter calling on worshippers not to vote and arranged bus trips and other events to keep churchgoers away from polling stations. (The Eisenach church had planned similar diversions to coincide with the 1951 referendum, but was persuaded not to implement them.)[23]

Though many Protestant clergy remained neutral, in 1951 the SED had to conclude that the 'progressive' evangelical pastors were not yet a majority.[24] Precise figures are unavailable for the 1951 referendum, but by the second of the three voting days only five of the thirty-six Protestant clergy in Erfurt, a Magdeburg church heartland, had voted. No great change occurred by 1954. Despite numerous conversations with church officials, the SED reported that: 'Only a few clergy, already known to be progressively minded, have called upon their parishioners to vote for the National Front candidates on 17 October … The church leadership was far more successful on the Sunday prior to the election in influencing the majority of clergy not to speak positively about the election in any way.'[25]

However, 'hostile church activities have not dominated … The vast majority of the clergy remained loyal and made no mention of the elections and party and state policies.'[26] Nonetheless, the SED was concerned that clergy should vote rather than remain passive. In contrast to Catholic clergy, most of Heiligenstadt district's Protestant clergy (mainly Magdeburg church) did not vote in 1954, some deliberately going away for the day. Those who remained at home but did not vote were subjected to repeated visits and hours of discussions with election agitators. These generally proved fruitless. The SED also discovered that pressurising clergy shortly before elections sometimes proved counterproductive.[27]

The Magdeburg church's continued defiance, and the discipline it exerted over its clergy, are reflected in the turnout figures of the various denominations' clergy in successive elections from 1957 to 1963:[28]

Figures (%)	1957	1958	1961	1963
Catholic clergy	84.0	74.3	96.4	90.1
Eisenach clergy	74.3	91.8	94.7	96.0
Magdeburg clergy	38.8	62.3	69.7	69.8
Smaller denominations	n/a	95.0	95.0	95.0

The 1957 elections marked a breakthrough for the state authorities with the Eisenach church. Even Bishop Mitzenheim voted (albeit in the privacy of the booth), and many other leading figures followed suit. The Catholic suffragan bishop of Erfurt, Dr Joseph Freusberg, did not himself vote, but did alter the date of the Corpus Christi procession to avoid clashing with the election.

Apart from denominational differences in voting patterns, clergy in small rural areas usually reacted more positively to SED policies at election time than those in urban centres. The state authorities speculated in 1951 that clergy in small villages were more worried about isolating themselves from their parishioners over the 'war or peace' question.[29] Equally, village priests were further removed from the influence of leading clergy and more easily preyed upon by local party functionaries.

Over the years, the clergy and the churches largely came to terms with the GDR and were prepared to support the elections as the highest symbol of their co-operation. By 1961, when even Dr Freusberg voted, in common with the entire local Catholic leadership and that of the Eisenach church, most of these churches' clergy also participated in elections. Two Eichsfeld priests and some Arnstadt vicars even appealed to the population to vote early, and the vicar of Breitenbach served on the *Bezirk* election commission in 1963. Other clerics also had official functions.[30] Only the Magdeburg leadership maintained its defiance. In both 1961 and 1963, following the church's instructions, only one of the eight Magdeburg superintendents in *Bezirk* Erfurt voted, and even he struck through the names of all but two candidates. The relatively low turnout among Magdeburg clergy suggests the influence of that church's leadership remained strong.

The battle for youth

As the 1950s progressed, the greatest disputes between the churches and the SED concerned the upbringing of young people. In the party's view, the SED's long-term future depended on new generations being raised as socialists with exclusive faith in the working-class movement and its Marxist-Leninist party. Young people were not to be distracted by supernatural beliefs, especially as the churches were connected with the SED's political opponents, principally the West German CDU/CSU, and more generally western capitalism. Equally, the churches' long-term future depended on new generations growing up believing in God and rendering institutional loyalty to the churches.

The incompatibility of these two mutually exclusive demands on youth quickly provoked a war of attrition between state and churches. The SED attached such significance to winning over young people to socialism that it began its campaign to secure their support very early in the GDR's history. It was well established even before Walter Ulbricht announced the building of socialism in 1952. Initially the battle centred on religious education in state schools, and on the SED's opposition to the *Junge Gemeinde* ('Young Congregation'). The SED felt this informal church association of young believers threatened the FDJ, which was designed to bring together all young people to support the socialist state and secure the SED's future. The later phase of this existential fight, the introduction in 1954 of the *Jugendweihe* as a secular and essentially socialist confirmation ceremony, also pre-dated crucial socialisation measures such as the completion of agricultural collectivisation (1960) and the nationalisation of the smaller private companies (1972).

The SED's objectives during the 1950s in youth policy as it concerned religion – the removal of religious education from state schools and its marginalisation in society, and young people publicly pledging themselves to the SED's goals – were for the most part realised, and with a speed which reflects the SED's strength in implementing policy, despite the general weakness of the party rank and file. The party's relative success also demonstrates the population's increasing preparedness, even before the Wall's construction, to conform to the expected patterns of outward behaviour.

In education, the SED had two main aims: first, to remove religious education from the classroom and hinder it elsewhere, and second to restructure the syllabus so that children were imbued with a purely materialist outlook as a basis for complete faith in SED policies. While the churches believed religion was 'not one subject among others but the fundamental principle of all instruction',[31] the SED accorded materialist principles and instruction in Marxism-Leninism the same importance. The churches quickly realised the scale of the long-term threat to their position these policies implied.

The Eisenach church negotiated with the Soviet authorities about the importance of religious education as early as October 1945. Bishop Mitzenheim optimistically told Kolesnitschenko, the first head of the Soviet administration for Thuringia, that all education rested on Christian foundations, and that, as more than 90 per cent of Thuringia's population belonged to a church, Christian schooling was democratically legitimate. The Soviet general pointed out that Christian schooling had not prevented the Third Reich and insisted on a clear division between church and state, underlining that religious education was purely a church matter.[32] The Eisenach church hoped to include a guarantee that 'religious education is a subject with equal rights and the concern of the religious institutions' in the 1946 Thuringian constitution,[33] but Article 72 merely guaranteed the churches' right to give religious instruction, without requiring state assistance. Schools were to educate young people 'to real humanity in the spirit of the peaceful and friendly coexistence of the nations and of true democracy'. Article 74 insisted that no-one should be compelled to participate in any religious activity, including religious education, while more mildly adding that no-one should be prevented from participating, other than on legal grounds. This last provision allowed the legislator, in practice the SED, to define when pupils should be prevented from receiving religious education. The stipulation in Article 37 of the GDR's 1949 constitution that schools would 'educate young people in the spirit of the constitution' again depended on how and by whom this was defined. The GDR's constitution did, however, guarantee the churches' right to dispense religious education in state classrooms and to choose their own teachers. As in Thuringia, no-one could be forced to attend or be prevented from so doing, but Article 48 ensured that parents could not insist on children attending religious education beyond their fourteenth birthday.[34]

The Magdeburg church quickly realised the threat of the new legal framework. Bishop Müller protested in April 1950 about the monopoly enjoyed by the materialist ideology in schools.[35] A pastoral letter specifically complained that schools, colleges and the FDJ pressurised children to speak and write in contradiction to their own feelings, that the Christian religion was being presented as 'contemptu-ous' and that teachers were trying to convince pupils that Christ had never lived.[36]

Even before the real battle began, the state's refusal to support religious educa-tion (RE), even though classes were held in state school buildings, caused admin-istrative difficulties for the clergy giving the lessons. These problems were often compounded by bad discipline as teachers encouraged children to regard RE as an unnecessary extra. At a 1951 parents' evening held by a Mühlhausen church, a cat-echist noted: 'The children are highly undisciplined because the RE lessons are no longer organised as part of the timetable.' Another described chaotic circum-stances: 'The children's behaviour is quite dreadful. We have literally to drag the children back from the toilets when it is time for the RE lesson. And while we are rounding up the last ones, the first ones have already got up and gone again. This is because we find so little sympathy among the teachers.' Another catechist said teachers helped him, but knew this was against their instructions.[37]

The churches also protested at the pressure exerted on children to join the FDJ or its children's wing, the Young Pioneers, against their conscience. The evangeli-cal superintendent of Erfurt complained that many cases of 'spiritual disturbance' resulted from this pressure. Some people gave into pressure and were ashamed of themselves. Others despised those who were won over by promises of outward advantage. However, many grew apathetic and were prepared 'cold bloodedly' to assume any disguise.[38] Here, arguably, lay the origins of the 'niche society' of out-ward conformity but private individualism, to which many of this first GDR gen-eration subscribed in adulthood twenty and thirty years later.[39] Inculcating behaviour patterns which lacked ideological foundations, and suppressing opposi-tion to the state and/or natural allegiances to alternatives such as religious belief, ultimately did not guarantee SED hegemony. However, the indifference that took root in this early period was sufficient in the long term to undermine traditional support for religion in eastern Germany.[40]

The Protestant churches used parish youth groups, known as the *Junge Gemeinde* to try to combat the encroachment of FDJ and Young Pioneer activities on their traditional position among young people. The *Junge Gemeinde* greatly con-cerned the SED throughout the 1950s and 1960s.[41] During the early 1950s in par-ticular, the state regularly protested that the *Junge Gemeinde* constituted an unauthorised organisation. The churches maintained this was not so, rather that the *Junge Gemeinde* merely represented a grouping of the youth of each parish. While most *Junge Gemeinde* groups had no membership cards or books, young believers did wear badges proclaiming their affiliation. The practical difference between formal organisation and informal grouping was minimal.

Much of the 'war' between state and churches was waged by proxy via the FDJ and *Junge Gemeinde*. Vicars and priests made great efforts to provide exciting enter-tainments and opportunities for young people to entice them away from the FDJ. These often had only minimal or auxiliary religious association. One Erfurt vicar even made himself popular by telling his youth group ghost stories. Church holiday camps, voluntary work missions, sports festivals and amateur dramatics were also organised in competition with similar FDJ activities, often attracting FDJ members and generally higher attendances than the 'unity' organisation achieved. Faced with the *Junge Gemeinde*'s overwhelming popularity, the party employed its own underhand tactics. SED members in the police were instructed to observe events carefully and intervene if meeting rooms became overfilled in breach of fire regulations; in Apolda, a headmaster arranged with the SED and FDJ for two committed FDJ members to join the *Junge Gemeinde* to ascertain its plans.

Both sides engaged in blackmail attempts: one primary school headteacher told FDJ members who also sang in the church choir that they would be unable to participate in FDJ events in the future. The children left the church choir and stayed with the FDJ. Meanwhile, the vicar of Plaue told confirmation candidates who had signed a greeting to Stalin that they must cross off their names or not be confirmed. Peer pressure clearly played an important role in both cases. A Bad Langensalza vicar played on international uncertainties by warning the parents of Christian children in the Young Pioneers' choir that the church could not allow children to belong to communist organisations: the Americans would arrive soon and 'discover everything'.

At a time when the churches generally maintained orthodox teaching on the Creation, biology classrooms were also central to the state's battle against religion. The state insisted that only the scientific theory of evolution was taught. Clerics regularly provided children with counter arguments for biology lessons, and taught biology and history in RE periods to undermine the teachers' position. The Catholic priest of Hüpstedt attacked the local biology teacher from the pulpit, while a Bad Langensalza priest reportedly incited Catholic school girls to accuse a biology teacher of indecent behaviour on a school outing. The teacher was imprisoned for six weeks before the girls withdrew the allegation.[42]

The many incidents of this sort foreshadowed increasing tensions between the state and the *Junge Gemeinde* after Walter Ulbricht proclaimed the building of socialism and the 'unavoidable' intensification of the class struggle in 1952 at the SED's Second Party Conference. An integral part of this 'struggle' was that against the churches and in particular against the *Junge Gemeinde*, to protect the FDJ. One strategy was to exchange FDJ membership books in early 1953, a move similar to the SED's purge of untrustworthy members in 1950–51.[43] Every FDJ member was questioned on his or her ideological commitment, with clear implications for those who also participated in *Junge Gemeinde* activities. Those who refused risked losing FDJ membership and thereby attracting personal disadvantages.

Meanwhile the SED's *Politbüro* began a campaign to remove pupils with 'bourgeois' backgrounds and known *Junge Gemeinde* activists from the high schools (*Oberschulen*). The party estimated that 50 to 70 per cent of high-school pupils were involved in the *Junge Gemeinde* and that numbers were rising.[44] Apart from hindering the FDJ's growth, the *Junge Gemeinde* was seen as divisive, dangerous and subversive. Members had, for instance, perpetrated such 'anti-republic' activities as disrupting SED-inspired protests at an Erfurt high school against the west's planned European Defence Treaty (designed to integrate the Federal Republic into the western defence alliance), regularly decried by the party as the 'General War Treaty'.[45] The campaign against the *Junge Gemeinde*, presented as a hotbed of West German and American agents, was centrally co-ordinated by FDJ chairman Erich Honecker and intended as a 'strong ideological battle'. Pupils' energies were to be diverted into the FDJ, which still appeared weak in March 1953.[46] The campaign led to a number of high school pupils being expelled that spring.

It would be mistaken to see these expulsions as primarily religiously motivated. In this early stage of the struggle with the *Junge Gemeinde* they affected politically active Christians who were seen to be agitating against the GDR and its developing socialist order. In the first instance the state was keen to neutralise the ringleaders, such as those being investigated by the *Stasi* in Teistungen for preparing to sabotage the 1 May celebrations.[47] The fervour and ideological commitment with which the campaign was waged in some high schools, and the reluctance with which it later had to be abandoned as part of the 'New Course' in June 1953, demonstrate the extent to which the SED had established a functioning hierarchy with strong party discipline by 1953, and the existence of 'class struggle' in the first phase of Ulbricht's construction of socialism.

Documentation survives of the witch hunt at the Buttstädt high school in Sömmerda district.[48] Here, three sixth formers with strong *Junge Gemeinde* connections, and another who had co-founded an opposition *Edelweißpiraten* group at the school,[49] were expelled on 17 March 1953, despite the one CDU teacher's protests. The school's FDJ organisation was virtually non-existent, while the *Junge Gemeinde* was very strong, boasting a display board in the town with slogans designed to embarrass the SED, such as: 'Though we must all wear masks, the Lord God can see into our hearts.' An investigative commission of nine SED members (including three functionaries) questioned several pupils and based its conclusions on allegations made by *Junge Gemeinde* opponents, in particular one SED pupil. They reported that a *Junge Gemeinde* newspaper, *Die Stafette*, published in 'imperialist' West Germany, was used in meetings, and that the local priest and a catechist were undermining and 'correcting' certain school lessons. As before, the *Junge Gemeinde*'s status was queried. While those involved claimed it was not an organisation as it collected no dues and issued no membership cards, and was therefore legal, one pupil added that money was collected to support 'Christian teaching'. Though these and other complaints (pupils had rejected an FDJ ball scheduled for Holy Week) might appear mild, the SED commission viewed them as of great potential danger in the charged atmosphere of the Cold War, as reflected in the report's sharp language: 'They [the members of the Pedagogical Council] uphold the expulsion of the elements who have consciously dragged the mass of the young people through the quagmire of political terrorist work by their active work in the *Junge Gemeinde* ... Comrade schools inspector R. [demonstrated] that the *Junge Gemeinde* is a front organisation of Anglo-American monopoly capitalism.'[50] This tone was similar to an article in the FDJ paper, *Junge Welt*,[51] which had described the *Junge Gemeinde*'s 'sabotage work'.

A Buttstädt catechist, the father of an expelled pupil, subsequently complained to the district council. He protested that the commission had breached Articles 42(3), 40 and 44 of the GDR constitution and noted that as the *Junge Gemeinde* was not an organisation, his daughter could not have been a functionary in it, as charged. The letter also revealed his daughter's record as an FDJ functionary, for which she had won a medal in 1950. This suggests that the action was designed not only to remove a committed Christian pupil from the school, but also to intimidate the catechist father and through him warn others.[52]

Although the GDR's interior ministry formally banned the *Junge Gemeinde* on 28 April 1953,[53] the Buttstädt case had a surprising outcome which casts light on far wider matters. The catechist's protest had no effect itself, but two of the four expelled pupils were reprieved in early May and sent to a different high school (where they would be carefully observed) after the intervention of the local Soviet commandant, who summoned the district education director for talks. Though the decision possibly resulted from the Soviet connections of one pupil's father, the intervention may be an early indicator of the more relaxed Soviet policy towards the GDR's building of socialism following Stalin's death, and of the direct intervention at the highest levels which led to the Soviet imposition of the 'New Course' in early June. In any event, the influence still exerted by the Red Army in the GDR's domestic affairs in May 1953 is very evident in the education director's meek acquiescence to the commandant's view. Consequently the Sömmerda district council requested the regional authorities to ensure no further action was taken in the case.[54]

The locally initiated reprieve for these two Buttstädt pupils anticipated a general amnesty for other expelled students in the SED's more moderate 'New Course', introduced on Soviet orders in early June 1953 as an (unsuccessful) attempt to defuse growing social discontent. Measures taken against teachers during the *Junge Gemeinde* 'investigations' were also to be reversed. Furthermore, all 'special measures against church institutions' were to be halted; 'democratic legality' was to be 'guaranteed', an admission that it had not been beforehand.[55] This U-turn, integral to the 'New Course', was directly linked to a meeting between government and church leaders on 10 June. It is indicative of the level of public and church opposition to measures against the *Junge Gemeinde* and religious education during 1953 that this meeting was the first practical action to follow the SED's announcement of the 'New Course' the previous day. But even as these momentous policy changes were being announced, on 9 June the Sömmerda high school's 'Pedagogical Council' was discussing the ninth form's essays on the *Junge Gemeinde*. The meeting unanimously decided to expel an actively Christian pupil who had disputed the *Junge Welt* reports on the nature of the *Junge Gemeinde* and preferred to trust the version presented in the West German *Stafette*. The pupil's behaviour was felt to 'greatly damage the respect of our democratic school and to hinder its social development'. The pupil's continued attendance would be 'incompatible with our educational aims'.[56]

As the Sömmerda example suggests, the *Junge Gemeinde* campaign could not simply be reversed by decree. Some pupils had already 'fled the republic'. At the Bad Berka high school two of fifteen expelled or suspended pupils were not asked to return as they were 'decided enemies who have carried out planned attacks against the occupation power and the Soviet Union'. Similarly, pupils in various classes at the Nordhausen high school opposed the return of students expelled for *Junge Gemeinde* contacts.[57] Such cases illustrate the differences between central regulations and local realities, but also that the SED's basic outlook towards the churches remained constant, even though the New Course had forced a premature end to the first phase of the party's efforts to restrict religious influence over youth.

Battle rejoined: religious education and the introduction of the *Jugendweihe*

As the SED regrouped and shook off the restraints of the 'New Course', the relaxation of hardline policies forced on the state by the Soviets' intervention after the June 1953 uprising proved to be of short duration for the churches, as for other parts of society. However, as openly aggressive attacks on religious organisations and individuals were no longer politically acceptable, the state and party introduced new tactics which less obviously but far more effectively undermined the churches and in particular their appeal to the younger generation. The SED's innovations in this period were the administrative difficulties placed in the path of religious education in state schools, and the introduction of the *Jugendweihe*.

The churches had already encountered problems in giving religious education in schools before June 1953. The church–state agreement of 10 June 1953 stipulated that the restrictions imposed on 1 January 1953 concerning religious education in school buildings would be reviewed.[58] The education ministry's new regulation of 3 August stated: 'Religious education may not be given before the beginning of timetabled education (8a.m.) … It can be given directly after the timetabled lessons of individual classes.'[59]

Within months, though, there were complaints about the regulation's interpretation. In practice schools refused to permit RE to be taught in the mornings to classes whose timetabled lessons began well after 8am, or to classes when their timetabled lessons were complete if classes elsewhere in the school were still being taught. One complainant understandably refused to accept an oral decision from the ministry that the entire school's timetable had to be complete first, as this represented a significant change to the published regulation.[60] At the Theo Neubauer high school in Erfurt, rooms were not made available for RE until 3 p.m. Headteachers regularly decreed that children should rest before extracurricular lessons, and that RE periods held immediately after timetabled lessons interfered with school needs such as detentions.[61] Religious instructors found it difficult to persuade children to wait for lengthy periods after their lessons for an RE class, especially in rural areas where children might have to travel several miles home and then return to school. As the fundamental differences continued between the churches' interpretations of human development in RE lessons and the version taught by school biology and history teachers, the conflict could only deepen.[62]

The dispute persisted for years. In February 1956 the regional council submitted a draft directive to Berlin designed to effectively outlaw RE in state schools. The regional council proposed that at least two hours should elapse between the end of schools' timetabled lessons and the start of RE classes, supposedly to avoid over-burdening children. Even where pupils in outlying villages would be forced to miss transport home if they attended RE classes, no exceptions were permitted. On the pretext of ensuring traffic safety, teachers were to accompany their charges out of the building and as far as the school gate after lessons, effectively meaning that the RE instructor would have to attempt to assemble the class again later. Even more restrictively for the churches, the decree stipulated that any extracurricular teachers must be suitable and have a 'positive attitude towards the workers' and peasants' state'. The decision about suitability would fall to the (invariably SED) district education director. Such teachers would require a permit, renewable every three months, which could be revoked without notice.[63]

On 12 February 1958, the GDR's education ministry issued a directive very similar to the Erfurt proposal. The so-called 'Lange decree' caused indignation and protest from the churches.[64] Clergy faced a dilemma. If they obeyed their churches' instructions to disregard the directive, they would lose their influence in the schools. However, on the point of inspection of RE classes by the headteacher, many clergy followed church instructions and immediately stopped the lesson when the head was present. No outcome could have pleased the SED more.[65]

In the following years, after a renewed church–state rapprochement of 1958, there was some local easing of the situation. In Eisenach discussions with the clergy produced a dispensation: the two-hour wait could be waived in schools where children had to travel long distances home. However, catechists were still not permitted to collect entire groups from their classroom or at the school gate.[66] Such concessions reflected a more rational approach by the SED, but also suggest a growing confidence that unpopular, hardline, class-struggle policies were less imperative given the progress already made in undermining the churches' mass following. However, the Eisenach arrangement was unusual. Although Bishop Mitzenheim could announce in 1960 that it was becoming easier for the religious instructors to teach in state schools again, the Lange decree's administrative obstacles succeeded in driving RE out of most schools and into church buildings.[67] This robbed the churches of their captive audience of the entire youth of a locality in compulsory lessons. They had to attract young people into the presbytery, or persuade their parents to send them. As contacts with the churches were frowned upon, and as a new generation of parents lacked religious education themselves, the churches' position was seriously undermined.[68]

The churches were even more concerned by the threat posed by the *Jugendweihe*. Before the Third Reich the *Jugendweihe* was a secular, atheist alternative to Christian confirmation, a coming-of-age ceremony in the German humanist, free-thinking and socialist tradition. It re-emerged in the GDR in November 1954 with the foundation of a 'Central Committee for *Jugendweihe*', theoretically independent but in practice established at the SED's behest and fully supported by state leaders and institutions. In the GDR, the *Jugendweihe* entailed several weeks of preparatory lessons on a materialist view of human development. To belittle the churches' view of the Creation and related topics, the preparatory course covered themes such as 'the start of life on earth' and 'the development of humankind'. This preparation culminated in a formal ceremony at which young people were welcomed into the adult word and swore an oath. In the first years, participants vowed to fight for and defend peace and a peaceful, democratic, independent Germany, and to work for progress in the economy, science and art.[69] By 1958, reflecting the GDR's stabilising international position, the oath had changed: young people, addressed as 'faithful sons and daughters of our workers' and peasants' state', were entreated to devote all their energies to the great and noble cause of socialism and to join the Soviet and all other peace-loving peoples in securing world peace. The aspects of the oath which emphasised the participant's membership of the socialist community were enhanced in later years.[70]

Whereas the churches had previously confronted only individual biology and history teachers, they were now faced with a state-sponsored scheme designed to spread atheist views amongst all fourteen year olds. By December 1954, the Catholic Bishop of Berlin, Weskamm, had already insisted in a pastoral letter that the '*Jugendweihen* now being planned can never be considered by a Catholic'.[71] Both Weskamm and his Protestant counterpart, Dibelius, already the SED's declared enemy, were equally firm in rejecting any compatibility of the atheist *Jugendweihe* with the confirmation ceremony.[72] As a secular ceremony, in which young people committed themselves to materialist atheism, the churches viewed the *Jugendweihe* oath as a rejection of God. The scene was set for a resumption of the bitter conflict.

Though the Thuringian bishop, Moritz Mitzenheim had (and retains) a reputation as the 'red bishop' for attempting to find a non-confrontational role for his church, he nevertheless quickly commented on the theological implications of the new secular ceremony. He emphasised the common church line on the *Jugendweihe* in his 1955 New Year message. Hoping to protect parents with religious convictions from reprisals, Mitzenheim pointed out that the church took seriously Luther's words that the 'church should not be turned into the town hall and the town hall should not be turned into the church'. Therefore, Mitzenheim emphasised, if parents decided not to send children to the *Jugendweihe*, that was a matter of conscience rather than politics and therefore protected by the GDR's constitution.[73] The bishop complained to the chairman of the regional council, the SED functionary Willy Gebhardt, about the *Jugendweihe*'s atheist character and declared that its effectively obligatory nature meant the state had abandoned religious neutrality and toleration. Though Gebhardt insisted the *Jugendweihe* was an entirely voluntary, independent institution, Mitzenheim cited examples of state schools actively promoting the *Jugendweihe* and of pupils who had been told they could only attend high school if they took the *Jugendweihe* oath.[74] In a further letter, Mitzenheim cited a notice from the Weimar education department about an obligatory teachers' conference to discuss supporting the *Jugendweihe*.[75] The movement's officially independent status was undermined by the fact that the Central *Jugendweihe* Committee's temporary address was the GDR's culture ministry, and that an SED directive called on education functionaries to involve teachers and headteachers in the *Jugendweihe* movement. Regionally, the campaign was implemented almost entirely by the SED's culture department and the regional council's education department.[76]

During 1955 Mitzenheim's sermons often carefully elucidated why religion and the materialist ideology were irreconcilable and how a proper understanding of science should lead to greater reverence for God rather than a renunciation of religion. On this basis, and stressing parents' responsibility for raising their children as Christians, he declared unambiguously that *Jugendweihe* participants could not be confirmed, as the *Jugendweihe* oath represented a rejection of the church. The choice, Mitzenheim insisted, was simply either confirmation or *Jugendweihe*. On this point, he claimed, all clergy were united.[77]

Apart from initial popular apathy towards the *Jugendweihe*, and signs that rural populations would need far more convincing ('they'll have a tough fight on here in the country!'), early in the campaign there was instinctive deep concern in some religiously minded children. Thus, a group of Mühlhausen school girls feared that participation in the *Jugendweihe* would deny them a church burial.[78] The SED's perception of young people's religious affiliations as a threat to the party's own long-term existence largely explains the great efforts invested in the *Jugendweihe* campaign. Additionally the party felt constrained to use the *Jugendweihe* to combat the *Junge Gemeinde* ('Young Congregation') which in 1955 still involved 8,236 young Protestants in *Bezirk* Erfurt. The Catholics' parallel *Pfarrjugend* ('Parish Youth') had 4,783 adherents. Though the proportions of *Junge Gemeinde* activists were fairly insignificant in some districts, the movement had strengthened somewhat since 1953. The SED worried about the churches' continued use of ruses, such as blackmail against confirmands involved in Young Pioneer events and outings timed to clash with FDJ occasions.[79]

Once the *Jugendweihe* campaign began in earnest, the churches' influence became decisive in many areas as clergy followed their own bishop's lead by fighting a war of attrition at parish level. Rarely had the church been so united. Reports flooded in of clergy threatening to exclude *Jugendweihe* participants from confirmation ceremonies, in line with the bishops' decisions; some clergy went from door to door collecting signed declarations from parents that their children would not attend the secular ceremony. Church influence was particularly apparent in Teistungen (Worbis district), where seven residents formed a *Jugendweihe* committee on 20 November 1954. After pastoral letters were read in the Catholic and Protestant churches, only one committee member was prepared to continue (also a member of the SED), and no parents agreed to co-operate with the *Jugendweihe* preparations. The priest of Haynrode (also Worbis district) declared that the *Jugendweihe* was only for the godless and that it was tainted with the swastika.[80] By 1956 the Magdeburg church also attempted to stigmatise the *Jugendweihe* by insisting that confirmands or their parents declared to the church if the confirmand would be attending the state ceremony. In such cases, the child's suspension from confirmation classes signalled the incompatibility of the two events.[81]

In the face of such fierce church opposition, the CDU, a theoretically loyal bloc party but also ostensibly a party for the Christian population, not surprisingly refrained at grass-roots level from actively supporting the *Jugendweihe*.[82] The CDU's position had not changed by late 1955 when *Jugendweihe* committees were formed for 1956. No CDU members served on the regional and district committees, and only two CDU members were known to belong to a town or village committee.[83] When the regional *Jugendweihe* committee declared in 1956 that anyone who refused to swear the *Jugendweihe* oath was 'against the unity of our German fatherland and against peace', the CDU responded that the party and non-party Christians regarded this as a great insult to non-participants.[84] Such reactions reinforce the view expressed in Chapter 2 that the CDU (at least below the national leadership) was not entirely a pliant tool of the SED by the mid-1950s.

The results of the first *Jugendweihe* campaign must have disappointed the SED, and clearly illustrate the churches' continuing influence even after ten years of socialist construction, as only 19.2 per cent of *Bezirk* Erfurt's Form 8 pupils participated. In the Eichsfeld the results were far worse (2.9 per cent in Heiligenstadt district and 5.2 per cent in Worbis district; the adjoining Mühlhausen district was also below average at 14.5 per cent). However, the churches' influence was not total, as some *Jugendweihe* participants had also been confirmed, despite the churches' insistence on the two ceremonies' incompatibility. In Sondershausen district as many as 91 per cent of those who took the secular oath had also been confirmed. Generally the churches did not immediately implement their threats to exclude *Jugendweihe* participants, though some cases were reported from Sömmerda and Nordhausen districts. Thus, one young Lipprechterode churchgoer was denied rights received through confirmation, such as communion and church marriage, but was told that devout attendance at services until the age of 18 would allow a review of the case. Ironically, the SED profited from such examples by accusing the churches of inflicting moral pressures on young people and preventing freedom of expression.[85] In fact, both the churches and the SED were using such pressures, though neither side accepted that the other was entitled to.

When campaigning began for the following year's *Jugendweihe* in late 1955, the churches responded immediately. Various reports noted the continuing greater reluctance to participate in the *Jugendweihe* in rural communities, where the churches were generally stronger. Apart from proven tactics such as anti-*Jugendweihe* declarations, some clergy spread rumours that, for instance, *Jugendweihe* participants would not receive a present that year. The vicar of Schön-städt sent every 1955 *Jugendweihe* participant a form with which they could renounce their secular oath. The churches also resorted to bribery. In Diedorf, where the priest forbade pupils who visited an exhibition entitled 'Agents, Sabo-teurs, Spies' to serve as altar boys, most of the population turned against the *Jugendweihe* and the school. The churches' influence was also visible in the nega-tive responses to the *Jugendweihe* of various teachers and even SED comrades, some of whose wives refused to allow their husbands to serve on *Jugendweihe* commit-tees.[86] Bishop Mitzenheim wrote personally to all Protestant teachers in his diocese in 1955 to highlight the *Jugendweihe*'s atheist nature, to warn of the consequences for confirmed participants, and to emphasise that assisting the *Jugendweihe* cam-paign was not an act of loyalty towards the state, given the ceremony's voluntary nature, despite the confusion the SED was trying to sow. Mitzenheim warned that teachers who persuaded pupils to participate in a ceremony which must be rejected on religious grounds would lose the respect of the community.[87] An SED report noted functionaries' 'lack of faith' in the party's ability to combat 'more aggressive' vicars, indicating that even those responsible for building socialism doubted they would succeed.[88]

The SED and the *Jugendweihe* committees it dominated and sustained increas-ingly concentrated their efforts on splitting and undermining the churches' oppo-sition. A report of October 1955 called for greater attention to 'loyal' clergy and parish council members and for stronger public protests against 'reactionary' vicars.[89] A letter from the regional *Jugendweihe* committee attempted to isolate par-ents from the churches by claiming that many parents wanted their children to par-ticipate in both confirmation and the *Jugendweihe*. The committee backed this view and attacked the 'impatience' of some clergy, whose view of the secular cere-mony was denounced as creating 'conflicts in the hearts of the faithful'. However, the letter could cite only two clergy, neither of them from the Erfurt region, who supported the *Jugendweihe*.[90]

Bishop Mitzenheim proved central to the SED's approach. Despite his con-tinuing theological aversion to the *Jugendweihe*, he failed to recognise the churches' strength in 1955 and, presumably seeing the SED's plans as unstoppable, attempted to preserve a climate in which the churches could retain influence among young people by beginning to equivocate on the incompatibility of confirmation with the *Jugendweihe*. On 23 November 1955 his sermon in Weimar attacked Marxism-Leninism, but included an assurance that participation in the secular ceremony would prevent churchgoers only from becoming godparents, holding church office and taking part in church elections, rather than denying them all church rights. 'No-one can say this is an intolerant and impatient attitude,' declared the bishop. 'Everyone must admit that this is a generous and charitable ruling which takes account of our young people's characters.'[91]

Though this reaction was arguably premature at a time when the *Jugendweihe* was not yet a standard part of young people's development and when the churches' battle against the new institution still enjoyed wide support, Mitzenheim had perhaps accurately recognised that in the long term the churches would be powerless to prevent the SED's success, given the party's domination of youth through the education system and the FDJ, and its control of young people's careers. By the late 1950s, these factors turned the *Jugendweihe* into an accepted milestone in young people's lives. Mitzenheim's Weimar sermon foreshadowed the debate which split the church between those who firmly believed the churches should (indeed could) not alter their theological position, and those who, like Mitzenheim, looked beyond the *Jugendweihe* issue in their concern for the churches' overall position and preferred to make some concessions rather than face probable extinction over their own 'either/or' dogma. The SED, which pursued a 'divide and rule' policy with the churches wherever possible, only benefited from these controversies. The internal wrangles undermined the churches in the public eye and enabled believers to salve their consciences when bowing to the growing pressures on their children to conform by taking the *Jugendweihe* oath.

Generally, Mitzenheim pursued a dual policy, trying to preserve both peace with the state and defending his theological positions on the *Jugendweihe* and confirmation. During the late 1950s he was attacked by the western press and many within the churches for his pragmatism and readiness to compromise, and by the SED press for fulfilling his role as bishop.[92] Eventually, faced with realities, his pragmatic desire for an arrangement with the state won over. In the meantime, despite indicating his readiness to compromise a little in November 1955, Mitzenheim continued to fight the *Jugendweihe*. In October 1956 he wrote privately to Paul Wandel, the SED's culture and education secretary, to protest that the state was using all possible means to promote the *Jugendweihe*, although it was supposedly an independent, voluntary institution. He referred to the campaigns being waged even within children's holiday camps, and complained that newly printed family bibles omitted space for confirmation details, but left plenty of room to record the *Jugendweihe*. Mitzenheim appealed for the pressure and conflicts of conscience heaped on young people to end, and warned that the churches' position would not change. Instead he suggested the state could introduce a different ceremony for all school leavers which was neither atheistic nor anti-Christian and did not clash with the timing of confirmation ceremonies. If such a ceremony had no oath and a different name, he promised the church would reconsider its position.[93] The state – aware that the *Jugendweihe* was slowly taking root and undermining the churches in an increasingly secular world, and no doubt fearful of humiliation – refused to make such a major retreat.

Thus, Mitzenheim's pragmatism did not extend to significant theological shifts. In a 1957 letter to clergy, Mitzenheim responded to a speech made by the SED's leader, Ulbricht, in Sonneberg by again denouncing the *Jugendweihe* and swore that the church would always protest against the ceremony's state support.[94]

However, his general position gained ground within his diocesan church and ultimately it was the Eisenach church which, during a synod meeting of January 1958,
took the first moves towards compromising with the state over the *Jugendweihe*.
Increasing numbers of parish clergy were also prepared to co-operate with the state,
in line with the more moderate synod line.[95]

The synod's January 1958 vote, which followed a change in the wording of the
Jugendweihe oath, was a major departure from previous policy as it allowed all children to attend religious preparation classes and be confirmed, irrespective of
Jugendweihe participation. However, the confirmation ceremony was altered to
exclude first holy communion, which was held separately a few weeks later. For
1959 the rules were again altered: now confirmands were only excluded from communion if they used the *Jugendweihe* deliberately to reject Christian teaching. Even
so, vicars were advised to reject intending communicants only after consulting the
parish council and the local superintendent.[96]

Although the causal relationship was circular to some extent, it is hard to
escape the conclusion that it was rising levels of *Jugendweihe* participation during
the late 1950s as the SED's organisational and persuasive techniques improved
which forced the church's eventual changes of principle on the incompatibility of
confirmation and *Jugendweihe*. As Mitzenheim had realised, the churches had little
option other than to react to the SED's success if they wished to retain any influence with the young. He upheld this view even though confirmation figures fell as
quickly in Thuringia as in provinces where the churches still rejected the
Jugendweihe.[97] Nevertheless, in the few areas where the churches' influence
remained paramount, the SED had little success in introducing the *Jugendweihe*.
This was notably the case in the Catholic Eichsfeld throughout the 1950s, where
even many SED members did not enter their children. In response, in 1957 the state
education service attempted to improve youth indoctrination by co-operating with
the SED on cadre policy in the Eichsfeld's schools, where there were 'too many'
CDU headteachers. Heads and other teachers were to be replaced with SED staff
over a two-year period to ensure the implementation of 'socialist education aims'
and to 'strengthen and more successfully structure ideological education'.[98]

Like the Catholic church, and in contrast to the Eisenach diocese, the Magdeburg church outwardly retained its harsh stance throughout the 1950s. A letter from
the Magdeburg bishop to parents of confirmands in January 1959 not only re-
emphasised his church's 'either/or' position, but sought to embarrass the SED in
much the same way as the party tried to embarrass the churches. The technique was
to quote prominent comrades who had departed from the official constitutional
ground of religious toleration, such as Werner Neugebauer, the SED's education
chief, who publicly announced: 'We Marxist-Leninists … are firmly convinced
there is no God. But when the religious believers repeatedly proclaim their religious
teachings and speak of God, sometimes our feelings are also hurt … ' His colleague
Kurt Hager was also quoted as saying that *Jugendweihe* preparations enabled 'young
people to see the world as it really is, free of any superstitious and mystical beliefs'.[99]

Most notably the Magdeburg church responded to Ulbricht's Sonneberg speech of September 1957, when he launched the 1958 *Jugendweihe* preparations, by writing to all parishes highlighting the speech's implicit attacks on the churches and on Christian beliefs.[100]

However, even the Magdeburg church was forced to acknowledge the *Jugendweihe*'s ubiquity by the late 1950s, and to refrain from placing parents in an impossible position between the intransigence of both state and churches. The Eisenach church's lead also embarrassed Magdeburg into change. Thus, while urging parents and young people to refuse the *Jugendweihe*, the Magdeburg church attempted to avert mass disobedience by effectively fudging the issue. Even if they attended the *Jugendweihe*, all children were to receive confirmation classes. Thus, Christian influence on them was to be preserved for as long as possible. Recognition would be given to all children who completed the course. This recognition would not, however, be equivalent to confirmation, which would be reserved for those children who had not attended the *Jugendweihe*. Those who participated in the secular ceremony would not, however, be excluded from communion forever, let alone excommunicated, despite some earlier threats. The church realised that those who attended the *Jugendweihe* needed most spiritual guidance. Therefore, these young people could be received fully into the church providing they proved they really belonged to their parish, rejected the anti-Christian, atheist path for about a year, and accepted *Junge Gemeinde* help. The new procedures would remain in force until a 'final resolution of the confirmation question'.[101] This compromise also amounted to a victory for the SED as even the Magdeburg church had tacitly recognised the socialist state's claim to instil dialectical materialism into children. The church leadership was perhaps reacting to signs that some Magdeburg vicars, faced with the problems of practical ministry, were increasingly prepared to deal with state authorities despite instructions to the contrary.[102]

This compromise, though a major concession by the Magdeburg church, still did not satisfy everyone. This quickly became clear in Bleicherode when confirmands' parents refused to accept that their children must wait an entire year for confirmation just because they had attended the *Jugendweihe*. Some parents threatened to leave the church altogether because of the new arrangement. Evidently their religious convictions did not run particularly deep. The dissent in the parish forced the superintendent to introduce a local compromise, in which all children would receive a special blessing on the traditional confirmation date. Those who had not attended the *Jugendweihe* would be confirmed on Ascension Day, while *Jugendweihe* participants could be re-educated by the church and prove their religious devotion in time for a confirmation ceremony by the end of the school year. The superintendent, Dr Schack, defended his position, saying: 'The individual pastor's Christian conscience must take precedence over the church authorities' regulations in times of complex conflicts and difficulties.'[103] Such a comment reflected a great, if reluctant, change of heart in Schack who in 1950 had continually referred to communism as a form of 'organised theft' and compared the GDR's development to the Third Reich's.[104] Elsewhere, the Magdeburg church's insistence on upholding its regulations about confirming *Jugendweihe* participants caused problems well into the 1960s, and highlighted citizens' readiness to conform to the norms demanded by the state, even at the expense of their own religion. This enabled the state to attack the Magdeburg church and pressurise clergy to abandon their stance. The state was, thus, practically encouraging children to demand confirmation to embarrass the church. The state also attacked the Magdeburg church with the 'good' example of its Eisenach counterpart.[105]

The Catholic church's unequivocal resistance to the *Jugendweihe* can be quickly sketched. Initially, while leaving individuals to make their own choice, the suffragan bishop of Erfurt, Freusberg, decreed that neither those who swore the *Jugendweihe* oath nor their parents could enjoy the sacraments until an official recantation supported by two referees was given in a priest's presence.[106] Later in 1955, a pastoral letter from Freusberg to all Thuringian Catholics warned that participants faced excommunication as the *Jugendweihe*'s organisers regarded Christianity as a fairy tale and did not observe the event's officially voluntary nature. Like other church leaders, Freusberg emphasised this voluntary nature in the hope that citizens would have the courage to resist the pressure exerted in the schools and elsewhere.[107] Local priests shared the bishop's hardline stance. The depth of feeling is illustrated by the Martinfeld priest (Heiligenstadt district), who reportedly said he would rather deal with a dead child than one who had been to the *Jugendweihe*.[108] However, there were some signs of Catholics leaving the church over the *Jugendweihe*, forcing the church to allow *Jugendweihe* participants to take communion six months after the state ceremony.[109] Overall, though, participation rates remained low in the Eichsfeld, bucking the trend elsewhere. Even in 1963, the state had to use underhand means to involve Eichsfeld children in the state ceremony, for instance by retrospectively announcing that a school trip to a factory had been the first preparation lesson.[110]

By 1960 the SED had succeeded in removing most young people from the churches' influence through the administrative expedients employed against religious education in state schools and the introduction of a ceremony which effectively countered confirmation. The *Jugendweihe* appeared relatively innocuous to most young people and their parents, and many perceived that the potential disadvantages of non-participation to career prospects far outweighed any theological considerations. As a consequence confirmation numbers quickly fell, and when the teenagers of the 1950s had children of their own in the 1960s and 1970s, across the GDR far fewer of them were baptised than in the early 1950s.[111] However, the SED's success in reducing the churches' influence did not increase young people's enthusiasm for socialism, as was to become clear in 1968 (see Chapter 7). For many young people, the *Jugendweihe* was merely an outward ritual to achieve societal acceptance, and with the immediate incentive of material reward in the way of *Jugendweihe* presents or money. The Protestant leaders were themselves partly responsible for allowing their churches' influence to wane, but their congregations' insistence on combining their temporal and secular duties forced them into compromises.

Clearly, Protestant parents were not prepared to go to the cross to protect their children from atheist influence. Catholic leaders, however, felt little pressure to conform from their adherents and steadfastly resisted the *Jugendweihe*. Here was a clear example of the limits of SED hegemony.

The churches in the 1960s

By the mid-1960s, the state felt far more secure in its relations with the churches. After the battles of the 1950s, there were no signs that church influence was regaining ground. Though various opponents still demanded the state's attention, some of the church leaders whom the state perceived as a threat had moved or retired. The Thuringian synod's support for the generally loyal Bishop Mitzenheim increased following the election of several new members. The churches' perceived need to organise events designed to initiate a more active parish life, particularly aimed at the young, suggest that the scale and societal importance of church life had dramatically diminished since the 1950s.[112]

One sign of this was that many officially left the church (which absolved them from church taxes) rather than simply letting their faith lapse. The trend was visible even among the generally more devout Catholic population: while only 255 Catholics in the future *Bezirk* Erfurt left their church in 1948, 1,284 did so in 1954. In the first nine months of 1955 alone, 7,250 people in the *Bezirk* had left the churches.[113] Between 1948 and 1960, 142,000 people left the Eisenach church, compared with 20,600 who joined. Mitzenheim noted that the highest rates were in years when the state fought the churches most actively, a reflection which may have influenced his conciliatory policy to avoid further attacks. It was also reported that the SED was pressurising people to leave the churches, principally its own members, but even groups in the state's pay such as firefighters.[114] Furthermore, mass emigration before the borders were sealed in 1961 robbed the Thuringian church of many believers and created a proportionally more secular society.

Church attendances were also poor. Spot checks in 1962 showed that well under 5 per cent of the population attended Sunday services in rural districts and even fewer in the towns.[115] Not surprisingly, the situation was significantly different in Heiligenstadt district where some 23 per cent of the whole population (around 30 per cent of church members) attended Sunday mass in Heiligenstadt and Ershausen, and as many as 57.6 per cent (63.1 per cent) in Uder. Churchgoers were predominantly female, usually young or old and not of working age, and often from 'bourgeois' backgrounds. As Sunday services apparently had a 'minimal' influence on the population, the churches also used other means, including personal visits, to reach the population.[116] In 1960 Bishop Mitzenheim reported that the Eisenach church's position was stabilising in rural areas (presumably in response to the church's resistance to agricultural collectivisation) after a period of stagnation. However, no ground could be won amongst the working class. Church choirs were also still active in 1961, though the number of singers had dropped to 14,500.[117] The church's popularity in villages often depended on local clergy.

Though by 1960 religious education was again permitted at acceptable times in some state schools, attendances had fallen. Mitzenheim blamed parents for this. He reported that in many rural parishes between 90 and 100 per cent of baptised children attended these classes, but only 50 per cent in the larger towns and around 30 per cent in industrial centres. However, as over half of the region's population lived in urban communities by 1964, and as the proportion of baptised children fell by nearly two thirds in the Thuringian diocese between 1950 and 1965,[118] a decline in RE attendance seemed inevitable. Confirmation numbers were also falling, even allowing for somewhat smaller year groups. Meanwhile, *Jugendweihe* figures grew steadily during the 1960s. In 1965, 16,043 youngsters (some 83 per cent of this age group) attended the ceremony in 1965.[119]

The FDJ could also claim by 1959 that many young believers were actively involved in the official youth organisation, despite a hard core whose religious affiliations prevented them endorsing even the official peace policy and who preferred to believe that God controlled the nuclear trigger. A larger group was concerned with such matters as the compatibility of religion and socialism, and of the church and the FDJ. Nevertheless, by 1959 very few young believers felt compelled to leave the FDJ on religious grounds. The *Junge Gemeinde* and *Pfarrjugend* never recovered from the 1953 campaign against them. Despite boasting some 14,000 regular attenders between them in 1959, that figure represented only 6.25 per cent of *Bezirk* Erfurt's 14–25 year olds. The *Junge Gemeinde* contracted to 7,500 followers in 1960, and 14–16 year olds proved increasingly difficult to attract. Nevertheless, the state permitted bible-study holidays after the churches' 1958 concessions, and young people's missions were also active. Although these activities were not threatening, the FDJ was worried enough to produce a thirty-four-page report. The FDJ was particularly concerned that the Protestant churches' youth work was often directed by the less 'progressive' clergy. As many as 90 per cent of church youth functionaries apparently supported Berlin's anti-SED 'atom bishop' Dibelius'.[120]

The churches were not content to watch their influence and future simply disintegrate and by 1962 redoubled their efforts to recruit young people by organising dances, sports days and the like, while playing down purely religious themes. The FDJ was reputedly 'on its knees' in some areas.[121] However, the churches did little to resist the introduction of conscription in 1962 and religiously minded young people enlisted normally.[122] Despite the SED's paranoid reactions, young people's marginally increased interest in religion still did not threaten the well established FDJ's existence in most areas, let alone imply that a theocracy was imminent. For most church communities, the 1960s were a period of stability yet steady decline.[123] The state's interest in steadily co-opting Christians via the NF's 'Christian Circles' and similar groups waned in some areas, perhaps reflecting a lost sense of urgency once the tide had been turned. Although some vicars attempted to retake the initiative, as in Bleicherode,[124] in most areas religion was not a dominant part of everyday life by the 1960s.

An exception was the Catholic Eichsfeld, which remained devout. Here the SED very noticeably changed its policy, and recognised Catholicism's strength. Local propaganda emphasised the 1959 'Call from the Eichsfeld', which symbolised the party's more realistic policy after the earlier, mainly fruitless, class struggle. The 'Call' was made by about 120 local Catholics at an NF meeting, and urged Catholics throughout the GDR to work for peace (the lowest common denominator) and collaborate in building 'our social order' which would give Christians, as other groups, a 'secure existence and future'. One Catholic at the meeting summed up the Eichsfeld's peculiar mixture of strong religious tradition and enforced deference to state authority (especially in the border area) by saying: 'there can be no co-existence between the ideology of Christians and atheists, but this must not and cannot prevent either Christians or atheists constructing socialism jointly in our German Democratic Republic.'[125] In other words, both sides would ignore their differences in a situation which could not be changed: both Catholics and the GDR were there to stay. This new line essentially marked the SED's recognition (via the NF and CDU) that it could not hope to establish the same degree of control in the Eichsfeld as elsewhere.

Yet the SED still attempted to gain ground in the Eichsfeld within this framework, and the church's accommodation with the secular power did not prevent it from defending its position when this seemed necessary. However, the dye of mutual toleration was essentially cast. Providing the faithful were generally working for socialism (at least outwardly), or at least not working against it, the party was satisfied and concentrated only on undermining those 'reactionary religious influences' who seemed particularly dangerous. Meanwhile, ordinary Christian citizens would not be 'insulted, disparaged or presented as morally substandard people or bad citizens'. Tact would underpin the 'atheist Enlightenment'. The Eichsfeld party had little practical alternative, as many functionaries were themselves committed Catholics prepared to overlook church events which would not have been so easily tolerated elsewhere. Many other Eichsfeld SED members were not natives of the area, but had moved or been moved there. They must have appeared to locals as colonial masters. Overall, though, 'ideological subversion' by the clergy declined markedly in the new climate.[126]

The new toleration encouraged the Catholic church to increase its religious activities. Sometimes this had political consequences. Following Bishop Freusberg's visitation to Mühlhausen district in 1962, during which he was attended by large numbers of the faithful and railed against state education and the *Jugendweihe*, children refused to sing pioneer songs and attendance at meetings of the official women's organisation (*Demokratischer Frauenbund Deutschlands*, DFD) fell sharply. More tellingly, in some areas SED members without their party badges joined those welcoming Freusberg. Similarly, visits after 1964 by Freusberg's successor, Hugo Aufderbeck, became major events in specially decorated Eichsfeld villages. The bishop was given a motorcycle escort to the church and was welcomed by the church choir. By early 1968, no priests and few parish-council members were prepared to participate in the 'Christian circles'.[127]

The Eichsfeld's many church festival parades were tolerated by the party, providing they were orderly and purely religious in nature. The events were carefully discussed with the state authorities in advance, who effectively gave a tacit state blessing on the ceremony. They remained major public events throughout the 1960s. In 1966, for instance, the Palm Sunday procession attracted 3,400 participants in Heiligenstadt, and some 9,000 joined the Klüschen pilgrimage. The state bitterly noted that the population showed much more spontaneous initiative on such occasions than on state festivals, but attendances kept rising.[128]

However, the question of legal recognition for church holidays remained an area of controversy between the Catholic church and the state throughout the 1960s. In 1966 only 41 per cent of pupils attended school on All Saints Day.[129] Though the situation improved in the following years, in 1968 only 70 per cent of Heiligenstadt district's school children arrived at school punctually on that day. Most of the remainder arrived only after mass. In some villages, however, around three quarters of school children were late. In Reinhotterode only 3.7 per cent attended on time, and in Birkenfelde there were no lessons before 8.20 a.m. In one Heiligenstadt school not even all staff were present.[130] Such conflicts of authority continued into the late 1960s and beyond and represented an issue of great emotional sensitivity to local Catholics.

The SED's failure to co-opt the Eichsfeld fully is perhaps clearest from *Jugendweihe* statistics for the 1960s. In 1965 only 221 young people took the state oath in Heiligenstadt and Worbis districts combined. This represented only 1.4 per cent of participants in *Bezirk* Erfurt, although the two districts represented 8.8 per cent of the region's population.[131]

The SED was undoubtedly right to conclude in 1962 that although 'the great majority of the Eichsfeld Catholics remain loyal to their church, as GDR citizens they carry out the duties required for the strengthening of the GDR in a disciplined way'.[132] By 1978, when the SED made its general pact with the (Protestant) 'church in socialism', the party had perhaps learnt from the Eichsfeld example that the socialist order was not threatened by even an active church. Though the party had not won hearts and minds, it had, crucially, won its citizens' obedience and could achieve better results by co-operating with the churches rather than seeking to crush them.

Notes

1 On the ideological background to the conflict, cf. R. Mau, *Eingebunden in den Realsozialismus? Die Evangelische Kirche als Problem der SED* (Göttingen, Vandenhoeck & Ruprecht, 1994), pp. 15–20.
2 Nine parishes in Nordhausen district belonged to the Hanover Evangelical-Lutheran Church.
3 Cf. R. Goeckel, *The Lutheran Church and the East German State* (Ithaca, NY, Cornell

University Press, 1990), pp. 16–17.

4 ThHStAW, Ki 3, fol. 57, 'Bericht … ', 1 October 1953.

5 ThHStAW, BdMP 863, fol. 198, Mitzenheim to Eggerath, 23 February 1950.

6 ThHStAW, BdMP 233, AfI, 'Bericht Nr. 554', 12 October 1950; BdMP 864, fols 87–96, meeting between Eggerath and the vicar.

7 *Ibid.*, fol. 358, SED, 'Informationsbericht Nr. 118/52', 24 June 1952.

8 LPA, BIV/2/14-006. This example is drawn from a seven-page report covering the last months of 1954, 'Feindliche Äußerungen durch Pfarrer … ', undated.

9 1 October 1953 report (note 4), fol. 60.

10 ThHStAW, Ki 18, fols 29–30, Magdeburg church pastoral letter, May 1951.

11 ThHStAW, BdMP 238, fol. 150, AfI, 'Bericht Nr. 273', 6 June 1951.

12 ThHStAW, MdI/20, 66, fol. 310, BdVP, 'Übersicht über die Lage … ', 26 June 1953; Ki 3, fol. 210, 'Informatorischer Bericht … ', 15 July 1958; LPA, BIV/2/13-008, RdB, 'Einschätzung über die Vorbereitung und Durchführung der Wahlen … ', undated [1957], p. 22; ThHStAW, Ki 7, fol. 77, 'Bericht über Besprechung mit dem Landeskirchenrat Eisenach … ', 7 August 1957.

13 Cf. H. Siebert, *Das Eichsfeld unter dem Sowjetstern* (Duderstadt, Mecke Druck und Verlag, 1992), p. 226. Even this virulent opponent of the GDR, a retired senior Catholic priest, provides no examples of arrested Thuringian clergy.

14 15 July 1958 report (note 12), fol. 211.

15 ThHStAW, NF 183, fols 37–8, 'Beschluss des Sekretariats der Bezirksleitung der SED Erfurt vom 10.12.1959, Nr. 256'.

16 ThHStAW, BdMP 228, AfI, 'Bericht Nr. 101', 12 May 1950; BdMP 229, AfI, 'Bericht Nr. 225/50', 17 July 1950; BdMP 863, fol. 271, 'Aktennotiz für den Herrn Oberstleutnant Mischtschenkow', 6 October 1950; *ibid.*, fol. 277, 'Niederschrift', 26 October 1950.

17 LPA, IV/L/2/3-047, SED Thuringia executive, 19 October 1950 minutes, pp. 4–5.

18 LPA, AIV/2/4-123, SED Mühlhausen, 'Bericht über Erscheinungen … ', 18 October 1950, p. 3; 6 June 1951 report (note 11), fols 148–9.

19 ThHStAW, MdI/20.1, 479, fol. 94, Heiligenstadt police report, 21 November 1961.

20 LPA, AIV/2/4-123, 'Analyse der Volksbefragung vom 3.-5.6.1951 … ', undated, p. 44.

21 ThHStAW, Ki 27, fols 22–5, 'Einschätzung der Geistlichen … ', 21 October 1954; LPA, BIV/2/14-002, 'Wahlanalyse über die Beteiligung der christlichen Bürger … ', undated [1961], p. 4; ThHStAW, Ki 27, fol. 111, RdK Heiligenstadt, 'Auswertung der Volkswahl 1958', 22 November 1958.

22 21 October 1954 report (note 21).

23 LPA, AIV/2/4-123, Magdeburg church letter to the prime ministers of Thuringia and Sachsen-Anhalt, 23 May 1951; ThHStAW, Ki 3, fol. 137, 'Information über Verhalten der Religionsgemeinschaften … ', 20 May 1957; undated report (note 20), p. 44.

24 Undated report (note 20), pp. 43–4.

25 LPA, BIV/2/13-006, 'Die Einschätzung der Volkswahlen … ', 20 October 1954, p. 13.

26 LPA, BIV/213-007, 'Einschätzung der Arbeit der Organe des Staatsapparates … ', 1 November 1954.

27 21 October 1954 report (note 21).

28 1957, 1958, 1961 results: ThHStAW, Ki 11, fol. 78, 'Wie verhielten sich die Kirchenleitungen 1958 und 1961?', undated [1961]; 1963 results: LPA, BIV/2/13-725, 'Entwurf! Analyse über die Vorbereitung und Durchführung der Volkswahlen … ', undated [late 1963?], pp. 51–2.

29 6 June 1951 report (note 11), fol. 148.

30 ThHStAW, Vs/St 571, fols 20, 39, police reports on election security, 2 and 13 September

1961; Ki 9, fols 4, 6, RdS Weimar, 'Niederschrift. Gespräch leitender Partei- und Staatsfunktionäre ... ', 17 September 1963.

31 According to the Catholic bishop of Aachen in 1960, cited in A. Hearnden, *Education in the two Germanies* (Oxford, Basil Blackwell, 1974), p. 135.

32 Siebert, pp. 185–6, gives various examples of early SMA involvement in religious education matters.

33 ThHStAW, BdMP 863, fol. 10, Mitzenheim to Frölich, 18 December 1946.

34 *Länderverfassungen 1946/47* (Berlin, Staatsverlag der Deutschen Demokratischen Republik, 1990), pp. 12–13; K.-H. Schöneburg (ed.), *Geschichte des Staates und des Rechts der DDR: Dokumente 1945–1949* (Berlin, Staatsverlag der Deutschen Demokratischen Republik, 1984), pp. 263–5.

35 ThHStAW, BdMP 863, fol. 203, Eggerath's meeting with Müller, 4 April 1950.

36 *Ibid.*, fols 220 ff, Magdeburg church, 'Kanzelabkündigung', 31 March 1950.

37 ThHStAW, BdMP 864, fols 294–5, AfI, 'Bericht Nr. 294', 3 July 1951.

38 *Ibid.*, fol. 311, AfI, 'Bericht Nr. 743', 29 December 1950.

39 For a discussion of the term 'niche society', cf. M. Fulbrook, *Anatomy of a Dictatorship* (Oxford, Oxford University Press, 1995), especially pp. 129–30.

40 Cf. Mau, *Eingebunden*, p. 26, and D. Pollack, 'Von der Volkskirche zur Minderheitskirche: Zur Entwicklung von Religiosität und Kirchlichkeit in der DDR', in H. Kaelbe, J. Kocka and H. Zwahr (eds), *Sozialgeschichte der DDR* (Stuttgart, Klett Cotta, 1994), p. 279.

41 The Catholic *Pfarrjugend* ('parish youth') played a similar role.

42 ThHStAW, BdMP 864, fols 365–6, 369, 371–2, 377, AfI, 'Bericht Nr. 344', 11 September 1951; LPA, BIV/2/14-003, SED Bad Langensalza, 'Tätigkeit der sogenannten Jungen Gemeinde', 1 December 1952, and 'Tätigkeit der Jungen Gemeinde', 11 March 1953, p. 4.

43 LPA, BIV/2/16-017, FDJ, 'Bericht über den Abschluß des Umtausches der Mitgliedsbücher ... ', 20 July 1953.

44 Cf. G. Besier, *Der SED-Staat und die Kirche: Der Weg in die Anpassung* (Munich, Bertelsmann, 1993), p. 115.

45 LPA, BIV/2/14-002, SED BL, 'Arbeit der Kirche und Junge Gemeinde (April 1953)', p. 4.

46 Besier, *Der SED-Staat*, p. 116; *Dokumente der SED*, III (1954), 279–92. On the SED/FDJ's descriptions of the *Junge Gemeinde*, cf. C. Stappenbeck, 'Freie Deutsche Jugend und Junge Gemeinde 1952/53', in H. Gotschlich (ed.), *"Links und links und Schritt gehalten ... " Die FDJ: Konzepte, Abläufe, Grenzen*, Die Freie Deutsche Jugend: Beiträge zur Geschichte einer Massenorganisation, 1 (Berlin, Metropol Verlag, 1994), pp. 141–56 (especially p. 151).

47 April 1953 report (note 45), p. 4.

48 ThHStAW, V 15, fols 47–51, RdK Sömmerda, 'Protokoll über die Maßnahmen gegen die staatsfeindlichen Kräfte an der Oberschule Buttstädt', 18 April 1953. A similar example is provided by A. Peter, 'Der Kampf gegen die Junge Gemeinde Anfang der 50er Jahre: Das Beispiel Guben', in Gotschlich (ed.), *"Links und links ... "*, pp. 198–205.

49 The *Edelweißpiraten* was also the name chosen by some opposition youth groups during the Third Reich: cf. D. Peukert, *Inside Nazi Germany: Conformity, Opposition and Racism in Everyday Life* (London, Penguin, 1989), pp. 154–65. The Buttstädt students clearly perceived that SED rule closely resembled NSDAP rule.

50 18 April 1953 report (note 48), fols 49, 50.

51 Cf. Stappenbeck, 'Freie Deutsche Jugend..... ', p. 151.

52 ThHStAW, V 15, fols 55–6, letter to RdK Sömmerda, 20 April 1953.

53 I. Spittmann and K. W. Fricke, *Der 17. Juni 1953: Arbeiteraufstand in der DDR* (Cologne,

Edition Deutschland Archiv/Verlag Wissenschaft und Politik, 1982), p. 9.

54 ThHStAW, V 15, fol. 53, RdK Sömmerda to RdB, 5 May 1953.

55 *Ibid.*, fol. 58, 'Maßnahmen auf dem Gebiete der Volksbildung … ', (undated).

56 *Ibid.*, fol. 88, 'Sitzung des Pädagogischen Rates der Oberschule Sömmerda am 9. Juni 1953'. The essays are in *ibid.*, fols 60–82.

57 *Ibid.*, fols 21–3, report on the 'New Course' in education in *Bezirk* Erfurt, 24 June 1953.

58 Text of the 10 June 1953 communiqué in Besier, *Der SED-Staat*, pp. 130–1.

59 ThHStAW, Ki 3, fol. 69, 'Arbeitsbericht des Ref. Religionsgemeinschaften … ', 9 November 1953.

60 *Ibid.*

61 ThHStAW, V 15, fol. 91, 'Christenlehre und Schulunterricht', 28 October 1953.

62 An Erfurt vicar told one class that he regarded God as the highest being, while others believed this role was filled by 'some SED functionary or other': *ibid.*, fol. 119, untitled report [spring 1954?].

63 ThHStAW, V 15, fols 237–9, 'Entwurf einer Anweisung … '; *ibid.*, fol. 236, covering letter, 23 February 1956. In 1968 all fifteen district education heads were SED members: ThHStAW, Ka 133, 'Gesamtanalyse … ', 22 March 1968.

64 The 'Lange decree' of 12 February 1958 is discussed by Besier, *Der SED-Staat*, p. 253.

65 LPA, BIV/2/14-002, 'Informationsbericht Nr. 12/58', 4 June 1958, pp. 7–8.

66 ThHStAW, Ki 10, fols 19–20, RdK Eisenach, 'Niederschrift über die Aussprache … ', 27 March 1961.

67 ThHStAW, Ki 20, fol. 173, Mitzenheim to the synod, 'Der Stand des kirchlichen Lebens in Thüringen', 2 May 1961. My observation relies on oral information provided by Thuringians after 1989.

68 Cf. Pollack, 'Von der Volkskirche … ', p. 281.

69 H. Dähn, *Konfrontation oder Kooperation? Das Verhältnis von Staat und Kirche in der SBZ/DDR 1945-1980* (Opladen, Westdeutscher Verlag, 1982), pp. 54, 215.

70 H. Dohle, *et al.* (eds), *Auf dem Weg zur gemeinsamen humanistischen Verantwortung* (Berlin, Union Verlag, 1967), p. 312; H. Zimmermann, H. Ulrich and M. Fehlauer, eds, *DDR Handbuch*, 3rd edn, 2 vols (Cologne, Verlag Wissenschaft und Politik, 1985), I, 693.

71 Cited by G. Lange and others (eds), *Katholische Kirche – Sozialistischer Staat DDR: Dokumente und öffentliche Äußerungen 1945–1992* (Leipzig, Benno, 1992), p. 73.

72 Cf. Dibelius's 7 January 1955 letter, cited in F. Kopp and G. Fischbach (eds), *SBZ von 1955 bis 1958*, Taschenausgabe (Bonn/Berlin, Bundesministerium für gesamtdeutsche Fragen, 1961), p. 8.

73 *Glaube und Heimat*, 2 January 1955, 'Wort des Landesbischofs zum neuen Jahr'. Copy in ThHStAW, Ki 19, fol. 41.

74 The January–February 1955 correspondence is cited by Dähn, *Konfrontation oder Kooperation?*, p. 56.

75 ThHStAW, V 15, fols 137–8, Mitzenheim to Gebhardt, 18 February 1955; *ibid.*, fol. 13, RdK Weimar circular to schools, 2 February 1955.

76 LPA, BIV/2/9.02-021, 'Vorbereitung und Durchführung der Jugendweihe', 1 December 1954, pp. 2–3; *ibid.*, 'Jugendweihe', 13 January 1955, p. 2.

77 ThHStAW, Ki 7, fols 91-8, Mitzenheim speech, 19 March 1955. Several similar sermons are recorded in ibid.

78 LPA, BIV/2/9.02-021, 'Bericht über den Stand der Vorbereitung der Jugendweihe … ', 13 December 1954, pp. 4–5.

79 ThHStAW, Ki 3, fol. 129, 'Bericht über die feindliche Tätigkeit der Kirche', 18 January 1956; LPA, BIV/2/14-002, 'Informationsbericht über die Tätigkeit der Kirche … ', 18

January 1955, p. 6.

80 13 January 1955 report (note 76), p. 4. Hitler Youth members swore an oath to the *Führer*, reproduced in J. Noakes and G. Pridham, *Nazism 1919–1945*, Exeter Studies in History, 3 vols (Exeter, University of Exeter Press, 1983–88), II (1984), 422.

81 ThHStAW, Ki 19, fol. 123, Magdeburg church, 'Rundverfügung Nr. 30/56', 3 February 1956.

82 13 January 1955 report (note 76).

83 LPA, BIV/2/9.02-021, Bezirksausschuß für Jugendweihe, 'Bericht über den Beginn der Jugendweihe 1956 … ', 14 October 1955, p. 3.

84 LPA, BIV/2/14-002, SED memo, 22 May 1956.

85 LPA, BIV/2/9.02-021, 'Direktive über die Ergebnisse der Jugendweihe 1955 … ', 11 August 1955, pp. 2–3, and Bezirksausschuß für Jugendweihe, 'Bericht über die Ergebnisse der Jugendweihe 1956 … ', 19 May 1956, p. 1.

86 LPA, BIV/2/9.02-021, Bezirksausschuß für Jugendweihe, 'Bericht über den Beginn der Jugendweihe … ', 8 October 1955, pp. 5–7, and 'Information über den Stand der Jugendweihe 1956', 29 November 1955, p. 2.

87 ThHStAW, Ki 19, fols 149–50, Mitzenheim, 'An die evangelischen Lehrer … ', 20 October 1955.

88 LPA, BIV/2/9.02-021, 'Gegenbericht zur Berichterstattung der Genossen des Bezirksausschusses … ', 17 October 1955, p. 3.

89 *Ibid.*

90 LPA, BIV/2/9.02-021, Bezirksausschuß für Jugendweihe letter, 1 February 1956.

91 29 November 1955 report (note 86), p. 2.

92 ThHStAW, Ki 19, FRG and GDR press cuttings about Mitzenheim.

93 ThHStAW, Ki 7, fols 44–6, Mitzenheim to Wandel, 27 October 1956.

94 ThHStAW, Ki 20, fols 154–5, Mitzenheim, '51. Rundbrief', 1 December 1957.

95 ThHStAW, Ki 3, fols 182–3, 'Einschätzung der Ev.-Luth. Kirche in Thüringen, Eisenach', March 1958.

96 ThHStAW, Ki 20, fols 48–50, 'Anordnung zur Durchführung des Synodalbeschlusses … ', 22 December 1958.

97 R. Henkys, 'Die Kirchen im SED-Staat zwischen Anpassung und Widerstand', in J. Weber (ed.), *Der SED-Staat: Neues über eine vergangene Diktatur* (Munich, Olzog Verlag, 1994), p. 205.

98 ThHStAW, NF 183, fol. 38; V 15, fol. 273 ff, see various correspondence and plans.

99 ThHStAW, Ki 19, fols 53–4, Bishop of Magdeburg to parents of confirmands, January 1959, pp. 1–2.

100 *Ibid.*, fols 90–3, Magdeburg church, 'Rundverfügung Nr. 45', 24 February 1956. The Sonneberg speech is in W. Ulbricht, *Zur Geschichte der deutschen Arbeiterbewegung* (Berlin, Dietz), VI (1962), 599–609.

101 January 1959 letter (note 99), pp. 3–4; ThHStAW, Ki 19, fol. 111, Magdeburg church, 'Rundverfügung Nr. 131/58', 27 November 1958.

102 ThHStAW, Ki 3, fol. 186, untitled March 1958 report.

103 ThHStAW, Ki 19, fol. 99, Schack to clergy, 7 March 1959.

104 ThHStAW, BdMP 228, AfI, 'Bericht Nr. 139/50', 23 June 1950.

105 ThHStAW, Ki 9, fols 70–3, RdK Eisenach, 'Niederschrift', 2 February 1962; *ibid.*, fol. 80, 'Protokoll über eine Aussprache in Rothenberga … ', 19 April 1961.

106 ThHStAW, V 15, fols 141–2, BdVP, 'Lagebericht Nr. 28', 15 February 1955.

107 ThHStAW, Ki 19, fol. 118a, 'Aktennotiz', 25 October 1955.

108 ThHStAW, V 15, fol. 343, 'Aktennotiz', 3 February 1958.

109 T. Raabe, *SED-Staat und katholische Kirche: Politische Beziehungen 1949–1961*, Veröffentlichungen der Kommission für Zeitgeschichte, Reihe B: Forschungen, 70 (Paderborn, Ferdinand Schöningh, 1995), pp. 202, 207.

110 ThHStAW, MdI/20.1, 485, fol. 40, VPKA [*Volkspolizei-Kreisamt*, District police office] Heiligenstadt, 'Lageeinschätzung … ', 27 April 1963.

111 ThHStAW, Ki 20, fol. 171, Mitzenheim to the snyod, 'Der Stand des kirchlichen Lebens … ' 2 May 1961; Pollack, 'Von der Volkskirche … ', p. 278.

112 ThHStAW, Ki 7, fol. 174, 'Verhältnis zur Thüringischen Landeskirche', undated [1964?].

113 ThHStAW, Ki 3, fol. 124, 'Bericht über die feindliche Tätigkeit der Kirche', 18 January 1956.

114 Speech (note 111); Ki 9, fol. 94, RdS Erfurt, 'Niederschrift über eine Aussprache … ', 11 December 1962; *ibid.*, fol. 101, RdK Eisenach, 'Niederschrift über die Aussprache … ', 13 November 1962.

115 Even in 1908 average attendance had been only 10–15 per cent , so the long-term decline was not dramatic: K. Nowak, 'Staat ohne Kirche? Überlegungen zur Entkirchlichung der evangelischen Bevölkerung im Staatsgebiet der DDR', in G. Kaiser and E. Frie, *Christen, Staat und Gesellschaft in der DDR* (Frankfurt, Campus Verlag, 1996), p. 25.

116 LPA, BIV/2/14-002, RdB, 'Kontrollmaßnahmen am 18.3., 25.3., 1.4., und 8.4.62 … ', 14 April 1962.

117 ThHStAW, Ki 20, fol. 46, 'Information über den Verlauf der Synode … ', 5 December 1960; Mitzenheim's 1961 speech (note 111), fol. 173.

118 Pollack, 'Von der Volkskirche … ', p. 285.

119 Mitzenheim's speech (note 111), fol. 172v; *Ein Jahr Jugendgesetz: Materialien zur Arbeit der Jugend und mit der Jugend im Bezirk Erfurt* (Erfurt, Staatliche Zentralverwaltung für Statistik, Bezirksstelle Erfurt, 1965), pp. 5, 43.

120 LPA, BIV/2/14-003, FDJ, 'Bericht über die Arbeit mit der religiös gebundenen Jugend … ', 17 October 1959, pp. 1, 3–4, 6–7, 23, 33; BIV/2/5-042, 'Zur Information', 20 October 1961; Mitzenheim's speech (note 111), fol. 173.

121 LPA, BIV/2/14-003, 'Analysierung der Tätigkeit konfessionell gebundener Jugend … ', 12 May 1962.

122 ThHStAW, Vs/St 571, fol. 75, BdVP, 'Information 28/62', 9 March 1962.

123 Cf. Pollack, 'Von der Volkskirche … ', pp. 272, 276–7.

124 LPA, BIV/2/9.02-654, 'Information zu einigen Problemen … ', 30 September 1965, pp. 3–5.

125 LPA, BIV/2/14-002, 'Einschätzung der Beratung mit katholischen Bürgern … ', 29 September 1959; 'Ruf vom Eichsfeld' [28 September 1959]. A less convincing 'Appell aus dem Eichsfeld' of 30 August 1961 welcomed the Berlin Wall: copy in ibid.

126 LPA, IV/4.06/150, 'Die Politik der Partei in Kirchenfragen … ', 9 October 1958; BIV/2/14-002, 'Auswirkungen des politischen Klerikalismus … ', undated [late 1959?], especially p. 3; IV/4.06/150, Staatsanwalt des Bezirkes, 'Bericht über die Tätigkeit der katholischen Kirche', 7 July 1962, p. 1.

127 LPA, BIV/2/14-002, Staatsanwaltschaft des Bezirkes, 'Einschätzung der Tätigkeit der kath. Kirche … ', 10 July 1962, pp. 2–3; BIV/2/14-006, BdVP, 'Tätigkeit des Kath. Weihbischofs … ', 10 July 1962, p. 4; IV/B/4.06/216, CDU Heiligenstadt, 'Informationsbericht', 9 January 1968, p. 6; ThHStAW, Ki 66, RdK Heiligenstadt, 'Vorläufige Einschätzung über die kirchlichen Handlungen … ', 13 September 1966, p. 1.

128 7 July 1962 report (note 126), p. 1; ThHStAW, Ki 66, RdK Heiligenstadt, 'Informationsbericht', 15 July 1966, p. 4, 'Einschätzung der Lage auf kirchenpolitischem Gebiet', 15 July 1966, p. 2, and 'Fronleichnamsprozession, 25.5.67', 26 May 1967, p. 2;

MdI/20.1, 485, fols 44-5, VPKA [*Volkspolizei-Kreisamt*, District police office] Heiligenstadt, 'Überwachung der "Maria Wallfahrt" … ', 15 July 1963.

129　See, e.g., LPA, IV/B/2/15-407, CDU, 'Information über die z.Zt. in den Eichsfeldkreisen geführten Diskussionen … ', 21 February 1968; ThHStAW, Ki 66, RdK Heiligenstadt, 'Jahreseinschätzung über die Probleme der kirchenpolitischen Arbeit', 15 December 1966, p. 9.

130　ThHStAW, Ki 66, RdK Heiligenstadt, 'Wertung über den Ablauf des 01.11.1968 … ', 4 November 1968, pp. 2, 4.

131　*Ein Jahr Jugendgesetz*, p. 43; *Statistisches Jahrbuch 1966: Bezirk Erfurt*, p. 3.

132　LPA, BIV/2/14-002, 'Einschätzung der Tätigkeit der katholischen Kirche … ', 13 July 1962.

6

Behind the Wall

The construction of the Berlin Wall in 1961 is generally regarded as a major caesura in GDR history. But viewed from the perspective of *Bezirk* Erfurt, some 250 kilometres away from Berlin, the event was of less central importance. Although party and state officials may have felt somewhat protected by the security the Wall offered, we shall see that patterns of conformity and non-conformity across the population were not particularly affected by its construction, and that after August 1961 life quickly settled back into the previously established contours.

1961: The borders are sealed

Although agricultural policies were the SED's main focus in early 1960, there were many other causes for concern, in terms of both popular attitudes (reflected in higher rates of citizens 'fleeing the republic'), and of the continuing weakness of local party and state structures. However, the 1960–61 period marked a turning point for the SED, not only because the GDR's borders were finally sealed after 13 August 1961, but also because the party's own structures began to stabilise. The party made more determined attempts to improve basic administration and to unmask the weak and oppositional elements within its ranks. Nonetheless, problems remained throughout the decade.

The political framework had changed in two significant ways since 1956. First, by 1960 western television was a significant disruptive political factor for the SED, despite the shortage of sets. The party attempted to deter this powerful new source of ideological 'poisoning' and 'border crossing' with campaigns in which citizens pledged to remove the part of the receiver which received the western channels. Second, food supplies, though still far from stable, were less of an issue. Instead worries centred more often on shortages of school textbooks, high textiles prices and the lack of checked shirts.[1] Despite the clear increases in industrial and food production, and production workers' wage rises since 1956,[2] perceptions of austerity persevered, suggesting lower tolerance levels. Sometimes there were severe difficulties, as in Heiligenstadt district where butter and bread were often unavailable in early August 1961 and hens were 102,200 eggs behind the state plan.[3] But one of the people's greatest economic complaints resulted directly from the SED's own misplaced optimism in claiming in 1958 that the GDR would overtake West

German standards by 1961. The population now realised this target was unattainable.[4]

There were some tentative signs that the GDR was gaining growing acceptance, if only because it had existed for eleven years. President Wilhelm Pieck's death in September 1960 evoked general sadness and some spontaneous displays of flags at half mast on private houses. However, the subsequent establishment of a Council of State under the SED's First Secretary, Walter Ulbricht, created some confusion. Some noted Ulbricht's accumulation of posts and feared he might 'follow in Stalin's footsteps'.[5]

More importantly, the ongoing 'German question' increasingly dominated public debate. The growing gulf between eastern and western Germany, and the difficulty in obtaining visas for travel between the GDR and FRG in either direction, had always been problematic for the SED, but assumed much larger dimensions in public opinion in the late 1950s as the West Berlin issue reached a head. In 1958, Khrushchev issued an ultimatum to the western allies that he would transfer Soviet responsibilities in West Berlin to the GDR government unless they agreed to West Berlin becoming a 'free city' within the GDR.[6] Many citizens of *Bezirk* Erfurt believed that 'Thuringia will return to the Americans if West Berlin becomes a free city', demonstrating the continuing potency of the brief American occupation over a decade later. Despite the SED's campaigns to send resolutions to that year's Geneva summit, few citizens believed they could influence the outcome, or that the summit would achieve anything. After Khrushchev and Kennedy failed to achieve a diplomatic breakthrough in mid-1961 and the USSR proposed a separate peace treaty with the GDR, some believed war would ensue. Only the more thoughtful pointed out that the real hindrance to German unity was that West German workers were better off than their GDR counterparts and consequently did not want socialism. The same underlying argument was more frequently heard in calls for 'free all-German elections',[7] or that the whole of Berlin should become a 'free city',[8] a development which would have fatally undermined the GDR state.

The SED's general position remained weak in 1960. Despite the party's perpetual anti-western propaganda, few East Germans believed the west wanted war or regarded the West German chancellor, Adenauer, as a danger. The SED's long battle against social democracy had also not prevented some workers from believing that the SPD mayor of West Berlin, Willy Brandt, 'is a good representative of the working class'. Although Soviet disarmament proposals were widely welcomed, this chiefly reflected general hopes for peace rather than devotion to the socialist camp. However, there was cynicism about the Soviets' motivations in some quarters, even among some presumably loyal local government officials. Understandably, plans to station nuclear weapons in the GDR caused some fear. By mid-1961 many felt: 'When they talk most about peace, then they want war. That's how it was under Hitler too.'[9]

Resistance to SED rule was also expressed in reactions to the recruitment campaigns for the National People's Army (NVA). Naturally, many young people wished to avoid military service (which remained voluntary until 1962). The NVA campaigns and GDR foreign and military policy were undermined by the general refusal to view West Germans as enemies, by the obvious contradiction between the SED's avowed peace policies and the simultaneous military expansion, and by fears that military expenditure would reduce living standards.[10] The Free German Youth's inefficacy was revealed when some FDJ members declared: 'We're pacifists and won't carry guns.'[11] Women were particularly reluctant to see their sons enlist.[12] Young people were reportedly fatalistic rather than keen to defend socialism, believing they could do nothing and the atom bombs would fall one day. The likely implications of a bilateral peace treaty for travel permits and world peace created a general 'fear psychosis'.[13] Even without the NVA problem, the party's work with young people was still highly unsatisfactory in some areas in 1960. In Dingelstädt, for instance, young people emulated western models by 'standing around on corners, watching western television and worshipping Presly [sic]'. The result of these 'demoralising tendencies' was rising youth criminality.[14]

There were also serious but isolated problems in factories, with occasional strikes over raised work quotas. Although this was essentially the reason for the 1953 disturbances, the much improved degree of SED control by 1961 was reflected in the speedy isolation of such strikes. Thus, a stoppage at an Eisenach car plant was limited to one department and concluded within four hours.[15]

Sometimes the Cold War's underlying uncertainties were reflected in the rumours which accompanied shortages. For instance, some believed that the chemicals needed for washing powder would instead be used 'for a new war', or that pigs were being purchased to ensure meat supplies in wartime.[16] Such comments suggested that many people still viewed the GDR as a provisional state and Europe's postwar borders as temporary.

In late 1960 many SED members shared the general public's perceptions. Meetings about 'ideological-political questions' were poorly attended in rural areas. It emerged that these groups had long since held no fundamental discussions on basic socialist policies. Comrades at one Erfurt factory 'underestimate the aggression of west German militarism to a dangerous extent'. At another, members were too busy fulfilling the economic plan to worry about ideological matters, suggesting a non-political motivation for party membership. Even in economic matters, however, comrades and non-SED workers alike doubted the economic plans were realistic and did not believe in the 'strength of the masses'. The economic situation was generally perceived to be 'worse now than years ago'. The SED's rank and file understood as little as most citizens of issues such as peaceful co-existence and the status of Germany. Even the 'fighting groups of the working class' seemed unreliable. One member said he would refuse to fight workers if they rebelled about food shortages. Some workers considered the 'fighting groups' the equivalent of Hitler's *Volkssturm*. Many grassroots members demonstrated 'liberal behaviour' and did not recognise the party's decisions as 'irrevocable'.[17] Comrade H., a KPD man since 1928, expressed many SED members' loss of faith: 'Your policies are wrong. Can't you see that all the workers and farmers are leaving your republic?' Echoing the fears of 1956, an Eisenach comrade believed: 'The comrades will soon be put through the mincer anyway. The trees to hang us all on are already marked out.'[18]

Thus, the SED seemed poorly placed to face the political challenges of sealing the GDR's borders. In July 1961 non-workplace party meetings attracted only around half the members, far fewer in some areas (only 29.1 per cent in Apolda district). Despite the looming elections, members lacked 'fighting spirit' and were often reserved on key issues. Though generally loyal, even the district party leadership in Erfurt-Land was not wholly reliable and had a 'serious deficit in political work with the masses'. Many district leaderships gave inadequate support to local groups, and in some areas attracted few new members. In the Catholic Eichsfeld, recruitment rates declined again during 1961.[19]

Against this background, the SED Central Committee's July 1961 call to 'further increase the fighting force of the [SED's] basic organisations' seemed highly necessary,[20] and quickly produced a rash of local self-criticism. The Erfurt party executive began an 'offensive battle to remove all forms of liberalism' in factories. 'Liberalism' and 'immoral behaviour' (often alcohol abuse) were now reported to have infected many party groups and diminished the party's image in Worbis district. The most notable result of the campaign was the sudden frequency of the word *Kampf* ('battle') in SED reports. However, there was little opportunity to raise the party's battle readiness before 13 August dawned. As a July report noted, the party's propaganda and agitation had not created clarity in key political questions, its argumentation was 'clumsy', particularly in the press, and lacking vigilance had enabled 'ideological co-existence' (in other words, tolerance) to grow, even among SED members.[21]

Most observers agree that the Berlin Wall's construction was principally caused by the high numbers leaving the country.[22] Though not as high as in the mid-1950s, this phenomenon increased again as international tensions worsened and fears grew that the doors would soon be closed ('*Torschlußpanik*').

Relatively few party members left: even in Heiligenstadt district they represented only 4 per cent of the total in 1960. However, some of these held important positions, such as a mayor, the district education director and the secretary to the SED's deputy district secretary. Often specific material difficulties caused people to leave, or threaten to. Typically, a combine harvester operator drunkenly threatened: 'If my flat problem isn't sorted, I'm going to Adenauer.' In rural border districts, collectivisation sometimes led to entire families leaving for the west. Frustration over refused visa applications was another frequent cause, even among otherwise loyal SED supporters.[23] Some complained the government was hindering 'human and family contacts'. Others threatened to relinquish party activities unless they received a visa. Some believed visas were only issued to those with personal contacts.

Torschlußpanik set in by mid-1961 when the border closures seemed almost inevitable. One comrade protested: 'We must not lock people in!' Others provocatively called on the government to 'decide that nobody can travel to or from West Germany any more'. Meanwhile, Ifta citizens felt it was high time they 'cleared off, before Berlin is shut'. Police stations reported citizens 'forcefully' insisting they be given visas immediately. The fear that visas would no longer be available was combined with actual and perceived grave economic difficulties. This generalised into widespread apathy and a 'feel bad' factor within the party which undermined many comrades' faith in socialism's future.[24]

Despite these inherent weaknesses, the SED organisation in *Bezirk* Erfurt rose to the challenge once the Berlin borders were closed on 12–13 August 1961. The party's regional executive met early on 13 August, with representatives of the security services and the mass organisations present. They dictated various measures which were quickly communicated to the districts.[25] In Erfurt, for instance, the city's SED leaders conferred with the chairs of the bloc parties and mass organisations, and acquainted functionaries with the official explanations. Officials visited key installations to explain the developments and prevent any disruption to water, gas, electricity and postal services by potentially disgruntled workers.[26] Similar procedures were repeated in every district and at *Bezirk* level. In factories, most SED members were reportedly on the offensive and directing discussions on 14 August.

The public's initial reactions to the Berlin Wall were often unusually positive, perhaps because the development had been foreseen.[27] Even in June 1961, bus passengers were overheard saying that 'Adenauer will close the borders' unless the West Berlin question is solved. Immediately after the borders were closed, numerous citizens felt the measures should have been taken much earlier and welcomed the end to the 'slave trade' of GDR workers taking jobs in the west. Others agreed with steps to prevent 'West Berliners buying up the GDR'.

However, these early responses suggest ignorance of the true scale of the measures. After all, the borders between the western and eastern sectors of Berlin had been closed before. In the first days after 13 August, few seemed to realise that visits to the west would now be forbidden.[28] Railway workers, for instance, felt it important to 'show people that traffic will still be maintained and these steps are only a series of security and control measures'. Thus, initial resistance was vague, with isolated calls for free elections or the return of the eastern territories, or complaints that the GDR's supplies would be better without the co-operative farms. The security forces were quick to dampen any outspoken resistance, and arrested six Eisenach youths for 'wild, rabble rousing propaganda'. But even on the first day, some feared the west's reactions. By 15 August, as western reports of tanks and barbed wire filtered through, numerous citizens began commenting that the measures were too harsh and could lead to war. The impact of western television became apparent: 'I'm not in favour of ripping up streets in Berlin to put up barbed wire. It's true, I saw it myself on western TV.'

As days passed, and clarity about the Wall's implications grew, so dissatisfaction increased. Calls for '"free", pan-German elections' continued. Many correctly foresaw that the Wall would deepen Germany's division. Some feared wages would fall with the borders closed. Ulbricht was personally blamed for the Wall, and some workers felt the deceased President Pieck and the sick prime minister and former social democrat, Otto Grotewohl, would have acted differently. Although many workforces and other groups were persuaded to sign resolutions welcoming the moves, compliance was not total. Some factories recorded significant levels of abstentions (40 per cent in the state owned enterprise (*Volkseigener Betrieb*, VEB) Holzbau, Erfurt). Young workers sometimes attempted to blackmail the SED by threatening poor election results in September if more visas were not made available. Graffiti artists depicted Ulbricht on gallows or daubed slogans, such as 'Ulbricht, the Russians' watchdog'. Nine protesters were arrested in Sömmerda district on 19 August alone; one had threatened to murder Ulbricht. Other crimes included ripping down the GDR flag or drawing swastikas. In response, the SED increased propagandist activity, often linked to the imminent Young Pioneers' Jamboree. Apart from house meetings, Pioneer delegations joined the general public in drafting resolutions welcoming the border closures and pledging support for the GDR and Ulbricht. Nonetheless, four weeks later the Wall remained central to popular discussion, and threats not to vote if visas to West Germany were refused increased.

Fears of war provoked more practical reactions. In some Worbis district villages, sales in shops increased by up to 600 per cent in the days after the Wall's construction, and panic buying continued into September. Thereafter rumours of future shortages encouraged hoarding, causing shortages and further unrest. There were also examples of unusually high cash withdrawals from banks.[29]

It was easier to achieve active support from workers in the state-owned enterprises (VEBs) than those in private or semi-private firms (HSBs), where discussions centred on 'personal matters'. In one HSB the staff spontaneously left a meeting at their normal clocking-off time, without electing a 'voters' representative'. Relations with HSBs were not eased by 'sectarian' attitudes among state officials who despised private businesses.[30]

Doctors and other medical staff were particularly dissatisfied. They had for years demanded privileged travel arrangements, for professional and personal reasons, and the SED had often complied to retain their services in the GDR. The Wall prompted an 'open, provocative attitude' from some doctors and nurses once its implications became clear.[31]

Despite the continuing general discontent engendered by the sealed borders, reactions were 'spontaneous, individual and generally helpless',[32] and therefore did not translate into any structured, meaningful opposition to the SED. This was most evident when local elections proceeded normally just five weeks later. The official results showed higher turnouts and fewer 'No' votes in every district compared to 1957.[33] As will become apparent, this result was achieved despite rather than because of good party organisation in many areas, but may represent an emergent trend towards making one's peace with the GDR after the escape hatch had been closed. Voting remained compulsory, and the Wall had created a greater inducement to conform to the rules of a country which one could no longer leave. By taking no action over the Berlin Wall themselves, the western allies had arguably set an example in upholding the status quo which individual GDR citizens could only follow.

The SED faced a still greater challenge shortly after the September elections when further measures became necessary to secure the border between Thuringia and the Federal Republic, to supplement the moves in Berlin. Between 13 August and the end of the month, eighty-one *Bezirk* Erfurt residents had fled the GDR in thirty incidents. Another ninety-seven had been arrested in the attempt and there were twenty cases of people entering the prohibited 'ten-metre strip' of land along the GDR's side of the border. (One hundred and twelve people were also arrested trying to enter the GDR illegally.)[34] The new regime included stricter rules about entering the 'prohibited areas' near the border, curfews to prevent escapes under cover of darkness and, later, evacuating apparently unreliable citizens from the villages closest to the border.

For the SED this meant further antagonising the Catholic community in the Eichsfeld: thirty-eight of the parishes in Heiligenstadt district were within five kilometres of the border. The public meetings to explain these measures were well attended, even by those who had never attended meetings before. The high turnout clearly reflects anxiety about the new measures. The party was quickly inundated with practical questions. How would doctors and vets enter the prohibited zones, and how would residents reach chemists outside it? How would essential services be available during the curfew? In some communities, the SED was pleased to note great willingness to assist border patrols, though some 'helpers' may simply have wished to reconnoitre border installations to facilitate later breakouts. Similarly, farmers perhaps had more than agricultural motives when they queried the use of fields directly adjacent to the border. The difficulty of obtaining passes for the 'restricted zone' caused increasing aggravation.[35]

Fuelled by memories of the expulsions of allegedly untrustworthy elements from the border areas in 1952, rumours about similar evacuations emerged almost immediately after 13 August. When the evacuations began on 3 October, the local population seemed resigned to them, providing they were not personally affected, and with few exceptions worked normally, merely expressing the hope that 'they've got the right ones'. Large assemblies to watch the evacuations were rare. Even the sister and fiancée of a deported Fretterode man made no complaint as 'he was no good anyway'. Few posed questions at explanatory meetings. Though tensions were relieved by the promise that the forcible removals were now complete, the population adopted an even more reserved attitude. However, people also began behaving more loyally, perhaps believing they could avoid further SED interference by keeping the peace. Residents in Eisenach district felt: 'It's better to accept some unpleasantness than be deported.' Thus the local population handed over would-be escapees to the authorities, and even readiness to remove the western channel from TV sets increased.[36]

Despite the stricter border regime and the evacuations, escapes continued, mainly involving villagers near the border. Most spectacularly, on 2 October twelve families numbering fifty-three people, including the chairman of the co-operative farm, fled from Böseckendorf, a village within 500 metres of the border. The date suggests that a desire to escape deportation was the direct cause. A further twelve members of two Böseckendorf families escaped on 23 February 1962.[37] Though the SED's district party inspectorate had reported serious internal personnel problems and local dissatisfaction in August, and a *Bezirk*-level report of September had already identified the village as one of six in Worbis district where there was no belief in the socialist perspective, the SED could not remedy the situation.[38] Analyses produced after the mass escape highlight the party's poor control of some areas. Only two SED members lived in Böseckendorf; they belonged to neighbouring Bleckenrode's party organisation which itself performed no real work due to 'personal squabbles and arguments'. One of the Böseckendorf members had 'gone so morally to pot' that he had to be expelled. The village co-operative farm, founded late after harsh disputes, was co-operative in name only and dominated by big farmers unfavourably disposed to socialist agriculture. In its first year, much farming work was deliberately neglected. Böseckendorf–Bleckenrode's complacent SED mayor and SED teacher had done little to improve the party organisation and received little support from higher levels, notably not from the local party secretary who was later removed. Nor did all local members of the strongest local party, the farmers' DBD, support the new border regime. The SED's position in Böseckendorf suffered further over irregularities in the disposal of goods belonging to the families who had left. Eventually the local mayor, teacher and policeman were arrested, even though the teacher had been solely responsible for achieving any SED presence or co-operative agricultural activity in the village at all.[39]

Though the Böseckendorf example represents an extreme, it demonstrates that the SED had many problems to resolve in co-opting the general population and establishing firm structures within the party after the Wall's construction. However, many of these problems predated the Wall.

Superficial stabilisation behind the Wall

After the SED Central Committee's July resolutions (see page 122) and the border closures, the party took a more offensive line within its own organisation, and more members were encouraged to conform to party statutes. Within a closed country with longer term prospects than before, membership of the leading party suddenly seemed more worthwhile. In the first days after the Wall's erection, attendance at party meetings rose to 75 per cent (though in at least one case a 6am emergency call was required to assemble otherwise unavailable members), and in Erfurt alone there were ninety-four applications to become SED candidate members between 13 and 28 August. Similarly, the Wall had the effect of galvanising 'ideologically weak' teachers into acknowledging the SED.[40]

Nonetheless, some comrades initially felt the Wall was a step too far and responded by refusing party work. Some men in the 'working-class fighting units' also refused duty, albeit with excuses about sick wives and time pressures; some comrades failed to contradict comparisons of the GDR with a prison. In the Volkenroda potash works comrades compared the GDR unfavourably with the Nazi era, and one member threatened to resign unless he received a visa. The chairwoman elect of the women's organisation (DFD) in Mühlhausen refused to assume her post after the border measures were introduced. In training colleges, 'despite the progress in the development of political consciousness, opportunistic, liberalistic, objectivistic and pacifist views have not been overcome among some training instructors.'[41]

However, the Wall enabled the SED to cleanse its ranks and make examples of dissidents within the party, some of whom were expelled, such as the local policeman in Stöckey who refused his duties and eventually flung down his police notebook and pistol declaring he wanted his freedom. Similarly, a Brehme member who 'imagined communism differently' was expelled and recommended for resettlement away from the border. In all, four members in Worbis district, including one local-party secretary, were expelled from the party for opposing the Wall, and various other members and non-members were arrested, imprisoned or expelled from the border area for dissident behaviour.[42] Although some districts, like Nordhausen, had to be encouraged to take seriously the personnel review of party groups located near the border,[43] such measures represented a clear disincentive to party members and the general population alike to oppose the new order. The SED's rank and file could be in no further doubt about the need either to resign membership, and risk personal disadvantages, or remain outwardly loyal.

The new border regime unmasked serious weaknesses within the Eichsfeld SED. The Heiligenstadt district party organisation numbered only 2,060 members and candidate members (some 4.7 per cent of the population, compared with 9.4 per cent nationally), of whom fewer than half were traditional 'workers'. This was barely more than the CDU's 1,528 members. Seven of the district's sixty-three communities, ten of the eleven Commercial Production Co-operatives (PGH), fifteen private firms and seventy-three of the ninety-one co-operative farms had no SED organisation. The party organisations in the co-operative farms were anyway considered unreliable, as their members were mainly religious and influenced by their relatives.[44] However, the SED profited from the border changes by attempting to strengthen its organisation. In line with the Central Committee's requirements, 'aggressive debates' were held with members and functionaries who 'fulfilled their party duties unsatisfactorily'. As not all comrades could be persuaded to toe the party line, 'cadre changes' were made in some groups' leaderships. By 11 October, seventeen party secretaries, fourteen mayors (including eight SED appointees) and nineteen National Front chairmen were removed in the district's five kilometre restricted zone. A further eighteen staff were to be removed from the district council. The reasons included a 'wavering attitude to the implementation of party and government decisions', 'weakly developed class consciousness', former membership of the NSDAP and 'immoral behaviour, sometimes repeatedly'. Overall the *Bezirk* needed to replace forty-nine party secretaries, twenty-four mayors and thirty-eight NF chairmen in border communities, but failed to supply the agreed replacement cadres to Heiligenstadt quickly.[45]

The Heiligenstadt party's district leadership was itself weak, giving inadequate help to local groups or even the party group in the district council. Membership of the border police also made no lasting impression, as 'due to marrying into Catholic families a large proportion of former colleagues give up their progressive attitudes and become keen churchgoers.' Thus, the party's 'leading role' was not assured in various border localities.[46] Though these problems were generally more extreme in the Eichsfeld than elsewhere, they existed across the *Bezirk*.

Exploiting the September 1961 elections in particular, loyalists began claiming the upper hand in local SED groups. Thus, 'discussions were held with comrades who have recently displayed liberal behaviour' in Sondershausen. Similarly, a deputy party group leader in Erfurt was officially warned about 'defeatist behaviour' after he neglected to persuade reluctant workers to sign a letter of support to Ulbricht. Pressure on members to conform became intense. Some comrades with dissident views were demoted to candidate status or removed from state posts. Aware of members' continuing ideological weaknesses, the leadership insisted on 'turning party organisations' membership meetings into forums of instruction'.[47]

However, the battle was not restricted to party members. Many offensives were waged against those who expressed dissident views. Thus a Sömmerda security officer was sacked for 'extolling' 17 June 1953. Similarly the party exposed as a 'fascist element' an Eisenach builder who incited his colleagues to call strikes. The builder was arrested, his workmates forced to denounce him, and the strike was averted. Elsewhere, the appearance of 'Soviet comrades' in key factories was a 'significant help' to the SED.[48]

Regular consumers of western broadcasts were also attacked, as when an Erfurt DFD group dismissed its chairwoman for refusing to dismantle her aerial. The anti-western television campaign was particularly necessary in border areas. Here the party began dedicated, systematic campaigns after 13 August, particularly after six people escaped from Ecklingerode, all apparently influenced by western television. Despite some apparent initial successes, however, continued complaints that there was nothing political with watching sport and music on western television suggested the argument had not been won. There was also evidence that aerials for western channels were reinstalled in attics after being removed from roofs.[49]

Army recruitment was a major battleground during 1961. In Weimar, more than 50 per cent of all youths between eighteen and twenty-three signed pledges to enlist either immediately or after their studies. However, the continuing prevalence of comments such as 'We want to live in peace and work, why do we need a National People's Army?' suggests that coercion rather than conviction had produced these successes. However, after 13 August the SED felt confident enough to demand 'clear and concrete statements' from each individual at meetings about enlisting. SED members not prepared to 'defend the homeland with a weapon in their hands' could expect intense discussions with superiors, and exclusion from the party if they still refused to enlist. The weak FDJ, many of whose functionaries refused to join up, was also targeted. Members of the FDJ district executives were removed in Apolda and Worbis for this 'weakness'. However, although pressure on individuals increased, ultimately there was no alternative to introducing compulsory conscription in 1962. Young people avoided the meetings where they were expected to enlist voluntarily, and relatively few FDJ functionaries were loyal enough to implement the campaign, particularly at local level where they often avoided difficult debates.[50]

It also quickly became apparent that the new tough line within the party merely silenced the loudest opponents, but did not significantly raise the party's 'fighting force'. After the election campaign, party activity receded. The Mühlhausen district leadership estimated that 'in all party organisations only some comrades stand up in public' and that 'the work of the party groups in the local councils, state organs, mass organisations and NF committees does not meet requirements'. 'Liberalism' was resurgent in Heiligenstadt district's party organisation, and party work at the border was still 'particularly weak'. The renewed debate about Stalin and the personality cult at the CPSU's Twenty-Second Party Congress of October 1961, culminating in the removal of Stalin's body from the Red Square mausoleum and of his name from numerous towns and street signs, further damaged the party's image, as some defended Stalin's memories and others renewed comparisons with Ulbricht.

In the wider population, the questions, problems and restrictions raised by the Wall's construction on 13 August were not quickly forgotten (as was shown when it was opened in 1989). In April 1962 Weimar's population still hoped for speedy reunification and easier east–west travel. The public exploited the principle of 'peaceful co-existence' to argue for compromise between east and west. However, the more immediate problem of food supplies also dominated much discussion. Some ironically wondered if West Germany's prosperity resulted from better weather, while others openly blamed the 'co-operative farm's fast development'. As 1961 ended, popular discussion again turned to material problems. Some felt that Christmas supplies had never been so 'dismal' and that, among other complaints, textiles and shoe supplies were worse than ever.[51] Slowly, these tangible problems displaced the Berlin Wall as the principal focus of discontent.

Despite the efforts at socialist education, young people remained a particular concern to the SED. Some had begun talking of a 'third way' between socialism and capitalism, and most remained ignorant of the SED's 'National Document', the party's latest justification of the GDR's existence and rejection of unification with a capitalist FRG. Those who knew of it felt it would change nothing, and some believed (despite the vigorous campaign for recruitment to the National People's Army) that West Germany was not a militarist threat anyway. Pupils' attitudes were partly explained by their teachers' 'false' views, demonstrating that the SED had still not appointed entirely reliable teachers. Parents did much to undermine the political education which was dispensed. Despite the SED's organisational advances in the Eichsfeld, there were 'still many uncertainties and false views' in practically all the border communities of Heiligenstadt district. Many 'underestimated' West German militarism and some were unafraid to describe the GDR's border soldiers as 'murderers', reflecting the continuing antipathy towards the state. The SED (and *Stasi*) had little choice but to tolerate such sentiment.[52]

Thus, although the Wall initially enabled the SED hierarchy to clamp down on opponents and the uncommitted, who suddenly found themselves unable to leave or to threaten to do so, the shock of the Wall as a symbol of discipline quickly receded. Party efficiency resumed its normal, often indifferent, levels, and the expression of public dissatisfaction and apathy towards the regime's political goals returned. Though the population had to make its peace with the GDR, the SED had also to find a modus vivendi with all those who remained in the country.

The GDR in the 1960s

During the 1960s, problems similar to those in the 'pre-Wall' era continued, but consolidation occurred to the extent that life became somewhat more routine. Many state functionaries, for instance, regarded preparations for the 1963 elections to the *Volkskammer* (the GDR parliament) as routine and relatively unimportant. Similarly, voters turned out later and later in successive elections between 1961 and 1965,[53] despite the SED's exhortations to vote early and thereby snub detractors of the GDR's electoral system. The sudden return to early voting in 1967 suggests a major SED offensive.

During the 1960s, political life increasingly settled into a routine, not only because of the Wall, but also because the GDR had existed for fifteen years by the mid-1960s, longer than the Third Reich. Between elections, political and ideological activities directed at the general population died away, just as in previous years. NF committees as high as district level had to be reactivated for the 1963 election campaign. Similarly, although Erfurt boasted 6,250 political agitators, only half of the 'agitation leaders' attended their scheduled instruction meetings between December 1963 and January 1964, and only around a quarter of the agitators attended their courses. Although 'family conversations' were a proven method of effectively influencing the population, these were held in only one ward in the town. For their part, Erfurt's NF committees had no oversight of the local 'house communities'. There were similar reports from Mühlhausen.[54]

Thus, the parties' and mass organisations' efficiency remained far from satisfactory. In early 1965, for instance, the SED regional executive was dissatisfied with the activity plans of the five district leaderships it checked at random. Only one had attempted to match its 'agitation' work to the actual state of ideological awareness in the population. The leadership quality of the FDGB, FDJ and DFD varied drastically from district to district, and many SED members were still not fully aware of their own party programme. Even in the state administration only around two thirds of SED members attended party meetings and participation in the party education programme was poor. Worryingly for the SED, even replacement leaders for the inadequate party groups seemed incapable of making improvements, and the work of many groups depended on just one or two people.[55] In this respect, little had changed since the 1950s.

Although the Heiligenstadt district party organisation was particularly weak, its experiences during the 1960s illustrate the SED's failure to consolidate its structures fully even after the Wall's construction. The situation within the Heiligenstadt party deteriorated during the decade. There were reportedly poor relations between the leading comrades in the district executive, whose various departments failed to report to one another. Meanwhile, party groups in industry and agriculture prepared meetings inadequately and concentrated on local economic and administrative matters, rather than 'ideological growth'. The local leaderships' ideological uncertainties were reflected in ordinary members' comments. In 1967 party inspectors noted that the Heiligenstadt SED was too self-satisfied and that its leaders did not check their work rigorously enough. Both the district secretary and his deputy worked apparently aimlessly and did not always propose the right solutions to the problems they recognised. The party appeared to be on automatic pilot and merely keeping the local peace. By late 1967, the regional executive felt compelled to install a new district secretary to reinvigorate the district party, though the deputy remained and worked as poorly as ever. Nonetheless, there was a wave of disciplinary procedures during 1967 when, for instance, fifteen senior and eight middle-ranking party functionaries were called to account. They even included the chairman of the district council, accused of 'petit-bourgeois' behaviour at his thirty-third birthday party, and the head of the district party organisation's economic department, whose 'damaging' comments made him unacceptable as a party member.[56] Even without dangerous challenges to its rule, therefore, the SED failed to govern as effectively as the *Politbüro* in Berlin would have liked during the 1960s.

Although open opposition to the SED is recorded less often in the mid-1960s than before the Wall's construction (a 1963 election-campaign report noted only two significant incidents), the SED had not yet secured popular loyalty. The same types of political questions cropped up during the 1960s as in the previous decade. By 1963, workers, farmers and the 'intelligentsia' had still not accepted the reasons for the Wall and the impediments to east–west travel. Few supported the GDR's official stance on the German question. Throughout the decade, people doubted the dangers posed to peace by the Federal Republic, or commented that as 'the majority in West Germany has voted CDU, things can't be so bad there'. There were also questions about the nature of GDR elections and why there was no opposition in parliament. More worrying were isolated comments in 1967, during the Six Day Arab–Israeli War, such as 'Hitler wasn't at all wrong to want to eradicate the Jews.' Though such views were rare, their expression at all revealed basic weaknesses in the SED's ideological renewal of eastern Germany.

Beyond these political questions, complaints persisted about poor living standards. These often peaked before elections as people tried to bargain for material improvements in return for their votes. Despite the good intentions of policymakers to resolve such problems, particularly to avoid electoral embarrassments, bureaucracy and even 'heartlessness' were commonplace in the local offices responsible for housing and other essential services.[57] Functionaries were often regarded as lazy and held in extremely low esteem. The priest of Böseckendorf was moved to announce from the pulpit: 'Thou shalt labour for six days and on the seventh day thou shalt rest. On the seventh day they shall labour who do nothing during the rest of the week.'[58]

A further sign of dissatisfaction lay in the surprisingly high level of illegal escapes, despite the tighter border regime. In 1965, for instance, 284 *Bezirk* Erfurt citizens succeeded in leaving the GDR and a further 578 made unsuccessful attempts. Nearly half these people came from the border districts, notably Worbis district. In 1966, 193 crossed the border illegally, and a further 582 were arrested in the attempt. In both years fewer than a fifth of the total were over twenty-five, suggesting a serious failure to convince teenagers and young adults of their prospects in the GDR. The motives recorded by the police include 'some culprits' poor opinion of the GDR', particularly where this coincided with their parents' attitudes, western radio and television making young people believe life was better in the west, frustrated job or career plans, poor school performance and fear of punishment for crimes. The party and police campaigns to improve border vigilance succeeded in reducing the successful breakouts along the Eichsfeld border between 1965 and 1967, but many citizens refused to help the authorities. In the Eichsfeld many adhered to the principle of 'one Christian does not betray another Christian'.[59]

Reports of the mid-1960s reveal the same uncertainties and ideological problems during the non-crisis years as during exceptional periods such as 1961 and 1968, and as during the pre-Wall years. This can be demonstrated using the example of two sections of the population: those involved in education (young people, teachers and education officials) and agricultural workers.

Chapter 7 considers young people's failure to absorb the official SED line during the 1968 crisis in Czechoslovakia. However, the questions posed by young people then were common throughout the 1960s. Why, they asked, was the GDR the 'fatherland of all Germans'? Why bother with elections if there is no choice between the parties? Why must we study the classics of Marxism-Leninism? Is there any hope of implementing the party congress's resolution to overtake West Germany? Doesn't our side represent everything too one-sidedly? In West Germany there's no sign of the dangers of militarism![60]

Often, though, young people, particularly from working-class backgrounds, attempted to avoid political discussions and thus hide their lack of basic socialist knowledge and politically unacceptable opinions. It became apparent that 'it is not just a small number of pupils whose class consciousness is insufficiently developed' and that 'civic education is not effective enough'. The fact that 80 per cent of children were involved in groups to expand their knowledge of Marxism-Leninism reflected compliant behaviour, but did not seem greatly to influence young people's practical political outlook. Youngsters craving western pop music alarmed the authorities, who attempted to encourage a greater interest in socialist pop and more traditional music. However, most participants at a youth forum in Ohrdruf during 1965 were unafraid to state openly: 'We won't let anyone forbid us to watch western television. We need to be comprehensively informed.' Clearly, western television was not watched only in times of crisis. A 1967 Bad Langensalza report on youth attitudes recorded that all these political, ideological and cultural problems were as prevalent in the district as in the region as a whole. This was particularly ironic given a 1958 resolution in the regional parliament to make Bad Langensalza the *Bezirk*'s first 'socialist' district,[61] and highlights how little popular convictions had changed by the late 1960s.

Although teachers were generally capable of explaining sensitive political issues, it was also noted that not enough of them used their initiative to represent the party line, and that not all studied party materials properly. Here, as throughout society, were signs of apoliticism. The routine, unthinking patterns into which many functionaries lapsed is also reflected in a report that 'some school functionaries consider the completion of comprehensive statistics and analyses more important than lively collaboration with educationalists in the schools'.[62] We can conclude that young people's ideological problems during 1968 were not born of the Czechoslovak crisis, but had existed for years.

A brief survey of agricultural developments during the 1960s also demonstrates that some consolidation occurred, but that farmers' basic attitudes towards the GDR hardly changed despite the Wall. The party enjoyed little presence in the sector: only 7.1 per cent of co-operative farmers belonged to the SED in early 1963, and only around a third of LPG chairmen were also party members who could attempt to assert the SED's 'leading role'. As many as 45 per cent of co-operative farms had no SED group at all. By 1966, the proportion of LPGs without SED groups was still 39 per cent, and only around half of the existing party groups were capable of working independently. In the comparatively well functioning party group at the Weißensee LPG, for example, only just over half the members attended meetings.[63]

Compared to 1962, when some LPG chairmen worked their own fields with their own machinery and ignored the rest of the co-operative,[64] significant advances had been made. Opposition on principle to the co-operative farms receded during the 1960s, and is rarely reported. However, farmers still resisted SED attempts to impose further reforms. Just as individual farmers had defended their independence in 1960, now individual co-operative farms defended theirs from the new 'co-operation treaties' with which the SED attempted to introduce economies of scale.[65] Although many LPGs did begin to adopt the new system, particularly those with relatively strong party groups,[66] profitable LPGs were reluctant to co-operate with unprofitable neighbours.[67] Some farmers borrowed socialist terminology to decry the new 'complex' programme as an invasion of internal co-operative democracy.[68] The 'New Economic System', which attempted to enshrine the concept of profitability into socialist economics and reduced somewhat the role of central ministries in economic planning,[69] was implemented slowly in agriculture because 'leading cadres do not understand the problems theoretically, shy away from their increased responsibility, manage in a routine manner and do not sufficiently involve the co-operative farmers in planning and management.'[70] Despite some successes, only 31 per cent of the *Bezirk*'s arable land was being farmed according to the new 'co-operation' principle by late 1968. The conversion rate depended on the efficacy of individual SED district leaderships. Again it is evident that the party organisation often failed to implement the 'leading role' to which it aspired.

Reports in the 1960s demonstrate that in some areas the SED was not in control, often because of internal failings. A 1963 report on Kutzleben-Lützensommern concluded that 'the work of the parish administration and parish council are insufficient to implement state authority or to involve all inhabitants in the struggle. The leading role of the party is ensured by the number of members on the parish council and in the parish administration, but not in the comrades' behaviour.'[71]

Hard on the border in Böseckendorf – scene of the mass escapes of 1961 and 1962 – the situation had barely improved by the middle of the decade. Local rivalries between Böseckendorf and neighbouring Bleckenrode jeopardised the re-election of the mayor in 1965. For his part the mayor complained that although his village was regularly visited by all manner of 'agitators' and functionaries, 'none of them gives concrete help'. The local party secretary had not worked out a plan for the election campaign only weeks before polling day, and the local NF had been non-existent. The 'election helpers' had yet to meet and had received no training. The chairman of the co-operative farm, an SED man, had no personal skills and resisted all criticism. Local residents called for the opening of the border, 'so that everything is normal again', and were sceptical about the GDR's avowed peace policies. Young people were particularly annoyed that all social activities had to finish by the 11 p.m. border-zone curfew, and were further frustrated when an initiative to form a photographic circle failed, due to a ban on photography in the border zone.[72] Clearly Böseckendorf, where the SED had little hold over the population beyond the fortified border, was an extreme example. However, these extremes do reflect symptoms which could be found to a greater or lesser degree in most parts of the *Bezirk*.

Although some consolidation occurred after the Berlin Wall's construction in 1961, this should not imply that the SED had achieved all its ends. Though behaviour patterns were largely conformist, ideological commitment had not been achieved. Just as before the Wall was built, people concerned themselves with their daily tasks and made the professions of loyalty demanded of them, but otherwise remained relatively aloof from political life. The parties, mass organisations and state apparatus functioned at least well enough to maintain the system, and their hold on power was not seriously challenged, though there were regular reports of functionaries' failure to fulfil higher political goals. Life descended into a routine after the border closures, in which both rulers and ruled realised there would be no radical developments in the German question and accepted their respective roles. A temporary stability was achieved, but on the basis of imperfect control of a population which was unconvinced of its rulers' legitimacy. This could not be a recipe for long-term stability. Eventually the challenge of 1968, discussed in Chapter 7, was to demonstrate how fragile was the SED's ideological hold on the population.

Notes

1   ThHStAW, OI 271, fol. 48, RdK Bad Langensalza, 'Informationsbericht … ', 18 January 1960; OI 273, fol. 59, RdK Weimar, 'Informationsbericht … ', 23 February 1960.
2   ThHStAW, Vs/St 577, fols 91–3, 'Die wirtschaftliche Entwicklung … ', July 1961.
3   LPA, BIV/2/5-041, 'Einige Probleme … ', 1 August 1961, p. 1.
4   *Protokoll der Verhandlungen des V. Parteitages der Sozialistischen Einheitspartei Deutschlands*, 2 vols (Berlin, Dietz, 1958), I, 70; LPA, BIV/2/9.01-13, 'Vorlage an das Büro … ', 18 July 1961, p. 7.
5   LPA, BIV/2/5-039, 'Kurzinformation', 8 and 13 September, 15 October 1960.
6   On Khrushchev's ultimatum and the Berlin crisis, see, e.g., D. Bark and D. Gress, *A History of West Germany*, 2 vols (Oxford, Blackwell, 1993), I, 435–40.
7   LPA, BIV/2/5-041, SED reports, 13 June, 22 and 31 July 1961; ThHStAW, S 515, fol. 68, '10./1959 Informationsbericht', 12 June 1959.
8   18 July 1961 report (note 4), p. 2.
9   LPA, BIV/2/5-041 and ThHStAW, OI 271 and 272, 1960–61 state and SED reports.
10 15 October 1960 report (note 5), p. 5; ThHStAW, OI 274, fols 5, 17, Apolda and Erfurt reports, 22 and 20 February 1960.
11 LPA, IV/5.01/144, SED Erfurt, 'Informationsbericht … ', 21 August 1961, p. 20.
12 LPA, BIV/2/17-006, 'Information über die Entwicklung der massenpolitischen und politisch-ideologischen Arbeit des DFD … ', 8 September 1961, p. 6.
13 LPA, BIV/2/5-039, 'Kurzinformation Nr. 66/60', 27 October 1960, p. 3; 22 July 1961 report (note 7), p. 3.
14 LPA, BIV/2/5-060, 'Kurze Einschätzung der Kreisparteiaktivtagung am 5.10.60 … ', p. 3.
15 LPA, BIV/2/5-041, 'Kurzinformation Nr. 27/61', 4 July 1961.
16 15 October 1960 report (note 5), p. 7.
17 27 October 1960 report (note 13), pp. 2–7; 22 July 1961 report (note 7), p. 3; LPA, IV/4.06/121, MTS Bornhagen SED, 'Wie entwickelt sich die Kampfkraft … ?', 5 November 1960, p. 1.
18 22 July 1961 report (note 7), pp. 4–5.
19 LPA, BIV/2/5-050, 'Einschätzung der politischen Führungstätigkeit … ', undated [early 1961?]; IV/5.01/144, 'Informationsbericht Nr. 22/61', 30 July 1961, pp. 1–2, 5–6; IV/4.06/116, SED Heiligenstadt statistical reports, 11 October 1960, p. 1, and 3 July 1961, p. 2.
20 G. Roßmann, *Geschichte der SED: Abriß* (Berlin, Dietz Verlag, 1978), p. 415.
21 LPA, IV/5.01/144, SED Erfurt, 'Informationsbericht … ', 21 August 1961, p. 1;

IV/4.13/192, 'Bericht der Kreisparteikontrollkommission Worbis ... ', 1 August 1961, pp. 3–4; 22 July 1961 report (note 7), pp. 1–2.

22 Cf., e.g., M. McCauley, *The German Democratic Republic Since 1945* (Basingstoke, Macmillan, 1983), pp. 101–2.

23 LPA, IV/4.13/192, KPKK Worbis, 'Republikfluchten ... ', 2 March 1961, p. 3, and 'Quartalsbericht über Feindarbeit', 30 June 1961, p. 2; *ibid.*, Graf (SED Worbis 1st Secretary) to Bräutigam, 28 April 1961; BIV/2/5-041, 'Zur Stimmung ... ', 31 July 1961, p. 5.

24 31 July 1961 report (note 23), pp. 8–10; 18 July 1961 report (note 4), p. 3; ThHStAW, MdI/20.1, 82, fol. 92, BdVP, 'Informationen durch Einsatzleitung ... ', 1 August 1961; MdI/20.1, 139, fol. 56, BdVP, 'Information 60/61', 29 July 1961.

25 LPA, IV/2/3-387, 'Sondersitzung des Büros am 13. und 14.8.1961'.

26 LPA, IV/5.01/144, SED Erfurt, 'Erste Meinungen ... ', 13 August 1961, pp. 1–2.

27 These paragraphs are principally based on 1961 SED reports in LPA, BIV/2/5-041; see also SED Erfurt reports in IV/5.01/144, and BIV/2/9.01-13, 'Vorlage an das Büro ... ', 5 September 1961, p. 3.

28 Berlin situation reports of 13–15 August 1961 suggest similar conclusions. Cf. H. Mehls (ed.), *Im Schatten der Mauer: Dokumente 12. August bis 29. September 1961* (Berlin, Deutscher Verlag der Wissenschaften, 1990).

29 IV/4.13/192, KPKK Worbis, 'Einschätzung der Situation ... ', 5 September 1961, p. 2, and 'Bericht über Feindarbeit ... ', 21 December 1961, p. 1; BIV/2/5-041, 'Kurzinformation Nr. 42/61', 20 August 1961, p. 4; 8 September 1961 report (note 12), p. 5.

30 LPA, BIV/2/5-041, 'Informationsbericht Nr. 24/61', 22 August 1961, p. 6; BIV/2/9.01-13, 'Vorlage an das Büro ... ', 6 September 1961, p. 7.

31 21 August 1961 report (note 21), pp. 11–12.

32 M. Fulbrook, *Anatomy of a Dictatorship* (Oxford, Oxford University Press, 1995), p. 192.

33 LPA, BIV/2/13-725, untitled report, undated [1961], p. 2.

34 5 September 1961 report (note 29), pp. 3–4.

35 LPA, IV/4.06/149, 'Bericht der Arbeitsgruppe Heiligenstadt ... ', 12 October 1961, p. 1; *ibid.*, RdK Heiligenstadt, 'Bericht über die Realisierung der Maßnahmen ... ', 10 November 1961, p. 4; *ibid.*, SED Heiligenstadt, 'Bürovorlage', 25 September 1961, pp. 4, 7; *ibid.*, RdK Heiligenstadt, 'Einschätzung der Lage ... ', 26 October 1961, p. 3; BIV/2/5-042, 'Kurzinformation Nr. 59/61', 23 September 1961, p. 4.

36 LPA, BIV/2/5-041, 'Kurzinformation Nr. 39/61', 17 August 1961, p. 5; BIV/2/5-042, 'Kurzinformation', 2 and 3 October 1961; IV/4.06/149, SED Heiligenstadt telephone messages, 3 October 1961, report, 4 October 1961, 10.00 and telex no. 55, 5 October 1961; 12 October and 10 November 1961 reports (note 35).

37 H. Bernd, *et al.* (eds), *Die Grenze im Eichsfeld* (Göttingen, Verlag Göttinger Tageblatt, 1991), p. 19; LPA, BIV/2/5-042, 'Kurzinformation Nr. 62/61', 3 October 1961, p. 2.

38 5 September 1961 report (note 29), p. 6; 1 August 1961 report (note 21), pp. 2–3.

39 LPA, IV/4.13/187, 'Bericht der KPKK ... ', (undated); LPG Böseckendorf/Bleckenrode SED group, 'Einschätzung der sozialen, ökonomischen und politischen Struktur ... ', 5 December 1961; *ibid.*, Kreisdienststelle Worbis, 'Situation in der Gemeinde Bösekendorf', 21 February 1962.

40 LPA, BIV/2/5-041, SED reports, 16 and 28 August 1961; ThHStAW, V 137, fol. 8, 'Vorlage laut Arbeitsplan ... ', 15 November 1961.

41 LPA, BIV/2/5-041, SED reports, 16 and 25 August, 17 October 1961; 15 November 1961 report (note 40), fol. 9.

42 LPA, IV/4.13/192, KPKK Worbis reports, 5 September, 23 October and third quarter, 1961.

43 LPA, BIV/2/5-042, 'Informationsbericht Nr. 27/61', 27 September 1961, p. 8.

44 12 October 1961 report (note 35), pp. 1, 9; H. Zimmermann, H. Ulrich and M. Fehlauer (eds), *DDR Handbuch* (Cologne, Verlag Wissenschaft und Politik, 3rd edn, 1985), I, 213, and II, 1185; PGH and private firm statistics in 11 October 1960 report (note 19).

45 25 September, 12 October and 10 November 1961 reports (note 35); LPA, BIV/2/5-042, 'Informationsbericht Nr. 31/61', 17 October 1961, p. 5.

46 12 October 1961 report (note 35), pp. 3, 6, 10; 5 September 1961 report (note 29), p. 6.

47 28 August 1961 report (note 40), p. 6; LPA, IV/5.01/145, SED Erfurt, 'Verbesserung der Leitungstätigkeit … ', 23 January 1962, pp. 1, 3.

48 LPA, BIV/2/5-041, SED reports, 17 and 22 August 1961.

49 8 September 1961 report (note 12), p. 5; 5 September 1961 report (note 29), p. 6; 27 September 1961 (note 43), pp. 3–4.

50 ThHStAW, Vs/St 577, fols 157–8, 'Einschätzung über die Durchführung der konstituierenden Sitzungen', 5 October 1961; 5 September 1961 report (note 29), p. 2; LPA, BIV/2/5-041, 'Einige Bemerkungen über die Stärkung der Kampfkraft … ', 31 August 1961, pp. 4–5; BIV/2/5-042, 'Kurzinformation Nr. 45/61', 2 September 1961, pp. 2–3, 6–8.

51 LPA, BIV/2/5-042, SED reports, 2 October, 8 and 16 November 1961.

52 LPA, BIV/2/9.01-13, 'Einschätzung der Stimmung … ', 2 April 1962, pp. 2, 7, 9–10; *ibid.*, FDJ, 'Stimmung der Jugend … ', 3 April 1962, pp. 1–2; *ibid.*, SED Heiligenstadt, 'Einschätzung der Stimmung … ', 6 June 1962, pp. 6–8.

53 LPA, BIV/2/13-725, 'Entwurf: Analyse über die Vorbereitung und Durchführung der Volkswahlen … ', undated [1963], p. 23, and statistical records.

54 LPA, BIV/2/9.01-654, 'Einschätzung des gegenwärtigen Standes der massenpolitischen Arbeit … ' [Erfurt], 22 January 1964; similar Mühlhausen report, 4 February 1964.

55 *Ibid.*, 'Einschätzung der Pläne … ', 5 February 1965; 1963 report (note 53), pp. 27, 29, 48; ThHStAW, J 8, fol. 58, FDJ, 'Informationsbericht', 6 December 1962; LPA, BIV/2/13-726, 'Information über die Arbeit … ', [14 February 1964], pp. 7, 9.

56 LPA, BIV/2/5-349, reports on SED Heiligenstadt, 1965–67; IV/B/4.06/100, KPKK Heiligenstadt, 'Fernschreiben Nr. 13 der BPKK [Bezirksparteikontrollkommission] … ', 10 January 1968.

57 LPA, BIV/2/13-725, SED election period reports, 1963, 1965, 1967.

58 LPA, BIV/2/13-726, 'Bericht über die Lage in der Grenzgemeinde Böseckendorf … ', 25 August 1965.

59 ThHStAW, MdI/20.1, 122 and 146, police statistics and reports, 1966–68. Some young people quickly returned to the GDR: V 223, 'Probleminformation … ', 20 January 1967, appendix p. 4.

60 LPA, BIV/2/16-737, 'Informationsbericht 31/63', 15 October 1963; *ibid.*, 'Einschätzung über die Durchsetzung der staatlichen Jugendpolitik … ', 21 March 1963; ThHStAW, V 223, 'Probleminformation … ', 15 March 1967, p. 4.

61 LPA, BIV/2/5-383, 'Kurzinformation Nr. 10/65', 4 September 1965; ThHStAW, V 249, 'Berichterstattung der Abteilung Volksbildung … ', 1 August 1968, p. 3; J 28, 'Analyse über den gegenwärtigen Stand der staatlichen Jugendpolitik … ', undated [summer 1964], pp. 6, 11; J 29, RdK Bad Langensalza, 'Analyse über die Durchsetzung der zehn Grundsätze … ', 27 November 1967; Vs/St 493, fol. 8, Speech by Hossinger to the *Bezirkstag*, 5 July 1958.

62 15 March 1967 report (note 60), p. 5; 1 August 1968 report (note 61), p. 9.

63 LPA, BIV/2/7-550, 'Auszug: Jahresanalyse zur Mitgliederbewegung v. 25.1.1963 … '; *ibid.*, 'Zu einigen Problemen … ', 3 May 1966, pp. 3–4; *ibid.*, 'Einschätzung der

Parteiorganisation … ', 31 May 1966.

64 LPA, BIV/2/7-6, 'Bericht der Arbeitsgruppe … ', 10 September 1962.

65 LPA, BIV/2/7-550, 'Erfahrungen und Schlußfolgerungen … ', 3 November 1965, p. 3. On SED agricultural policy, cf. Zimmermann, *et al.* (eds), *DDR Handbuch*, I, 804–5.

66 LPA, IV/B/4.06/117, SED Heiligenstadt, 'Berichterstattung über Erfahrungen … ', 20 February 1968.

67 ThHStAW, Vs/St 900, 'Informationsbericht Nr. 19/66', 24 August 1966.

68 LPA, BIV/2/5-383, 'Informationsbericht Nr. 30/65', 4 October 1965, p. 8.

69 On the New Economic System, cf. McCauley, *The German Democratic Republic*, pp. 107–16.

70 ThHStAW, Vs/St 900, 'Vorlage für das Politbüro … ', 5 October 1967, pp. 5–6.

71 LPA, BIV/2/7-550, 'Kurzeinschätzung über die Situation der Parteiarbeit … ', undated [1963?], p. 4.

72 25 August 1965 report (note 58).

7

East Germany between socialist constitution and Prague Spring

We have seen that the construction of the Berlin Wall did little to bolster public perceptions of the legitimacy of SED rule. Even though this final sealing of the borders forced those who might otherwise have emigrated to make their peace with the GDR, patterns of conformist behaviour had already been established rather before 1961 and were not significantly affected by the new situation. This penultimate chapter attempts to determine the extent of political and social stability by 1968, and therefore to assess whether the GDR's political and social structures stabilised further over the longer term.

The year 1968 – in which the GDR embarked on its twentieth year, with a first generation of young adults who had not known any other state form – allows us to gauge popular reactions to two contradictory developments: the adoption of a new, 'socialist' constitution following a lengthy public debate (*Volksaussprache*) and plebiscite, and the events surrounding the 'Prague Spring' and subsequent invasion of Czechoslovakia by the Warsaw Treaty powers.

Both events tested GDR citizens' loyalty after two decades of SED rule. The plebiscite of 1968 required them for the first time explicitly to recognise and legitimise both Germany's long-term division and the socialist system. The socialist states' response to the Prague Spring also demanded active rejection of the Czechoslovaks' 'third way' alternative. While the construction of the Berlin Wall represented a physical watershed in the GDR's development, 1968 was its ideological equivalent and a new test of the SED's progress in socialising its subjects and its own ranks. If the late 1960s and early 1970s were the zenith of the GDR's stability, as historians have generally concluded, the snapshot of 1968 can help to determine its true extent. However, 1968 alone did not determine the GDR's ultimate fate. This depended on other, later factors which fall outside the remit of this book, not least international economic developments and the west's readiness in the early 1970s to reach an understanding with the Soviet bloc in the process of *Ostpolitik* (see Glossary on p. x). Nevertheless, the extent of popular acceptance or rejection of SED policies regarding the new constitution and the Czechoslovak crisis indicate the extent to which the SED had consolidated its power and influence by 1968.

The constitutional debate

In 1967 the SED decided to draft a new constitution which would unambiguously commit the GDR to socialism and delineate restricted criteria for re-establishing German unity. The new constitution not only formally codified the political structures which had developed in the GDR since 1949 – principally by constitutionally enshrining the SED's leading role – but also reflected changes in the shifting international situation. The SED leadership was well aware that the GDR and its own power were the product of the Cold War. They viewed cautiously West Germany's emergent *Ostpolitik* and the superpowers' cautious steps towards détente, and therefore attempted to strengthen the symbols of GDR sovereignty so that the 'German question' would not be solved by dissolving the GDR and disempowering the SED.[1] Thus the public debate (*Volksaussprache*) in February and March 1968 and the plebiscite which approved the amended draft constitution were designed to demonstrate that the GDR's population had exercised self-determination in confirming SED rule. Article 8(2) of the new constitution effectively declared that German unity could only occur if the western Federal Republic acceded to the socialist GDR, though the party was careful (until the 1974 amendments) to maintain German unity as a long-term goal for fear of alienating public support.[2]

During the *Volksaussprache*, and the short period before the hastily announced plebiscite, the parties and mass organisations embarked on a concentrated period of heightened activity. Prior to the plebiscite, 716,077 (57 per cent) of *Bezirk* Erfurt's citizens attended 34,054 special, mainly differentiated events between 28 March and 3 April alone. In *Kreis* Bad Langensalza almost 20,000 participated in National Front 'family discussions', and 2,261 NF events involved 58,362 participants.[3] Considering the *Kreis* electorate numbered 34,362, NF activities alone represented blanket coverage. The *Volksaussprache* also involved the usual pledges to join the SED or army, and attracted 34,000 productivity pledges valued at 32 million Marks.[4] Yet despite the apparent organisational efficiency, many local party members and functionaries could not explain the constitution's ideological message and required assistance from higher authorities. When the Prague Spring began, coinciding with renewed disturbances in Poland, many local SED secretaries were again unable to provide suitable explanations without guidance.[5]

Common reactions and concerns about the constitutional draft recur in reports compiled by various sources about the *Volksaussprache* and the plebiscite preparations. Fairly clear conclusions can be drawn fron these about popular attitudes.[6]

Comments on the political system itself were surprisingly scarce. Though historians regard the enshrining of the SED's leading role in the constitution as the key innovation,[7] the numerous reports never specifically mention this point. However, private discontent was perhaps reflected in a vicar's cynical comment that Article 2 was wrong to claim that 'the people' exercised all power. A Förtha teacher's proposals that the electoral system be constitutionally defined could be construed as an attempt to reduce SED power or embarrass the party, but they were apparently unique in the *Bezirk*. Although NDPD members expressed interest in raising such matters before the draft's publication,[8] and despite occasional queries about the reduced minimum voting age and the status and role of the bloc parties and the National Front, the GDR's power mechanisms were rarely mentioned. The SED's virtual power monopoly was widely regarded as unalterable and any challenge to it was taboo by 1968.

However, worries and complaints about other matters raised during and after the *Volksaussprache* suggest continuing widespread dissatisfaction with SED rule on significant policy matters, even though the party's hegemony was not directly attacked. Three topics of direct existential relevance to the GDR were repeatedly raised, namely the 'German' question, travel restrictions and socialist economics. Personal freedom, freedom of the press, religious tolerance and a range of personal material problems were other regular topics. These are discussed in turn below.

The organisations' and parties' reports regularly speak of commitment to the GDR as a socialist fatherland, and note a wide understanding of the true, imperialist nature of the Bonn republic. However, questions such as 'Is there still a German nation?' featured regularly. One assessment noted an 'insufficiently class-based standpoint' on this issue, revealed in frequent comments such as: 'The constitutional draft will deepen Germany's division.' Many citizens used *Volksaussprache* meetings to ask why Germany was divided, possibly seeking to embarrass agitators, or to suggest the GDR make compromises for German unity to match the compromises of West Germany's new *Ostpolitik*. Some citizens queried which Berlin, constitutionally, was capital; others maintained that West Germans wanted peace as much as the GDR. Less frequently, more thoughtful residents wondered whether the new preamble, which spoke of 'leading the entire German nation to a future of peace and socialism',[9] suggested a GDR *Alleinvertretungsanspruch*, that is a claim to represent the whole German nation which would compete with the west's. Was this interference in West Germany's internal affairs, they wondered. Others felt the GDR had little opportunity of changing the FRG's politics, implying that unification would not be achieved via SED socialism. Embarrassingly, a young Gotha worker felt that a new GDR constitution was superfluous if the aim was really to achieve unification.[10]

Among the bloc parties, LDPD and NDPD members most frequently raised doubts about the SED's national policy. Some older Liberal Democrats in particular doubted that socialism could achieve German unity and advocated more compromise on both sides. In Heiligenstadt, CDU members and farmers specifically criticised Ulbricht's comments on the 'constitutional treason of the West German bourgeoisie' and insisted that even West Germany's monopoly firms paid their workers well.[11] Despite years of propaganda, the SED had failed to convince much of the population of the strength of the 'socialist world system', or the dangers posed by the Federal Republic, and thus to legitimise Germany's division and its own rule.[12]

The related question of freedom of movement was also frequently raised, often in connection with Article 18(2) which guaranteed 'personal freedom'. The discussion centred both on the right to travel to the west, widely discussed, particularly among young people, and the restrictions on travel into and within the border zones. This latter topic was raised particularly, but not exclusively, in the border districts. Border issues provoked lengthy discussions following a staff meeting at the Erfurt railway goods depot. While the main meeting discussed less controversial matters, the real concerns were expressed informally afterwards, with searching questions about regulations concerning visitors from West Berlin and the FRG. These deep concerns had not, however, prevented the main meeting from unanimously endorsing the new constitution in a public resolution, highlighting the well internalised understanding of the difference between public and private opinions by the middle GDR period.

While the SED's leading role was not directly attacked, many of the party's ideological and economic policies were. Sometimes the constitution's wording was criticised: NDPD and DBD members wondered whether formulations such as 'in accordance with the law' were designed to restrict constitutional guarantees, while a proposal to formally designate the new text as the 'socialist constitution' perhaps aimed to create disquiet rather than express support. The true extent of personal freedom produced 'extremely lively' discussions throughout the population. The FDJ had to curtail one meeting because young people complained so bitterly about their lack of freedom. Elsewhere young people insisted real freedom would only come if they were allowed beat music.[13] The absence of a constitutional right to strike also provoked criticism, with some craftsmen seeing strikes as a legitimate way of fighting for higher wages. They clearly failed to recognise the SED's argument that workers struck only against themselves in a workers' state.

The draft constitution's emphasis on socialist forms of ownership and production, though central to SED policies, produced much worried reaction among craftspeople, small businesspeople and co-operative farmers. The NF devoted great attention to pacifying such people. Many artisans feared that the development of trade co-operatives (PGHs) would now inevitably be accelerated, and claimed that continued private competition was essential for quality goods and services. In agriculture, fears were widespread that co-operatively farmed land would cease to be privately owned and that inheritance rights were endangered. Understandably, there was much uncertainty and scepticism in the NDPD, whose membership of small business owners would be among those most affected by further socialisation measures.

The draft constitution raised many other issues. The concept of equality led to numerous queries, debates and complaints. While some women complained they still felt unequal, a Heiligenstadt member of the Democratic Women's League (DFD) raised the prospect of female conscription in the interests of equality, presumably to provoke unrest. The article guaranteeing personal freedom sometimes led youngsters provocatively to suggest they should have the right to 'loaf around' (*gammeln*), but more often provoked questions about freedom of expression. School children sometimes asked if this existed at all. Article 23, which guaranteed press, radio and television freedom, similarly encouraged demands to hear and watch western media freely.

All these points raised fundamental questions about the GDR's socialist order, albeit sometimes indirectly. However, two social policy issues – religion and education – also caused much debate and thereby effectively diverted attention from the purely political aspects.

Much controversy surrounded the apparently restricted guarantees of religious freedom in the draft constitution. Whereas the 1949 constitution devoted eight articles to religion, the new text referred specifically only once to religious freedom (in Article 38), and omitted the explicit right to freedom of belief and conscience. Though the draft did not rescind the churches' specific rights and their independence from the state, guaranteed in 1949, it did not restate them.[14]

Although most vicars of the generally loyal Eisenach church were reticent, the remaining strength of religious feeling amongst the general public became very apparent. It was principally Catholics who criticised the new draft, fearing that the absence of specific guarantees seriously threatened religious life. Catholics' complaints increased in the Eichsfeld after pastoral letters were read in the churches. The state authorities noted there had been little discussion of the question before the church's intervention and that the church had obviously carefully organised the campaign, which involved petitions and directions from the clergy to parishioners to write personal letters and to ask questions at meetings. Nonetheless, the population readily supported the church's entreaties. Heiligenstadt district council found it easier to note the public meetings which had *not* discussed the controversial Article 38. Indeed, in most places the religious provisions were the main topic of discussion.[15] At some meetings the church's organised campaign was supported by the grass-roots of the supposedly loyal CDU, despite the party leadership's clear line. Across the GDR, some 40 per cent of suggested amendments to the draft came from religious circles.[16] In particular, various clergy individually proposed the constitution should reiterate the church–state division.

Though the churches ultimately failed to preserve the existing constitutional guarantees, the strength of popular feeling, especially in Catholic areas, both among the general population and, more importantly, among key members of society (such as leading CDU members, co-operative farm chairmen, etc.) ensured that two demands were incorporated into the final version of the constitution before the plebiscite. Article 38 was slightly altered to suggest greater independence for the churches to decide their own affairs, while Article 19 was extended to include specific guarantees of freedom of belief and conscience, and equality of religious and ideological beliefs.[17]

It is unlikely that Ulbricht had intended the constitutional changes to initiate a new church struggle, for which there was patently no need by 1968, or to undermine the churches' position. The more probable intention was simply to treat the

churches as insignificant organisations by largely ignoring them in the new constitution. Thus, the minor modifications cost the party little but greatly improved
sentiment among those upon whom the system relied for support, and were exem-
plary in foreign relations as signs of a more liberal approach to human rights. Perhaps the proposed Article 38 was deliberately intended to provoke the criticism
which overshadowed discussion of political structures. The amendments also
achieved much greater support from the religious communities than might have
been achieved had Christians not believed they had achieved a victory along the
way. The Worbis CDU reported that its own members and non-party Christians
welcomed the changes. Whereas some clergy had threatened not to vote in the
plebiscite, in the event some did for the first time. Only four clergy in *Kreis* Nordhausen abstained.

In education, the raising of compulsory school age from 14 to 16 created foreseeable, normal reactions. Clearly children in classes seven and eight disliked the
prospect of two extra school years, but propagandists often needed persistence to
explain the new requirement to parents too, though most teachers were in agreement. The issue was the main topic at DFD meetings, which attracted numerous
non-members. Some mothers were concerned that two additional school years
would financially disadvantage families which needed an extra wage earner. Other
parents feared their children simply would not cope or that the entire scheme was
financially unviable. These fears notwithstanding, many others supported higher
educational achievement. Nevertheless, the government heeded certain concerns,
and the revised Article 25 permitted some children to complete their education as
apprentices rather than in school.

Finally, alongside questions of political or social principle, many saw the *Volksaussprache* as an opportunity to complain about personal and material worries,
mostly linked only vaguely to the new constitution. Would the constitutional right
to work ensure adequate creche provision in Apolda? Why was land inheritance
dependent on joining a co-operative farm? Why, given constitutionally guaranteed
equality, did wage levels vary between towns, and why should the 'intelligentsia'
receive better treatment? Why did child-benefit levels vary between categories of
workers? Why did parcels from the west go missing if postal secrecy was protected?
All of these important day-to-day problems were raised, along with continual complaints about housing shortages.

The wide participation in the constitutional debate has already been noted.
However, some felt there was little point making proposals, or that ordinary people
could make few sensible suggestions about a document which experts had already
discussed. While some NDPD members welcomed the plebiscite as a sign of true
democracy, others viewed the whole *Volksaussprache* as a 'democratic mirage'
(*Scheindemokratie*).[18]

The points of complaint and query raised skirted wider issues, and though an
NDPD report regretfully noted a tendency to *Artikeldiskussion* – critical examination of individual provisions which lost sight of the wider points – the lack of an

existential discussion on the GDR's future undoubtedly spared the SED many problems. Nevertheless, despite western publications which highlighted the reprisals for GDR citizens who expressed dissatisfaction and opposition, the population, including the supposedly loyal parties' and mass organisations' rank and file, was still keen to discuss matters of concern publicly in 1968, albeit within the limits of the SED's framework.

The examples above focus mainly on doubts and criticisms. However, the files also document many positive reactions and a disaffection among many citizens with the Federal Republic, which in 1968 seemed to have abandoned the moral high ground with its support for American aims in Vietnam and its attempts to introduce potentially authoritarian 'emergency legislation'.[19] Few believed that SED socialism could achieve German unity, and many regretted that the idea of the German nation was being abandoned just as West Germany's *Ostpolitik* was emerging. But crucially many were still prepared to accept the GDR's continued existence. The *Volksaussprache* records suggest no attempts to identify alternatives. The unspoken truth behind the *Volksaussprache* remained that the USSR still underwrote the SED's hold on the GDR. However, within this framework the SED used the *Volksaussprache* to achieve a more acceptable modus vivendi with the population, and the various sectors of the population accepted this as an opportunity either to improve the aspects of socialism with which they agreed or (often successfully) to reassert their existing rights. In this sense, the SED's 'dictatorship' was qualified by a recognition of the need to respond to at least some public demands. This suggests a certain attempt at paternalism, despite the local inefficiencies in providing adequate housing and supplies.

Voting in the plebiscite on 6 April 1968 passed mainly uneventfully in *Bezirk* Erfurt, despite the appearance of graffiti and leaflets calling for a 'No' vote in Gotha, the work of disgruntled youths, and incidents such as vandalised plebiscite posters in several areas.[20] The plebiscite was a novelty in that for the first time since 1949 voters were required to mark the voting slip by crossing either a 'Yes' or a 'No' box. As the SED's First *Bezirk* Secretary, Alois Bräutigam, noted: 'This time everyone must decide, yes or no.'[21] In the bloc meeting at which he was speaking, the minutes record only that the SED dictated its instructions. It appears that no other members spoke: it seems the SED had by now installed reliable supporters in the other parties and organisations and that it had thereby achieved total control over them.

Most people still voted as the SED required, even under these slightly freer conditions. 94.49 per cent of the GDR's population approved the constitution. Even excluding Berlin, where the result was 90.96 per cent, the average was only slightly higher at 94.75 per cent. The *Bezirk* Erfurt average only just underperformed this (94.72 per cent) on a turnout which was the highest anywhere (98.51 per cent) and reflected much preparatory work with individual voters. Only 0.27 per cent of cast votes were invalid.[22] However, a lower proportion voted 'Yes' in the Catholic areas, reflecting remaining dissatisfaction over the religious settlement and, in the Eichsfeld, with the border situation.

Nonetheless, the encouraging results represented a high degree of ritual conformity. Some NDPD members commented that no-one should directly deduce individual citizens' political attitudes and morale from the percentage of 'Yes' votes. *Bezirk* level functionaries concurred. An Apolda member claimed many people nodded approval during the *Volksaussprache* without daring to discuss particular problems, or were simply ignorant of the SED's proposals. Given the level of dissent already recorded in the *Volksaussprache*, this evidence of more, unexpressed problems suggests three possible conclusions. First, the population had simply learned the outward forms of obedience by early 1968; second, many nonetheless inwardly rejected either the division of Germany, SED rule, or both; third, some were still heavily influenced by the churches. For the SED, in the short term at least, only the first of these points was significant.

Prague Spring and Thuringian autumn

The new constitution was debated against a tense background in eastern Europe and in east–west relations. Specifically, the leadership change and adoption of liberal socialist policies in neighbouring Czechoslovakia, alongside student protest in Poland, worried the SED leadership for two related reasons. First, the SED feared Czechoslovakia's rapprochement with West Germany: as GDR citizens could travel freely to Czechoslovakia, the GDR's border regime would be threatened if Czechoslovakia's borders were opened to the Federal Republic. Any formal recognition by Czechoslovakia of West Germany would also undermine the GDR's diplomatic position.[23] Second, and potentially more serious, was the fear that the Czechoslovak party's reformist ideas might also inspire SED members and the general public.

Alexander Dubček's reform process – which threatened a break with Moscow and the renunciation of traditional communist policies and power structures – was already underway in Czechoslovakia during the *Volksaussprache*, but the Prague Spring hardly impacted on the constitutional debate, beyond tacit comparisons between the ending of the constitutional right to strike in the GDR and the strikes permitted in Czechoslovakia and Poland.[24] Nonetheless, early and mid-1968 saw much discussion about developments in Czechoslovakia. Many feared and denounced the threat to Czechoslovak socialism, and voiced surprise that people in a socialist country were attracted by the west.[25] Those committed to the cause or with a personal stake in the system mainly hoped that 'the Czechoslovak working class will succeed in defending socialist conditions'. This category saw the dangers of a repeat of the events in Hungary in 1956 and hoped for quick action lest 'comrades' blood flow uselessly in Czechoslovakia'. Most Eisenach SED members did not expect that Czechoslovakia would be allowed to return to 'bourgeois conditions'.[26] After June 1953 and the invasion of Hungary in 1956, they presumably felt the status quo was assured. With uncanny accuracy, Heiligenstadt members predicted the socialist states would intervene to crush the counter-revolution at the invitation of a group of loyal Czechoslovak comrades.[27] Such opinions were not restricted to those with a stake in the system and who hoped for this outcome. The expectation of such a development in Czechoslovakia was fairly widespread. Workers in a Nordhausen firm asserted in May that Czechoslovakia was a free country and that the USSR and the GDR had no business to intervene.[28] By late July, many people expected Soviet military intervention.[29] Such attitudes naturally dissuaded GDR citizens from attempting a similar course. Real anxieties about war existed before the socialist states appeared to reach agreement with Dubček on 3 August.[30]

However, there were also worrying signs for the SED. By May many citizens believed that socialism's days were numbered in Czechoslovakia, and that a 'bourgeois' constitution was imminent there. The Prague Spring's ideological innovations proved attractive in many circles. Workers greeted the concepts of democracy and freedom, and understood by the latter an opportunity to travel. Some expressed the opinion that the GDR was too closely allied to the USSR and should build its own socialism as the Czechs and Yugoslavs were doing. Young workers, meanwhile, were attracted to the Czechs' concept of a market economy.[31] Anti-Russian feeling was also expressed in rejections of 'Russian communism' in favour of the Czechoslovak version.[32] By late May the SED concluded: 'There is currently a wavering among all sections of the population ... Some citizens consider Czechoslovakia's liberalisation process is appropriate in the GDR too.'[33]

As this report subtly indicated, similar problems existed within the SED's own ranks, partly because members' faith was shattered by the developments within the Czechoslovak communist party (KPČ). A picture of inadequate SED party work emerged as many problems were blamed on poor communication of the SED Central Committee's explanations of the situation. In Gotha, for instance, local groups had neglected party education programmes and fabricated reports of meetings which had not occurred. However, the SED's ideological problems had far more serious causes than poor administration. Rather they reflected individuals' lack of conviction in party policies and often opportunistic reasons for party membership. These failings revealed themselves in numerous incidents. For instance, an SED economist in Sömmerda announced he favoured Czechoslovakia's free market economy and would now rejoin the church as that was again possible in Czechoslovakia. A young engineer commented: 'Dubček's doing the only right thing, and it must be possible here too.' He continued: 'I have nothing in common with the SED, can't I resign?'[34] Despite many resolutions of support for the official line, the SED was clearly not united behind its leadership over the fundamental issues raised by the Prague Spring. A state official who escaped to West Germany from Osterburg-Altmark was clearly right to note that the desire to democratise socialism still existed both among SED members and in the rest of the population.[35]

Bloc-party members also displayed independence of thought before the invasion, demonstrating that the SED had not yet fully achieved its ideological goals with these groups either. Reports of NDPD discussions demonstrate this point. Some members were committed to the system and felt that the mistakes revealed by Dubček in Czechoslovakia had not been made in the GDR. Others, however, doubted the SED's wisdom and extended the criticism made of the Czechoslovak bloc-party system to circumstances in the GDR. Some NDPD members even felt the Warsaw demonstrations represented true democracy of a type impossible in the GDR, a state which pursued policies with which they did not always entirely agree. On the eve of the invasion of Czechoslovakia, some NDPD members felt they would do better without Russian interference and gleefully wondered whether they had founded their trade co-operatives too early as socialism's future now seemed in doubt. The first signs of ideological spillover also appeared as NDPD artisans, who had just approved the GDR's constitutional commitment to national ownership, supported Czechoslovakia's economic liberalisation, and as three of the party's district organisations reported that members saw the new Czechoslovakia as a model for the GDR, especially in cultural policy.[36]

The Prague Spring also highlighted the desire of many, particularly young people, to leave the GDR. The possibility of eased restrictions at Czechoslovakia's western border provoked much interest, and brought an increase of applications to visit the country in case exit to the west became possible. In May 1968 there were 3,556 private trips to Czechoslovakia from *Bezirk* Erfurt, compared with 2,492 in May 1967, a rise of 42.7 per cent. Most applications were made by young people, but four vicars from Eisenach district also applied in August. SED loyalists understood the potential for a new escape hatch and suggested restrictions at the border with Czechoslovakia to avert the danger.[37]

It would be wrong to assume that the GDR was gripped with enthusiasm for Dubček's liberal socialism. Indeed, some traditional German prejudices emerged among those who felt Czechoslovakia and Poland's problems reflected economic backwardness. Notwithstanding P.-C. Burens' suggestion that the population's interest was aroused by Czechoslovakia's developing rapprochement with the FRG,[38] many GDR citizens were critical of West Germany's capitalism and its alliance with the United States, the aggressor in the Vietnam War. However, the ideological content of the Prague Spring made a significant impact in *Bezirk* Erfurt and doubts grew about the socialist bloc's cohesiveness and strength, with implications for the credibility of the SED's incantation that socialism would triumph as the world's strongest political force.[39] Some felt that Czechoslovakia must decide its own future, a view with ominous implications for the GDR. There were also widespread complaints about the poor reporting of Czechoslovak developments in the GDR media. Most dangerously, people who had visited Czechoslovakia, received visits from Czechoslovaks or listened to Radio Prague's German broadcasts, believed the SED was wrong to condemn the Prague Spring and viewed the reforms favourably. The SED was particularly anxious about Czechs working in the GDR who spread the new message among GDR workers and even described the GDR as 'Stalinist'. School exchange groups also concluded from Czechoslovak contacts that the GDR's media were giving false information.[40]

Against this already unsettled background, troops of the GDR's National People's Army participated in the invasion of Czechoslovakia on 20–21 August

1968, designed to remove Dubček from power and to maintain Moscow's hold over its satellites. The crushing of the Prague Spring had immediate and far reaching ramifications for GDR popular opinion, but Thuringians' reactions to the invasion also demonstrated how effective the SED's control mechanisms had become by 1968.[41]

Leading state functionaries met in Erfurt at 3 a.m. on 21 August to determine and implement emergency control measures. Various other staff spontaneously arrived by 5.30 a.m. to assist. Over eighty staff from the regional administrative headquarters were sent into the districts and key firms to direct political work. Special emphasis was placed on the border districts. Early meetings of the district councils were also convened and their officials were dispatched to the localities. State functionaries and party executives met during the day, and all mayors were informed of events and instructed to staff their offices continuously. The SED also informed the bloc-party district leaderships early on 21 August; the CDU and LDPD *Bezirk* executives summoned their respective district secretaries that afternoon. Meanwhile, attempts were made to acquaint the wider population with the official line on Czechoslovakia by organising workplace gatherings to hear broadcasts of the official statements.[42] Workplace meetings, some led by members of the SED regional executive, were still being organised more than a week after the invasion.[43]

The state authorities remained on special alert for a fortnight. The regional council aimed to organise political discussions systematically with all sections of the population in every district, particularly at the border, while the district councils were to encourage young people to assist in building works and thus keep them occupied and less likely to revolt. To encourage popular restraint, an extra 190 tons of meat were made available in the shops on the first weekend of the crisis. Party and state officials were available over the weekend for political discussions with the population as required. In Weimar, all major events were 'secured' to prevent their use as 'platforms for enemy agitation'. Regional council members and staff were also present at parish council, factory committee and National Front meetings to intervene if necessary. In the key area of education, district SED leaders attended special headmasters' conferences on 23 August. By 29 August every school's 'Pedagogical Council' had met to ensure teaching staff toed the ideological line. Fifty-two staff from the regional education department supervised these meetings in the districts. Many *Bezirk* staff remained in schools to check lessons and FDJ meetings once term began. So comprehensive was political control by 1968 that time was even found to remove film of Dubček from the current newsreel. This level of control was only possible because so many people's careers by now depended on maintaining the status quo.

The authorities aimed to ensure a display of outward acceptance of the invasion by forcing people to give their opinions. However, they could not prevent widespread negative reactions, even open protests. Ominously, even before the invasion there were unusual gatherings of young people playing western music on transistor radios in Mühlhausen on 19 and 20 August. Following the invasion two hundred people assembled in that town on 21 August for a 'silent march' following an FDJ meeting attended by only forty at which 'provocative questions' were asked.[44] Twenty arrests were made after this spontaneous demonstration was disbanded by police and Soviet soldiers, an incident which blighted some participants' careers.[45] Similarly, two hundred young people gathered in Erfurt on 22 August, including some from Gotha and Weimar. Of the thirty-six arrested, two were SED members. Although the gathering appeared essentially unplanned, and most participants were attracted by the music, as in Mühlhausen, and as in 1953, it inspired copycat actions. On 23 August 250 youths gathered, of whom only five were arrested for provocative behaviour. The authorities finally regained control on 24 August when a further gathering was prevented. Twenty-five people were arrested. The city authorities employed intimidation by holding direct talks with the families and employers of sixty-four young people involved in the Erfurt gatherings. Though order was restored, these incidents were not forgotten. Some Erfurt workers drew consequences about GDR society by commenting that arresting youngsters was not 'freedom'. Similar questions were raised in Arnstadt.

The detailed GDR records do not record the marches which westerners claimed had occurred in Eisenach (allegedly with three or four thousand participants), Gotha and elsewhere,[46] but there were numerous other examples of open, individual protest, such as the Sömmerda youth arrested for running around in a jumper showing the West German eagle, and the applause by the staff of Nordhausen's theatre whenever the director mentioned Dubček's name in his explanatory speech. Other isolated incidents included the intimidation of SED members who were forced to remove their party badges on Erfurt station, and the drunken youths outside Bad Berka town hall (whom the FDJ persuaded to perform voluntary community service the following day). The only signs of organised protest were in Weimar, where leaflets called for a sit down strike, and young people encouraged passers-by to participate in it.

Unlike 1953 and 1989, however, August 1968 was principally characterised by the many anonymous actions. Leaflets and graffiti, mainly supporting Dubček and calling for the Russians to leave, were found in most districts from 22 August onwards. Thuringia seems to have been a centre of protests; compared to the 272 slogans which appeared in East Berlin between 21 August and 8 September,[47] fifty-six slogans were daubed in one night in central Erfurt alone, and the words 'Long live Dubček, Russians out!' were painted on the steps of a Weimar school.[48] Yet anti-Ulbricht slogans were rarely reported.[49] Most leaflets were handwritten, but in Arnstadt they were mass produced, and large numbers ('Freedom for the ČSSR [Czechoslovakia] with Dubček!') were also seized in Erfurt. Villages were also affected.

Nonetheless, *Bezirk* Erfurt was outwardly quiet and most people worked normally during the crisis. In the period immediately following the invasion, the *Bezirk*'s police recorded only 122 connected 'incidents', including forty-eight of 'libel of the state'.[50] Meanwhile, over two hundred mainly young people demonstrated their loyalty by joining the SED in the fortnight following the invasion.[51] There was practically no panic buying (though the sales of the SED paper, *Neues Deutschland*, increased) and business remained normal, albeit with fewer bank deposits immediately after the invasion.[52] Despite widespread fears of war, especially among older residents, and the concerns of those with relatives in the army, cynical comments such as 'The next butter will come on ration cards' and 'Wars always start in September' were extremely rare.

Although there was little outward protest, the regional council's special 'Czechoslovakia information group' discovered that the unorganised minority's actions reflected widespread opinions. Well into September, critical comments were heard throughout the *Bezirk* and across the population, especially among younger people. Most frequently people observed that the action was reminiscent of Hitler's invasion of Czechoslovakia in 1938, and that therefore German troops should not be involved, views which struck at the heart of the GDR's (and socialism's) antifascist legitimation. As no names were published, there was great scepticism about which Czechoslovak leaders, if any, had called for intervention. One SED member doubted the legitimacy of such an appeal anyway, by noting that counter-revolutionaries could just as easily have appealed to the western powers for assistance.[53] Related complaints that Czechoslovakia's sovereignty had been violated were widespread. The socialist camp's much vaunted unity was also queried, as Romania and Yugoslavia had not participated in the invasion, leading some to ask why Czechoslovakia should not go its own way as Yugoslavia, Albania and China had done. Many felt that Dubček should have had more time to comply with the socialist camp's requirements. Some wondered if the GDR had little independence either, given the National People's Army's participation in the invasion. Defenders and opponents of the action alike asked how the Czechoslovak situation could have arisen after so many years of socialist development there.

All these general questions highlighted the inconsistencies of the SED's ideological position in the world socialist camp and undermined the concept of the inevitability of socialism developing according to Marxism's natural laws. Some individuals tried to embarrass party activists with trickier questions. Would the GDR or USSR also march into Yugoslavia and Romania, or even China, if called upon?[54] Was there any difference between the Warsaw Treaty Organisation's actions in Czechoslovakia and the US's in Vietnam?[55] Supposing an imperialist Czechoslovak government had called for help from the west? Was the USA equally entitled to occupy Cuba? Could a country leave the Warsaw Treaty Organisation to pursue its own path to socialism? As the days passed, the contradictions worsened. Why had Dubček, yesterday's traitor, been restored to power?

Despite the SED's administrative efficiency, the party's rank and file was as affected by the invasion as the rest of the population. Although the party's weaknesses are generally sparsely reported, this is clearly the implication of repeated reports that 'all sectors of the population' had doubts or condemned the invasion.

However, in one frank report the SED noted that some members were 'softening'. One member felt the GDR should be ashamed of participating, while another compared the invasion to Hitler's. SED railwaymen in Nordhausen refused to attend party meetings because of the invasion, and complained: 'We can't say anything in meetings because the police is there too.'[56] Various problems in the Catholic Eichsfeld illustrate the party's difficulties. There, the Lindewerra party secretary told a public meeting that he disagreed with the invasion, which he regarded as unconstitutional. He was supported by a visiting district official of the NDPD.[57] In Marth, two comrades known as dissidents bought their colleagues brandy to encourage them to make 'negative' comments. In Heuthen, only four members attended an extraordinary meeting on 27 August while their comrades were drinking in the co-operative farm. But although many members expressed significant doubts about the invasion or rejected it, the Heiligenstadt district party felt only seventeen members had made comments requiring further investigation. Doubts and wavering were not classified as damaging or opposed to the party line. Many members who had spoken too freely were also prepared to conform once party authorities began to intervene.[58] By not taking more rigorous action, the SED leadership seemed to be tacitly admitting that it could not expect the entire membership's unequivocal support. A 'party check' as rigorous as that of 1950–51 would have significantly weakened the party, and therefore SED hegemony, had it removed all those with any doubts about the correctness of the intervention in Czechoslovakia. It is also important to note that some SED members went on the offensive in party meetings against those who echoed arguments from the western media.[59] The existence of a strong core of loyalists who supported official policies either out of conviction or as a pragmatic opportunity to display their loyalty undoubtedly strengthened the SED's 'leading role' in the localities.

Bloc-party members also generally posed the same awkward questions as the rest of the population, and made as much use of western media. CDU members seem to have been particularly reserved on the topic. The Weimar CDU organisation implied that most of its members still disagreed with the measures almost a week later. Three weeks later the regional leadership felt the need for the measures was more clearly understood, but presumably, therefore, still incompletely. Many Heiligenstadt members also felt papal condemnation rendered the invasion illegitimate. However, some CDU members were also prepared to sign supportive resolutions and to defend the measures to their colleagues.[60] Similarly, not all LDPD members were convinced by September that a counter-revolutionary situation existed in Czechoslovakia and were also 'influenced' by western media. One report claimed the Czechoslovaks' liberalisation measures had no support among LDPD members, but also noted ideological uncertainties and that old anti-Soviet sentiments had been strengthened.[61]

Many NDPD members also shared the general concerns, and avoided discussions of Czechoslovakia in their meetings. In some cases supportive resolutions were adopted without discussion, but concrete pledges of economic performance were more difficult to obtain. Official resolutions apart, first reactions, when expressed, ranged from total rejection of the military intervention to conditional, but not total, support. Many were still unconvinced in early September that the Czechoslovak issue was resolved. Still more significantly, some members of the town leadership in Gebesee and the district leaderships in Erfurt-Land and Heiligenstadt wavered in their support, causing the loyal regional executive to intervene.[62]

In summary, bloc-party members shared the general doubts, but these more politically minded citizens' energies were consumed by parties whose leaderships loyally supported SED policies and intervened on the rare occasions when it became necessary to ensure that lower party organs conformed.

Young people were the population group most mutinous and unreceptive to the official line. Even the SED recognised that young people had most 'ideological uncertainties',[63] despite the GDR's emphasis on ideological education. After 21 August, Erfurt-Land officials reported young people's great interest in developments but neglected to claim they showed support, an unusual omission in such reports. Most school pupils demonstrated the enforced dual personality common to many GDR citizens. On one hand they displayed outward conformity by arriving at school in FDJ or Young Pioneer uniforms. Even the older, more rebellious students changed out of their western jeans and into FDJ garb in school toilets for FDJ gatherings and changed back before resuming their private lives.[64] On the other hand they posed the usual unanswerable questions. Some particularly asked why the GDR permitted only one youth organisation. By 23 August one report concluded that extra political work was required with young workers who were 'asking questions resulting from failure to recognise the context'. A brigade of young workers in Bad Langensalza said openly what others hinted at: 'We are not interested in politics, but in other things, and we condemn the invasion.' It is surely significant that the ideologically dissatisfied teenagers and young adults of 1968 were at the vanguard of the *Wende* (the 'change') in 1989.[65]

The reports stated that young people's questions were resolved, though not how, but their teachers often seemed uncertain or unconvinced of the official line themselves. This was undoubtedly a contributory factor to young people's ideological confusion. Though very few teachers outwardly protested, and some demonstrated great loyalty, many expressed doubts or raised the usual questions in 'Pedagogical Council' meetings; 'repeated discussions' were necessary with some colleagues, while some meetings attempted to avoid the Czechoslovak issue altogether. Despite the presence of district council members at such meetings in Arnstadt, some questions remained unresolved, suggesting that the ideological certainty and loyalty of even high-ranking state officials were overtaxed. In 1968 the minority of committed teachers and the direct political pressure from the attendant state and party officials ensured teachers' conformity once term began, but the level of ideological support from those entrusted with securing future generations' loyalty to socialism was clearly inadequate. In contrast, unreliable FDJ officials are rarely reported, and few members resigned.[66]

The Czechoslovak crisis demonstrated that the churches had been somewhat tamed, perhaps by their partial victory in the constitutional debate. There are no reports of turbulent priests damning the Czechoslovak invasion from the pulpit. Rather, most clergy, parish councillors and churchgoers exercised great reserve and remained silent unless asked.[67] This silence was similar to that after 17 June 1953, but marked a great victory for the SED compared to the churches' earlier public campaigns over other issues. The churches' silence did not, however, signify acceptance. The National Front and CDU carefully organised explanatory discussions on Czechoslovakia with clergy, but vicars typically regretted or condemned the invasion, or saw it as inevitable. More significant to the SED than these privately expressed views, however, was the highly supportive and morally upstanding public statement issued by the vicar of Altenbergen (*Kreis* Gotha), a member of the CDU's regional executive.[68]

The most significant casualty of the Czechoslovak invasion on GDR soil was, again, the SED's credibility. The population's doubts and questions were not resolved by the armies of party and state instructors, though their presence perhaps dampened open discussion and dissent. As the GDR's media were slow to provide any information (accurate or not) about the Czechoslovak crisis, the population turned en masse to western information sources.[69] This was nothing new: the western media had undermined the SED for over twenty years. However, the perceived scale of the crisis encouraged many citizens to say that GDR news was not credible,[70] and that they were forced to use western sources once the crisis began. Local functionaries in Dienstedt shared their view. As the crisis deepened, so the audience for western news grew. Reports that western stations were turned up loud in public suggest that the population did not perceive repression as total. Although the official political 'instructors' could claim the moral high ground by insisting that the public was being influenced by western imperialist propaganda, it was hard to counter young workers' cynical questions about what GDR television had to hide by showing less footage from Czechoslovakia, or an NDPD member's comment that the west's pictures 'speak for themselves'.[71] The Czechoslovak crisis finally established the bankruptcy of the GDR's own media in the public's perception and confirmed the long-standing trend towards reliance on western broadcasts, another highly significant factor before and during the 1989 revolution.

By far the most dominant reaction was reserve. Most people were reluctant to comment on the invasion, and noticeably ceased conversation if functionaries approached. In many public meetings, only functionaries spoke.[72] Life remained mainly normal. Most people wanted simply to work and then go home to normal life. Though the reports do not record that the spectre of 1953 was mentioned, they do include comparisons to Hungary in 1956. The renewed repression of 1968 seemed to preclude any alternative to building socialism in the GDR. Therefore most people kept quiet, publicly pledged themselves to work harder for the cause, and life continued. Only in isolated incidents did people refuse to sign party resolutions, despite claims that 'in Saxony and Thuringia alone tens of thousands of workers refused to agree resolutions supporting the intervention at their work-places.'[73] However, their difficult questions and unwillingness to accept official explanations clearly show that the SED had failed to win the masses' support for Marxist dogma by 1968. Indeed, ideological doubts were inevitable for a party which claimed a scientific understanding of political developments but was unable to provide a clear analysis of the Czechoslovak situation. Nonetheless, it is also clear that the SED had established patterns of societal conformity by 1968 which few actively opposed,[74] and that the state and party apparatus had so perfected its tech-niques that it could easily quell any real or potential dissent. Equally, practically all state and party functionaries could be relied upon to uphold the existing order, whether from conviction or vested interest. Though the bases of this compromise between party and people were somewhat unstable, they at least ensured the sta-bility of the regime for as long as the external parameters remained unaltered.

Notes

1 Cf. K. Dawisha, *The Kremlin and the Prague Spring* (Berkeley, University of California Press, 1984), pp. 29–30.
2 The full text of the 1968 constitution is in K. Sorgenicht, *et al.* (eds), *Verfassung der Deutschen Demokratischen Republik: Dokumente/Kommentar* (Berlin, Staatsverlag der Deutschen Demokratischen Republik, 1969); cf. G. Neumann and E. Trümpler, *Der Flop mit der DDR-Nation 1971* (Berlin, Dietz, 1991), pp. 28–38.
3 ThHStAW, NF 558, fols 25, 109, NF reports, April 1968. Unless otherwise stated, the archival reports in this chapter are all from 1968.
4 ThHStAW, NF 559, fol. 123, NF Erfurt, 'Informationsbericht', 14 March; SED Bezirksleitung Erfurt, 'Entwurf zur Geschichte der Bezirksparteiorganisation Erfurt der SED, 1945–1985' (unpublished manuscript), Chapter 7, p. 89.
5 LPA, IV/B/2/5-183, 'Kurzinformation Nr. 2/68', 23 January, p. 5; *ibid.*, 'Stimmung und Meinungen … ', 20 March 1968, p. 3.
6 Unless otherwise stated, this section is based on reports in ThHStAW, NF 558, 559, 560.
7 Cf., e.g., H. Weber, *Geschichte der DDR* (Munich, dtv, 1985), p. 387.
8 ThHStAW, NF 835, fol. 194, NDPD Bezirksvorstand, 'Halbmonatsmeldung Nr. 24/67', 20 December 1967.
9 Sorgenicht, *Verfassung*, p. 43.
10 ThHStAW, J 28, 'Bericht über Meinungen … ', 11 March, p. 3.
11 LPA, IV/B/4.06/002, SED Heiligenstadt, 'Informationsbericht', 15 January.
12 Cf. LPA, IV/B/2/5-183, 'Welche Hauptprobleme und Hauptargumente gibt es gegenwärtig … ', 16 January.
13 ThHStAW, J 28, 'Bericht über Meinungen … ', 22 February, p. 2.
14 The draft articles concerning the churches and religious affairs are cited in G. Besier, *Der SED-Staat und die Kirche* (Munich, Bertelsmann, 1993), pp. 651–2.
15 ThHStAW, Ki 66, RdK Heiligenstadt, 'Informationsbericht', 27 March.
16 Besier, *Der SED-Staat*, p. 660.
17 The final version of the 1968 constitution is in Sorgenicht, *Verfassung*. Draft articles 19 and 38 were renumbered 20 and 39.
18 LPA, IV/B/2/5-183, 'Kurzinformation', 22 January and 5 February; IV/B/4.06/218, NDPD Heiligenstadt, 'Halbmonatsmeldung 7/68', 5 April.

19 Cf., e.g., LPA, IV/B/2/15-410, DBD Bezirksverband, 'Neuwahlabschlußanalyse', 3 January, p. 20.

20 ThHStAW, OI 940, 'Information über den Stand der Vorbereitung … ', p. 7; V 223, 'Probleminformation … ', 20 May, appendix 2.

21 ThHStAW, OI 941, 'Protokoll der Blocksitzung am 27.3.1968', p. 4.

22 Figures compiled from Sorgenicht, *Verfassung*, p. 191; ThHStAW, OI 942, fol. 34, 'Schlußbericht'.

23 Dawisha, *The Kremlin*, pp. 30–1, 53; V. Mastny (ed.), *Czechoslovakia: Crisis in World Communism* (New York, Facts on File, 1972), p. 25.

24 ThHStAW, NF 560, fol. 27, NF Arnstadt, 'Bericht über die am 7.3.1968 in Bruchstedt Krs. Bad Langensalza stattgefundene Einwohnerversammlung'; NF 558, 4 April referendum report, fol. 28.

25 ThHStAW, NF 559, fol. 70, NF Erfurt, 'Informationsbericht', 21 March.

26 ThHStAW, MdI/20.1, 81, fols 144, 146, police reports, 20 and 24 May.

27 LPA, IV/B/4.06/119, SED Heiligenstadt, 'Kurzinformation … ', 21 May.

28 20 May report (note 26), p. 3.

29 LPA, IV/B/2/5-183, 'Information über die Stimmung … ', 30 July, pp. 4–5.

30 E.g., ThHStAW, I 127, fols 155, 188, Eisenach and Erfurt reports, August 1968.

31 LPA, IV/B/2/5-183, 'Information über Stimmung … ', 17 May 1968, p. 4, 21 May, pp. 3–4, and 11 June, p. 5.

32 ThHStAW, I 127, fol. 178, 'Information über Stimmungen … ', 8 August.

33 LPA, IV/B/2/5-183, 'Wertung der Diskussionen … ', 28 May, p. 2.

34 *Ibid.*, 'Information über Aufweichungserscheinungen … ', 13 June, pp. 2–3.

35 Cited in P.-C. Burens, *Die DDR und der "Prager Frühling"*, Beiträge zur Politischen Wissenschaft, 41 (Berlin, Duncker & Humblot, 1981), p. 78.

36 ThHStAW, NF 559, fols 145-6, NDPD report, 20 March; NF 836, fols 31, 102–3, NDPD reports, 7 May and 21 August, pp. 2–3.

37 ThHStAW, MdI/20.1, 81, fols 144, 150, 156, police reports, 20, 31 May and 14 June; Vs/St 1076, 'Information über Stimmungen … ', 8 August, pp. 4–5; LPA, IV/B/2/5-183, 'Information … ', 12 May, p. 2; 4 April report (note 24), fol. 28.

38 Burens, *Die DDR*, pp. 81–2.

39 Cf. P. Bühner and K. Itau, 'Dubček-Rufe auf dem Steinweg', *Mühlhäuser Beiträge zu Geschichte, Kulturgeschichte, Natur und Umwelt*, 16 (1993), p. 142.

40 ThHStAW, NF 560, fols 159–60, NF Sömmerda, undated, untitled report; NF 559, fol. 145, NDPD report, 20 March; V 223, 'Probleminformation … ', 17 July; LPA, IV/B/2/5-183, SED reports, 11 May, 13 June and 13 July.

41 Unless otherwise noted, the following paragraphs are based on August–September 1968 reports in ThHStAW, Vs/St 917, 918, 919 and 1076.

42 ThHStAW, NF 839, fols 105–7, CDU, 'Informationen zu den Massnahmen … ', 22 August; NF 831, fol. 186, LDPD, 'Situationsbericht 22/68', 22 August, p. 3.

43 Sieber, *Chronik 1962 bis 1970*, p. 213.

44 ThHStAW Weimar, I 262, 'Information über die Vorkommnisse durch Jugendliche in der Stadt Mühlhausen … ', 21 August. Similar events were reported in Prenzlauer Berg (Berlin): A. Mitter and S. Wolle, *Untergang auf Raten* (Munich, Bertelsmann, 1993), p. 393.

45 Bühner and Itau, 'Dubček-Rufe … ', pp. 141–3.

46 Mitter and Wolle, *Untergang*, p. 461; Burens, *Die DDR*, p. 72.

47 Mitter and Wolle, *Untergang*, pp. 459–60.

48 ThHStAW, V 223, 'Probleminformation … ', 19 September, appendix 2.

49 However, FDGB reports elsewhere in the GDR did record them: M. Fulbrook, *Anatomy of a Dictatorship* (Oxford, Oxford University Press, 1995), p. 197.

50 ThHStAW, MdI/20.1, 81, fols 26–7, undated, untitled police speech [autumn 1968?].

51 Sieber, *Chronik 1962 bis 1970*, p. 213.

52 ThHStAW, MdI/20.1, 139, fol. 244, BdVP, 'Bericht Nr. 10/68'.

53 LPA, IV/B/2/5-183, 'Dritte Information über Stimmung … ', 21 August, p. 2.

54 19 September report (note 48), IV, p. 3.

55 ThHStAW, V 223, 'Information', 22 August, p. 2.

56 LPA, IV/B/2/5-183, 'Information über die Stimmung … ', 24 August, pp. 5–6.

57 LPA, IV/B/4.06/101, 'Auszug aus dem Bericht über Informationen vom 23.8.1968'.

58 *Ibid.*, KPKK Heiligenstadt reports, 29 August, 4 September and 4 November.

59 LPA, IV/B/4.06/119, SED Heiligenstadt, 'An Parteiinformation', 28 August.

60 ThHStAW, NF 839, fols 105–11, 129, CDU reports, 22 and 27 August, 17 September; LPA, IV/B/4.06/216, CDU Heiligenstadt, 'Information', 29 August, p. 2.

61 ThHStAW, NF 831, fols 208ff, LDPD, 'Situationsbericht 27/68', 19 September.

62 ThHStAW, NF 836, fols 120 and 127–33, NDPD reports, 22 August and 2 September.

63 SED Bezirksleitung Erfurt, 'Entwurf zur Geschichte der Bezirksparteiorganisation Erfurt der SED, 1945–1985', Chapter 6, p. 106.

64 Bühner and Itau, 'Dubček-Rufe … ', p. 141.

65 This conclusion is also drawn by Mitter and Wolle, *Untergang*, p. 370.

66 A rare example concerned three members in Witterda: ThHStAW, Vs/St 918, RdK Erfurt-Land report, 2 August, p. 2. The upward membership trend is confirmed by figures in D. Zilch, *Millionen unter der blauen Fahne* (Rostock, Verlag Jugend und Geschichte, 1994–), I (1994), pp. 40, 53.

67 ThHStAW, NF 839, fols 127–8, CDU, 'Zur Lage in der ČSSR', 10 September, pp. 2–3.

68 22 August CDU report (note 60), p. 3.

69 Burens, *Die DDR*, pp. 66–7, suggests up to 95 per cent of the population regularly watched western television news.

70 22 August CDU report (note 60), p. 2.

71 ThHStAW, NF 836, fol. 132, NDPD, 'Halbmonatsmeldung Nr. 17/68', 2 September, p. 6.

72 LPA, IV/B/4.06/119, SED Heiligenstadt, 'An Sektor Parteiinformation', 23 August, p. 3.

73 Burens, *Die DDR*, p. 73.

74 This general conclusion is also reached by H. Dähn, 'Jugend, FDJ und Religion am Vorabend des 21. August 1968', in H. Gotschilk (ed.), *"Links, links und Schritt gehalten … " Die FDJ: Konzepte, Abläufe, Grenzen*, Die Freie Deutsche Jugend: Beiträge zur Geschichte einer Massenorganisation, 1 (Berlin, Metropol Verlag, 1994), p. 267.

8

Conclusion

As Mary Fulbrook notes in the conclusion to her *Anatomy of a Dictatorship*, an examination of the history of a country such as the German Democratic Republic either uniquely from above or from below cannot alone provide a rounded explanation of why the GDR operated in the way that it did, and why its population allowed it to do so.[1] Although the temptation at the end of this investigation of Thuringia between 1945 and 1968 is to attempt a full examination of all the large questions of interpretation of GDR history, such an exercise would clearly be beyond the remit of this volume. The wider political framework of the GDR's existence was dictated in Berlin and Moscow, sometimes in response to policies pursued by Bonn, Washington, London and Paris. The fortunes of the GDR's economy depended on all these players and other factors such as climate and world recession. The GDR's ultimate collapse, the short-term product of the opening of the Berlin Wall, depended on all these ingredients and others besides, rather than solely on the societal structures and the efficacy of regional and local functionaries discussed in the preceding chapters. However, though we cannot produce answers to all the unanswered questions about the GDR here, the conclusions which can be drawn from the above examination of popular opinion and the examples of the internal dynamics of power structures may contribute to a better understanding of the national whole from the perspective of the local part.

The questions posed in the introduction were underpinned by an attempt to define and categorise the nature of the GDR's societal and political forms. What sort of a country was the GDR? What sort of lives did its citizens lead? The perhaps surprising principal answer to these questions is that the GDR was quite a normal country, despite its unusual international and domestic political setting, and that its citizens for the most part led normal lives, dominated as in most countries by family life and concerns about work and material welfare. Naturally, Thuringians were directly affected by shortages and hardships in the initial postwar period. They then experienced the uncertainties and fears of the Cold War and their lives were also affected by the SED's political and economic objectives, such as the land reform and nationalisation. However, many of these conditions and fears were common throughout the Northern Hemisphere after the Second World War. For instance, West Germans were similarly affected by the introduction of the 'social market economy' and Britons by the radical innovations of the landslide Labour government of 1945.

As the Cold War division of Europe persisted, so Thuringians grew as accustomed to their lot as Bavarians, South Tyroleans or Britons, and led their lives within this new, postwar framework. None of these populations was necessarily entirely satisfied with the situation in which they found themselves as, for instance, Bavarian independence remained unattainable, Italian rule persisted in the German-speaking Tyrol, and the British Empire receded. But despite these frustrations, the tangible needs and worries of everyday life dominated most Thuringians' experience of everyday life. This is most immediately obvious in the way that life quickly returned to normal after each of the political upsets of the years examined in the preceding chapters. Though the sealing of the borders and the deportations of some citizens away from the border areas were unusual political events, they did not dominate the overall experience of life in the GDR, even if they were highly influential in forming individual citizens' underlying perceptions of the state, and of its 'leading party', the SED. Though these comments may stand to reason, they bear repetition as the GDR is often considered to have been a somehow 'abnormal' state, particularly as it was dismantled after only forty years. In fact, the GDR's fate was not particularly unusual: change is the norm. Since 1806, few German state forms have lasted as long as the GDR. On a still larger scale, there are few states anywhere in the world which exist now in the same form as they did a hundred years ago. However, within the flux of political development, individuals' lives continue.

Leaving aside for the moment the question of approval and/or disapproval, this framework of general normality presupposes a general acceptance of the GDR by its citizens, a view reinforced by the general lack of concerted opposition to SED rule before 1989, especially since even the uprising of June 1953 was supported only partially in *Bezirk* Erfurt. Conditions were made favourable for popular acceptance of almost any postwar German regime by various factors which were entirely independent of SED activities. Chief among these was Germans' awareness of being a defeated nation at the allies' mercy. The perception of being unable to control their own destiny underpinned many political outlooks well into the 1960s, and was reflected in the apathy which met the SED's repeated initiatives to swing public opinion behind campaigns to remove the western powers from Germany and to reunite the country in a form acceptable to Moscow. Thuringians remained well aware that Germany's destiny depended on the western powers too, and that the 'small man' would achieve nothing no matter how many petitions were signed, unless the allies and Germany's leaders, both east and west, agreed. Although the party regretted the apathy connected with its rallying calls, in the early years it was also this political apathy which eased the transfer of power into the SED's hands. Though the common epithet of the SED as 'the Russian party' was not intended to be complimentary, it signified that most Thuringians accepted that they could do little but accept their new masters, however cynical they remained about the SED's claims to popular legitimacy.

The perception of being powerless cogs in a larger system had roots which went back further than the war. Apart from the *Gleichschaltung* of the Nazi period, when local power had been removed to the *Führer* in Berlin and his NSDAP party subordinates, Thuringians had also experienced the removal of the democratically based SPD–KPD coalition government by *Reich* forces in 1923, and the progressive disintegration of the Weimar Republic's supposed democracy into effective rule by unelected bureaucracy by 1930. An older generation could remember the Kaiser's similar regime. After 1945 there was little incentive to believe that a defeated nation would be permitted democratic self-rule. After the SED emerged from a propaganda campaign reminiscent of the tactics of 1933, and once the principle of 'unity list' elections was in place after 1950, many Thuringians must have perceived that the *status quo ante* had been restored.

Furthermore, the harsh material conditions which prevailed at the end of the war also facilitated the ease with which the SED assumed power. The mass of the population had to contend with uncertain food and fuel supplies, while the many settlers from the lost eastern provinces had to make an entirely new life with few possessions and usually in accommodation rented from unwilling locals. In this situation, many people had neither the time nor the inclination to take a great interest in the developing political landscape, which seemed to many to be beyond their own control anyway. Thus relatively abstract events of the early years, such as the founding of the SED and the creation of the GDR, passed almost unnoticed by many Thuringians. This general disinterest caused the SED some problems in establishing political and societal structures at the grass-roots, where, for instance, the mass organisations and bloc meetings were often slow to begin meaningful activity; however, it also enabled the party to seize the key levers of political control without much organised domestic opposition. Such serious opposition as was mounted often had, or appeared to have, western roots and could be dismissed or countered by the SED for this reason alone in the worsening international climate of the Cold War.

Finally, the KPD/SED's takeover of power was facilitated by the considerable moral legitimacy which many believed had accrued to the party as a result of Nazi rule. The communist and social democratic martyrs of the Third Reich, not least Ernst Thälmann, murdered in Buchenwald, but also the Thuringians Theodor Neubauer and Magnus Poser, served as potent symbols of the evils of fascism and of the socialist forces which existed to ensure Nazism never returned. In the black and white political landscape of the crucial initial postwar phase, during which the key structures were established, the KPD/SED effectively used these symbols to maximum advantage in its publicity and propaganda work, deepening the convictions of those already sympathetic to socialism, and winning new adherents, particularly those who had once represented alternative political courses but who now pursued the goals of socialist unity from within the bloc parties.

These various factors combined to galvanise the pro-socialist sections of society and to neutralise much of the rest of popular opinion once the SMAD began favouring the KPD/SED. Thus we can to a certain extent relativise the role of the Soviet occupying powers in achieving the stability of the developing socialist system in the SBZ/GDR. Clearly, the Soviet Union dictated the parameters of its zone's development and increasingly enabled the SED to become the leading political force, as the option of uniting Germany on terms favourable to the USSR receded. The Soviet forces also intervened at decisive moments and in decisive places to ensure that its favoured path was not threatened. Examples of this are easier to find at zonal level (for instance, the removal of the CDU's leaders in 1945 and 1947) than regionally or locally, though clearly the deposing of certain elected German district officials by SMAD commandants in the early years and the clear Soviet military presence at striking factories in June 1953 fall into this category. A further example would be the favouring of the SED over the other parties with newsprint and other supplies. However, the Soviet Union's direct interventions as an occupying power to ensure SED hegemony in society were surprisingly rare. Indeed, as the years progressed the Soviet Union intervened more frequently to ensure that the SED's central leadership fulfilled its allotted tasks in domestic and foreign policy than to exert pressure on the GDR's population to conform.

To a very large extent, the GDR system was created and maintained by Germans themselves rather than by the Soviet Union, the latter having first created the essential conditions for socialism to develop and then withdrawn to a supervisory role. From the first KPD meetings in Buchenwald and the first SPD gatherings in private houses, German communists and social democrats laid the foundations for the state which emerged in 1949. Albeit with Soviet approval, they made the key personnel decisions for the developing party and state apparatus, established the mass organisations and took policy initiatives. Early police records, for instance, show quite clearly that German officials, mainly communists, established the new force themselves. The Soviet Union had no shortage of willing helpers in Germany who took advantage of the unique opportunity to create the socialist system both sides desired.

As the system grew and stabilised over time, more and more Germans became involved in the maintenance of SED hegemony, either directly through their membership of a political party and their consequent acceptance of its statutes (including, in the case of the bloc parties, recognition of the SED's leading role), or indirectly through membership of the NF or one of the mass organisations. On election days only a very small proportion of the population refused to vote or voted 'No'. Voters were not marched into the polling stations at gunpoint by Soviet soldiers. Most went compliantly, signifying either acceptance of or an accommodation with the prevailing political system. A few had to be sought out and persuaded to vote, but this political pressure was exerted by fellow Germans with an interest in preserving the system. From a variety of motivations, East Germans themselves created and perpetuated SED hegemony while the Soviet forces normally remained at a distance.

What were these motivations? For some, there was a sincerely held conviction that the SED was pursuing the correct policies towards a desirable goal. Such sympathies were particularly important in creating a sizeable core constituency of favourable opinion during the initial phase of constructing the state and party apparatus. Among and alongside the true believers were those whose careers depended on loyalty to the party and state apparatus they served. For these groups, preservation of SED hegemony was akin to self-preservation. This was increasingly the case the longer the system persevered, but also as public dissatisfaction with these officials increased. The obvious reaction of functionaries faced with reports of citizens preparing trees to hang them from, as in 1956, was to redouble their efforts to preserve the system. However, the degree of ideological commitment as opposed to personal material interest of the functionaries in the system was doubtful in many cases. These were the so-called 'wallet communists'. This became particularly apparent after the *Wende* (the 'change') of 1989 when the SED/PDS could no longer afford to pay its party functionaries. In Mühlhausen, and no doubt elsewhere, staff at the party's district headquarters resigned their party membership once it no longer provided them with a job.[2]

The fact that the voluntary work required to establish and maintain the various organisations was usually concentrated in very few, overworked hands, suggests that only a minority of the population actively supported the system, irrespective of the high proportion of SED members in the population (one seventh by 1968). For far more people, the motivation for allowing the political regime to continue was the desire to lead a quiet life in a situation which they (correctly) perceived to be unalterable. In some cases this motivation was born of fear of repression by the Soviets dating back to rapes and other crimes of the early occupation period. In other cases, personal fears of reprisals were related to the examples of persons deported from the border zones or arrested and imprisoned for misdeeds such as embezzling materials during the early years of extreme shortages or for allegedly failing to implement the land reform correctly. But for the majority of the population, political stability also meant personal economic stability. The memories of war and economic depression were still recent enough to act as a powerful disincentive against provoking further radical change, particularly in a situation characterised by two well-armed opposing camps. The persistent and general expectation of war in the 1950s and the comparisons between Czechoslovakia 1968 and Czechoslovakia 1938 certainly represented popular discontent with the prevailing political situation, both domestically and internationally, but were also symbolic of several generations' urgent desire to avoid renewed conflict, even at the cost of maintaining a regime with which few were particularly satisfied.

To return to the question of the extent and nature of popular approval or disapproval of the GDR, the local materials discussed here entirely bear out Mary Fulbrook's assertion that the GDR 'failed to produce a new, intrinsic legitimacy of its own', thus undermining the state's stability.[3] Despite the existence of a section of the population which was entirely or mainly sincerely committed to fulfilling the official policy goals of the central leadership, and despite the general conformity of behaviour to the norms expected of the population by the state and party organs, the records of popular opinion between 1945 and 1968 unambiguously show that the SED never succeeded in winning the arguments that socialism in the colours of the GDR was the only scientific and morally acceptable way forward; that the SED and in particular its *Politbüro* and First Secretary were therefore entitled to rule; that it was legitimate to pursue socialism in only one part of Germany, cut off from the other; that the 'progressive, peace-loving' Soviet Union was the GDR's greatest friend and protector rather than a somewhat backward country with unjustifiable imperialist and militarist ambitions; and that unity list elections were the most democratic way of securing Germany's future, to name only a few of the SED's more prominent assertions which the majority of the population never accepted. To judge by the range of opinion reports, belief in these principles of SED rule barely increased between the GDR's founding in 1949 and the adoption of the new socialist constitution of 1968.

Rather, and ironically given the bombardment of political propaganda in practically all the media and the importance attached to ideological education and outward displays of political symbolism, most of the GDR's population became essentially apolitical where internal GDR politics was concerned. This was reflected in the propensity of standard responses to milestones and initiatives in the GDR's political life, generally comments which sounded loyal but said and meant little, and the cynical comments of the smaller number who preferred not to express the standard lines of support. Popular opinion reports show few examples of comments where the speakers are truly engaging in reflective thought about the latest developments in political life. This was hardly surprising as most developments in the GDR's annual political round merely concerned yet another Soviet peace proposal or still more calls to raise productivity and overfulfil the state plan. Apoliticism is also, for instance, reflected in the sparsity of comments on the proposals for political structures in the 1968 draft constitution.

The general abandonment of political interest in the running of the GDR by the mid-1950s and up to at least 1968 was symptomatic of a widespread readiness to relinquish political control to the SED, thereby facilitating the party's implementation of its 'leading role', but also of an essential failure in wide sections of the population to identify with the GDR as their own state. Notwithstanding this lack of interest in internal affairs, the population remained keenly interested in international developments, even though in early 1967 nearly 60 per cent of *Bezirk* Erfurt's inhabitants believed there would be no developments in the German question for some time.[4] Such interest can be interpreted as hope that a change might one day occur which would at least allow travel to and from the west, if not German unification, another indication of the population's failure to identify with the GDR state by the late 1960s.

If it is clear that GDR citizens failed to identify with their state, it is also clear that they generally failed to take decisive action to undermine it. The widespread grumbling and cynicism translated into strike action relatively rarely, and into political opposition – as for instance expressed through boycotts of elections – hardly ever. During the 1950s and 1960s opposition was not systematically organised even at local level, so that even widespread grievances did not threaten the SED's grip on political life. Instead, most of the population participated in the mass organisations (even if they did no more than carry a membership card) and marched in parades to demonstrate their loyalty to the socialist course as required.

This combination of often contradictory factors suggests that most of the GDR's citizens did not particularly support their political system. Equally, however, to say they merely tolerated or suffered it would be to paint too negative a picture. The degree of participation in the GDR's social and political structures without the open application of force suggests at the very least a willingness to make the best of a bad job. Particularly in the years considered in this volume, before the stagnation of the late 1970s and 1980s set in, many contributed willingly to help make postwar Germany a success, either through specifically political or organisational activities or through schemes such as village enhancement programmes.

Despite the limitations of a regional study in answering larger questions, the material presented in this volume does allow some contribution to the wider debates concerning GDR history. The question of whether the GDR was always or from an early point doomed to failure has concentrated many minds since the *Wende*, particularly since the publication of Mitter and Wolle's important book on the topic, *Untergang auf Raten*. As Mary Fulbrook notes, the question is inextricably linked to the wider question of the viability of 'real' communist systems per se,[5] and as such cannot be fully answered here. However, material from Thuringia suggests that rather than being on an inevitable downward curve from June 1953 onwards, after the crushing of the attempt at revolt, instead structures stabilised and popular tolerance and acceptance of the GDR grew alongside an increased preparedness on the part of many citizens to be co-opted or *gleichgeschaltet* to the prevailing political and societal forms. The fact that complaints on all manner of topics continued throughout the period under review did not necessarily mean that the GDR would collapse. Indeed, widespread societal discontent does not necessarily translate into radical political upheaval, as even a cursory glance at recent British political history reveals.

One could say that the quick resumption of 'normal' life after the events of June 1953 means that the GDR was essentially stable by this point, though this stability was still underpinned by the open escape hatch to the west. By the time this was closed in August 1961, the absence of significant oppositional reaction to even the radical move signified by the building of the Berlin Wall suggests that regime stability was a well established phenomenon.

However, the issue of stability is perhaps more complex. Given the SED's underlying failure to 'win the argument', outlined above, it would perhaps be more appropriate to speak of a situation of 'stable instability'. In other words, the population was by and large prepared to accept its lot for the foreseeable and perhaps unforeseeable future, but nonetheless remained alive to the idea that the GDR's existential parameters were abnormal and might be changed if a number of external factors altered. Here the comparison to the United Kingdom breaks down. Despite the dissatisfaction felt in many quarters with successive British governments of various compositions, few question the overall legitimacy of the United Kingdom's political system. This has tended to be an issue for academics and a small proportion of the educated middle classes. In the GDR, by contrast, the majority of the population perceived a question mark to be hanging over the state and the SED's hegemony, irrespective of whether they personally wished SED rule to continue or not. Such perceptions were inextricably linked to the Central European fear and expectation of international upheaval and war, noted earlier. This is reflected both in the immediate rumour-mongering and cynicism which accompanied every Soviet bloc crisis or superpower summit meeting, and in the removal of party badges by SED members if things appeared difficult.

The notion of stable instability also calls for a re-evaluation of the normal periodisation of GDR history. The traditional view has been that the GDR remained unstable, particularly economically, until the closure of the borders in 1961, but that the erection of the Berlin Wall enabled a significant consolidation of the country's structures and of popular behaviour. While the economic aspect of this interpretation seems statistically unquestionable, the materials utilised for this volume call for some qualification of the theory of post-1961 political consolidation. On the one hand, the absence of serious political threats other than *Republikflucht* ('fleeing the republic') after 1953 suggests that the process of political consolidation and co-option of the population had long since begun and had already succeeded in cementing SED rule. On the other hand, the continued failure long after 1961 to recognise the ideological legitimacy claimed by the SED, the opposition of groups such as farmers to particular measures, the resistance of young people to the behavioural norms expected of them and the existential questions raised by the Czechoslovak crisis of 1968 all suggest that political stability within the population was not significantly greater than it had been before the Wall. Indeed, the strict border regime was inevitably an additional focus of discontent which undermined the SED's political message and claim to legitimacy. In terms of political consolidation, then, the importance of the Berlin Wall as a watershed in the GDR's domestic history must be relativised.

In summary, the GDR was not doomed to failure by societal discontent. There were, from a very early point, enough reasons and even incentives for the population to accept the GDR system, and these increased over time. However, from the outset there simultaneously existed a number of public perceptions about SED rule and the GDR's place in the international context to potentially undermine the entire system. From our post-*Wende* perspective, it appears that it was the flux of external rather than internal forces that determined which was the dominant set of societal forces at a given time.

Another major concern in GDR historiography has been to define and categorise the state as a political system. It would be inappropriate on the basis of the regional material considered here to embark on a lengthy comparison between the GDR and regimes such as the Third Reich, but the local perspective does permit some contributions to the wider debate. First, it seems clear that the notion of 'totalitarianism' should be applied extremely cautiously to the GDR. While the SED initially attempted to claim total acceptance by the entire population, and to exert total control, this 'totalitarian' desire was significantly relaxed by the later 1960s, when the insistence on participation in neighbourhood NF groups and the campaigns against the western media had been scaled down. Instead, the SED increasingly contented itself with the opposite approach, a total ban on opposition rather than a demand of total loyalty. This trend, already apparent by 1968, became the norm during the 1970s and 1980s as the 'niche society' became more acceptable. This subtle but significant alteration of SED demands reflected the party's failure, repeatedly recorded in the preceding chapters, to achieve total allegiance among the population.

The notion of 'SED dictatorship' is also problematic, as it makes various assumptions about the nature of the SED itself. Who or what was the SED? While it is indisputable that the SED dominated the GDR's governmental and institutional structures, it would be wrong to imagine that the SED consisted entirely of dedicated socialists all eager to do the *Politbüro*'s bidding in the regions and localities. As has become apparent at various points, the SED was itself a broad church whose members had joined the party from a range of different motivations. The party resources devoted to policing the opinions and actions of rank and file members, particularly in the early period, are testimony to the level of both divergent thought within the party and the inability of many of its functionaries to achieve political results, particularly in inculcating the population with socialist thought. Many of these problems undoubtedly resulted from the large influx of non-socialists into the party once it became clear that the SED would become the major patron of eastern Germany's civil service. If there is any moral basis for discussions of guilt in respect of the GDR's history, other than for specific events such as the shootings at the Berlin Wall, then it would seem inappropriate to judge complicity in maintaining SED rule solely on the criterion of SED membership. Conversely, many of those who were actively involved in maintaining SED rule did so from within the bloc parties. Some of these loyalists retained important government positions in the eastern *Länder* of united Germany, but harangued their erstwhile SED colleagues for having belonged to the 'leading party'.

The term 'SED dictatorship' also assumes a high degree of efficiency in the party's administration of the GDR. This presumption also needs serious qualification, at least insofar as it refers to most of 1949–68 period. Although specific police tasks such as clearing the border zones of suspected subversives on particular days were normally completed to order, much was lost in the translation of the more routine requirements of political and economic administration between the SED's Central Committee or a GDR ministry in Berlin and the district or local party headquarters or local mayoral office. Thus the incidence of illegal border crossing remained high during the 1950s and there was a surprisingly high rate of *Republikflucht* even after 1961. Membership drives normally failed to meet their targets, the FDJ regional and district executives were rarely informed of their local groups' activities (if any) and speakers at village meetings could not always be relied upon to say the right thing. Although matters generally improved during the 1960s, especially in respect of internal party discipline, consolidation of the structures of power was still incomplete by 1968. This improvement in efficiency in part resulted from the lower performance levels expected by the SED compared to the 1950s. However, despite the failure to fulfil the leadership's political and administrative goals completely, the high levels of compliant behaviour noted above combined with the administrative success which was achieved were enough to ensure that regime stability was preserved.

Beyond the confines of the party system, as we have already noted many Thuringians from all manner of backgrounds played their part in maintaining SED rule, often simply by failing to object to it and by perpetuating it at the ballot box. While Walter Ulbricht and in his turn Erich Honecker clearly dictated the outlines of the GDR's reality, this was a dictatorship in which most East Germans participated in their daily lives, despite their lack of faith in the very system which they were passively upholding. Even in the Eichsfeld, where the unusual circumstances of a tightly knit majority with its own alternative legitimacy made a special type of accommodation necessary between rulers and ruled, SED rule was not openly challenged once the ground rules of mutual toleration and respect between the local Catholic church and the SED had been established. In summary, the notion of 'dictatorship' must surely be qualified by the widespread preparedness to participate in the forms of the dictatorship, either by publicly declaring an allegiance which did not necessarily exist, or by staffing, often in a voluntary capacity, the state, party and mass-organisation offices at all levels which implemented and perpetuated the dictatorship of the SED *Politbüro* and the Kremlin. The role of the armies of *Stasi* informers, a much discussed topic since the *Wende*, can also be mentioned here.

Perhaps the ultimately defining characteristic of the GDR was apathy. In a state which seemed to be an accident of history, a temporary solution to the knotty problems of the postwar settlement, based on an ideology which found only limited sympathy with the mass of the population, only a minority showed the necessary commitment to make the new state a true success. The frequent absence of work plans, the recurrent necessity for replacement cadres in party and state offices, the poor ideological level of members of the SED and the other parties, all suggest that apathy was almost as prevalent in the structures which were supposed to uphold the system as in the population at large, from which, ultimately, the cadres were drawn. This apathy was the basis of the 'stable instability' which underpinned Thuringia's experience of socialist rule between 1945 and 1968.

Notes

1 M. Fulbrook, *Anatomy of a Dictatorship* (Oxford, Oxford University Press, 1995), p. 274.
2 N. Mros, 'Von der SED zur PDS', in J. Lütke Aldenhövel, H. Mestrup and D. Remy (eds), *Mühlhausen 1989/1990: Die Wende in einer thüringischen Kreisstadt*, (Münster, [n.pub], 2nd edn, 1993), p. 245.
3 Fulbrook, *Anatomy*, p. 279.
4 H. Niemann, *Meinungsforschung in der DDR: Die geheimen Berichte des Instituts für Meinungsforschung an das Politbüro der SED* (Cologne, Bund-Verlag, 1993), p. 219.
5 Fulbrook, *Anatomy*, p. 269.

SELECT BIBLIOGRAPHY

Archival sources

***Thüringisches Hauptstaatsarchiv, Weimar*, ThHStAW**
Land Thüringen 1945–52: Amt für Information (AfI); Büro des Ministerpräsidenten
  (BdMP); Landrat Worbis; Landtag (LT); Ministerium des Innern (MdI);
  Oberlandesgericht Weimar (ObLW)
Ministerium des Innern, Landesbehörde der Deutschen Volkspolizei (LdVP)
Bezirkstag/Rat des Bezirkes Erfurt 1952–90: Inneres (I); Jugendfragen (J); Kader (Ka);
  Kirchenfragen (Ki); Organisation-Instrukteur (OI); Sekretär (S); Volksbildung (V);
  Vorsitzender/Stellvertreter (Vs/St)
Ministerium des Innern, Bezirksbehörde der Deutschen Volkspolizei Erfurt (BdVP)
Nationale Front der DDR, Bezirkssekretariat Erfurt (NF)

***Landesvorstand Thüringen der PDS, Landesparteiarchiv Erfurt* (now a separate
collection within the *Thüringisches Hauptstaatsarchiv, Weimar*), LPA**
KPD and SPD collections
SED collection: *Landesleitung* Thüringen; *Bezirksleitung* Erfurt; *Kreisleitungen* Gotha,
  Heiligenstadt, Bad Langensalza, Mühlhausen, Nordhausen, Sömmerda,
  Sondershausen, Weimar, Worbis; *Stadtleitungen* Erfurt, Weimar
Documents collection
Erinnerungsberichte (Ernst Egert, Karl Kuron)
Nachlässe (August Frölich, Heinrich Hoffmann, Georg Schneider, Adolf Helbing)

***Public Records Office*, PRO:**
Foreign Office (FO)

Newspapers and journals

Erfurter Wochenzeitung (1965)
Statistische Praxis, Monatszeitschrift des Statistischen Zentralamts (1946–49)
Thüringer Volkszeitung (*Organ der KPD, Bezirk Großthüringen/Land Thüringen*) (1945–46)
Tribüne (Erfurt, 1945–46)
Das Volk (Erfurt, 1946–90)

Published works

Agsten, R. and M. Bogisch, *Bürgertum am Wendepunkt: Die Herausbildung der
  antifaschistisch-demokratischen und antiimperialistischen Grundhaltung bei den
  Mitgliedern der LDPD 1945/1946* (Berlin, Buchverlag Der Morgen, [1970])
Agsten, R. and W. Orth, *LDPD 1945 bis 1961 im festen Bündnis mit der Arbeiterklasse und
  ihrer Partei* (Berlin, Buchverlag Der Morgen, 1985)
Anweiler, Ä., *Zur Geschichte der Vereinigung von KPD und SPD in Thüringen 1945–1946*,
  Beiträge zur Geschichte Thüringens (Erfurt, SED Bezirksleitung
  Erfurt/Bezirkskommission zur Erforschung der Geschichte der örtlichen
  Arbeiterbewegung, 1971)
Badstübner, R., *Geschichte der DDR* (Berlin, Deutscher Verlag der Wissenschaften, 1987)

Baring, A., *Uprising in East Germany: June 17, 1953* (New York, Cornell University Press, 1972)

Benser, G., *Die KPD im Jahre der Befreiung* (Berlin, Dietz, 1985)

Berichte der Landes- und Provinzialverwaltungen zur antifaschistisch-demokratischen Umwälzung 1945/46 (Berlin, Akademie Verlag, 1989)

Besier, G., *Der SED-Staat und die Kirche: Der Weg in die Anpassung* (Munich, Bertelsmann, 1993)

Besier, G. and S. Wolf (eds), *»Pfarrer, Christen und Katholiken«. Das Ministerium für Staatssicherheit der ehemaligen DDR und die Kirchen*, Historisch-Theologische Studien zum 19. und 20. Jahrhundert [Quellen], 1, 2nd edn (Neukirchen-Vluyn, Neukirchener Verlag, 1992)

Bessel, R. and R. Jessen (eds), *Die Grenzen der Diktatur: Staat und Gesellschaft in der DDR* (Göttingen, Vandenhoeck & Ruprecht, 1996)

Bouvier, B.W. and H.-P. Schulz, *"… die SPD aber aufgehört hat zu existieren": Sozialdemokraten unter sowjetischer Besatzung* (Bonn, J.H.W. Dietz Nachf., 1991)

Braun, G., '"Regierungsangelegenheiten" in Thüringen im Spannungsfeld von sowjetischer Deutschlandpolitik und SED-Kalkülen 1947: Die Sekretariatssitzung des SED-Landesvorstandes Thüringen vom 30. April 1947', *Beiträge zur Geschichte der Arbeiterbewegung*, 34 (1992), 67–91

Broszat, M. and H. Weber (eds), *SBZ-Handbuch* (Munich, R. Oldenbourg, 1990)

Burens, P. -C., *Die DDR und der "Prager Frühling": Bedeutung und Auswirkungen der tschechoslowakischen Erneuerungsbewegung für die Innenpolitik der DDR im Jahr 1968*, Beiträge zur Politischen Wissenschaft, 41 (Berlin, Duncker & Humblot, 1981)

Büttner, H., *et al.* (eds), *Handbuch der Deutschen Demokratischen Republik* ([Berlin], Staatsverlag der Deutschen Demokratischen Republik, 1964)

CDU Bezirksverband Erfurt, *Das Wirken christlicher Demokraten im Bezirksverband Erfurt: Erlebnisse Erfahrungen Erkenntnisse* (Erfurt [n.pub.] [1980?])

CDU (Sekretariat des Hauptvorstandes), *Thesen zur Geschichte der Christlich-Demokratischen Union Deutschlands*, Beiträge zur Geschichte ([Berlin?], Christlich-Demokratische Union Deutschlands, 1970)

Černý, J. (ed.), *Wer war wer: DDR. Ein biographisches Lexikon*, 2nd edn (Berlin, Christoph Links, 1992)

Černý, J., D. Keller and M. Neuhaus, *Ansichten zur Geschichte der DDR* (Eggersdorf, Verlag Matthias Kirchner, 1993–), V (1994)

Childs, D., *The GDR: Moscow's German Ally*, 2nd edn (London, Unwin Hyman, 1988)

Dähn, H., *Konfrontation oder Kooperation? Das Verhältnis von Staat und Kirche in der SBZ/DDR 1945-1980* (Opladen, Westdeutscher Verlag, 1982)

——, ed., *Die Rolle der Kirchen in der DDR: Eine erste Bilanz*, Geschichte und Staat, 291 (Munich, Olzog Verlag, 1993)

Dawisha, K., *The Kremlin and the Prague Spring* (Berkeley, University of California Press, 1984)

Deutscher Bundestag, *Bericht der Enquete-Kommission "Aufarbeitung von Geschichte und Folgen der SED-Diktatur in Deutschland"* (12. Wahlperiode, Drucksache 12/7820, 31 May 1994)

Diedrich, T., *Der 17. Juni 1953 in der DDR: Bewaffnete Gewalt gegen das Volk* (Berlin, Dietz, 1991)

Dokumente der SED (Berlin, Dietz), IV (1954)

Dressel, G., *Wahlen und Abstimmungsergebnisse 1920–1995*, Quellen zur Geschichte Thüringens, 4 (Erfurt, Landeszentrale für politische Bildung Thüringen, 1995)

Eggerath, W., *Die fröhliche Beichte* (Berlin, Dietz, 1975)

Faulenbach, B., M. Meckel and H. Weber (eds), *Die Partei hatte immer recht: Aufarbeitung von Geschichte und Folgen der SED-Diktatur* (Essen, Klartext Verlag, 1994)

Finn, G., *Buchenwald 1936–1950: Geschichte eines Lagers*, 3rd edn (Berlin, Westkreuz-Verlag, 1991)

Fricke, K.W., *Politik und Justiz in der DDR* (Cologne, Verlag Wissenschaft und Politik, 1979)

Frölich, J, ed., *»Bürgerliche« Parteien in der SBZ/DDR: Zur Geschichte von CDU, LDP(D), DBD und NDPD 1945 bis 1953* (Cologne, Verlag Wissenschaft und Politik, 1995)

Fulbrook, M., *Anatomy of a Dictatorship* (Oxford, Oxford University Press, 1995)

Goeckel, R., *The Lutheran Church and the East German State: Political Conflict and Change Under Ulbricht and Honecker* (Ithaca, Cornell University Press, 1990)

Gottwald, H., *Der Thüringer Landtag 1946–1952: Ein politischer Abriß*, Schriften zur Geschichte des Parlamentarismus in Thüringen, 5 (Erfurt, Thüringer Landtag, 1994)

Gradl, J.B., *Anfang unter dem Sowjetstern: Die CDU 1945–1948 in der sowjetischen Besatzungszone Deutschlands* (Cologne, Verlag Wissenschaft und Politik, 1981)

Grebing, H., *et al.*, *Zur Situation der Sozialdemokratie in der SBZ/DDR 1945–1950* (Marburg, Schüren Presseverlag, 1992)

Günther, G. and L. Wallraf (eds), *Geschichte der Stadt Weimar* (Weimar, Hermann Böhlaus Nachfolger, 1975)

Gutsche, W., ed., *Geschichte der Stadt Erfurt*, 2nd edn (Weimar, Hermann Böhlaus Nachfolger, 1989)

Hagen, M., *DDR – Juni '53: Die erste Volkserhebung im Stalinismus* (Stuttgart, Franz Steiner Verlag, 1992)

Heiden, D., and G. Mai (eds), *Thüringen auf dem Weg ins »Dritte Reich«* (Erfurt, Landeszentrale für politische Bildung Thüringen [n.d.])

Herbst, A., W. Ranke and J. Winkler, *So funktionierte die DDR*, 3 vols (Hamburg, Rowohlt, 1994)

Jahnke, K.H., ed., *Geschichte der Freien Deutschen Jugend*, 2nd edn (Berlin, Verlag Neues Leben, 1983)

Kaelbe, H., J. Kocka and H. Zwahr (eds), *Sozialgeschichte der DDR* (Stuttgart, Klett Cotta, 1994)

Kaiser, G. and E. Frie (eds), *Christen, Staat und Gesellschaft in der DDR* (Frankfurt, Campus Verlag, 1996)

Keller, D., H. Modrow and H. Wolf, *Ansichten zur Geschichte der DDR* (Bonn, PDS/Linke Liste im Deutschen Bundestag, 1993–), I (1993)

Klemm, V., *Korruption und Amtsmißbrauch in der DDR* (Stuttgart, Deutsche Verlags-Anstalt, 1991)

Klonovsky, M. and J. von Flocken, *Stalins Lager in Deutschland: Dokumentation, Zeugenberichte 1945–1950* (Munich, dtv, 1993)

Kolesnitschenko, I.S., *Im gemeinsamen Kampf für das neue antifaschistisch-demokratische Deutschland entwickelte und festigte sich unsere unverbrüchliche Freundschaft*, Beiträge zur Geschichte Thüringens (Erfurt, SED Bezirksleitung Erfurt/Bezirkskommission zur Erforschung der Geschichte der örtlichen Arbeiterbewegung, 1985)

Konzentrationslager Buchenwald: Bericht des internationalen Lagerkomitees Buchenwald (Weimar, Thüringer Volksverlag [1949])

Krippendorff, E., *Die Liberal-Demokratische Partei Deutschlands in der Sowjetischen Besatzungszone 1945/48: Entstehung, Struktur, Politik* (Düsseldorf, Droste Verlag,

[1963?]])

Krisch, H., *German Politics under Soviet Occupation* (New York, Columbia University Press, 1974)

Kulbach, R. and H. Weber, *Parteien im Blocksystem der DDR: Aufbau und Funktion der LDPD und NDPD* (Cologne, Verlag Wissenschaft und Politik, 1969)

Länderverfassungen 1946/47 (Berlin, Staatsverlag der Deutschen Demokratischen Republik, 1990)

Lange, G., *et al.* (eds), *Katholische Kirche – Sozialistischer Staat DDR: Dokumente und öffentliche Äußerungen 1945–1990* (Leipzig, Benno, 1992)

Leonhard, W., *Spurensuche: 40 Jahre nach Die Revolution entläßt ihre Kinder* (Cologne, Kiepenheuer & Witsch, 1994)

Mählert, U., *Die Freie Deutsche Jugend 1945–1949* (Paderborn, Ferdinand Schöningh, 1995)

Malychka, A., *Auf dem Weg zur SED: Die Sozialdemokratie und die Bildung einer Einheitspartei in den Ländern der SBZ*, Archiv für Sozialgeschichte, Beiheft 16 (Bonn, J.H.W. Dietz Nachfolger, 1995)

Mau, R., *Eingebunden in den Realsozialismus? Die Evangelische Kirche als Problem der SED* (Göttingen, Vandenhoeck & Ruprecht, 1994)

McCauley, M., *The German Democratic Republic since 1945* (Basingstoke, Macmillan, 1983)

Mehls, H., ed., *Im Schatten der Mauer: Dokumente. 12. August bis 29. September 1961* (Berlin, Deutscher Verlag der Wissenschaften, 1990)

Mitter, A. and S. Wolle, *Untergang auf Raten: Unbekannte Kapitel der DDR-Geschichte* (Munich, Bertelsmann, 1993)

Moraw, F., *Die Parole der »Einheit« und die Sozialdemokratie*, Schriftenreihe des Forschungsinstituts der Friedrich-Ebert-Stiftung, 94 (Bonn/Bad Godesberg, Verlag Neue Gesellschaft, 1973)

Müller, H., ed., *Beiträge zur Geschichte Thüringens 1968* (Erfurt, Museen der Stadt Erfurt, 1968)

——, *Beiträge zur Geschichte Thüringens* (Erfurt, Museen der Stadt Erfurt), II (1970)

Naimark, N., *The Russians in Germany: A History of the Soviet Zone of Occupation, 1945–1949* (Cambridge, MA, The Belknap Press of Harvard University Press, 1995)

Neef, H., *et al.*, *Die Nationale Front der DDR: Geschichtlicher Überblick* (Berlin, Dietz, 1984)

Neumann, G., and E. Trümpler, *Der Flop mit der DDR-Nation 1971* (Berlin, Dietz, 1991)

Neumann, T., *Die Maßnahme: Eine Herrschaftsgeschichte der SED* (Hamburg, Rowohlt, 1991)

Niemann, H., *Meinungsforschung in der DDR: Die geheimen Berichte des Instituts für Meinungsforschung an das Politbüro der SED* (Cologne, Bund-Verlag, 1993)

Niethammer, L., ed., *Der »gesäuberte« Antifaschismus: Die SED und die roten Kapos von Buchenwald* (Berlin, Akademie Verlag, 1994)

Overesch, M., *Hermann Brill in Thüringen 1895–1946: Ein Kämpfer gegen Hitler und Ulbricht* (Bonn, J.H.W. Dietz Nachf., 1992)

——, *Machtergreifung von links: Thüringen 1945/46* (Hildesheim, Georg Olms, 1993)

Patze, H. and W. Schlesinger, *Geschichte Thüringens*, Mitteldeutsche Forschungen, 48 (Cologne, Böhlau), V, Part 2: *Politische Geschichte in der Neuzeit* (1978)

Raabe, T., *SED-Staat und katholische Kirche: Politische Beziehungen 1949–1961*, Veröffentlichungen der Kommission für Zeitgeschichte, Reihe B: Forschungen, 70 (Paderborn, Ferdinand Schöningh, 1995)

Richter, M., *Die Ost-CDU 1948–1952: Zwischen Widerstand und Gleichschaltung*, Forschungen und Quellen zur Zeitgeschichte, 19, 2nd edn (Düsseldorf, Droste

Verlag, 1991)

Ritscher, B., *Speziallager Nr. 2 Buchenwald* (Weimar/Buchenwald, [n.pub.], 1993)

Rosner, F., *et al.* (eds), *Vereint sind wir alles: Erinnerungen an die Gründung der SED* (Berlin, Dietz, 1966)

Rossmann, G., ed., *Geschichte der SED: Abriß* (Berlin, Dietz, 1978)

Sandford, G., *From Hitler to Ulbricht: The Communist Reconstruction of East Germany 1945–6* (Princeton, NJ, Princeton University Press, 1983)

Schaefer, A., *Lebensbericht: Landrat im Eichsfeld, Zeuge der Besatzungszeit*, 2nd edn (Heiligenstadt, F.W. Cordier, 1994)

Schöneburg, K.-H., ed., *Geschichte des Staates und des Rechts der DDR: Dokumente 1945–1949* (Berlin, Staatsverlag der Deutschen Demokratischen Republik, 1984)

Schöneburg, K.-H. *et al.*, *Vom Werden unseres Staates: Eine Chronik*, 2 vols (Berlin, Staatsverlag der Deutschen Demokratischen Republik, 1966, 1968)

Sieber, H., G. Börnert and G. Michel-Triller, *Dokumente und Materialien zur Geschichte der Arbeiterbewegung in Thüringen 1949–1952*, Beiträge zur Geschichte Thüringens (Erfurt, SED Bezirksleitung Erfurt/Bezirkskommission zur Erforschung der Geschichte der örtlichen Arbeiterbewegung, 1978)

Sieber, H. *et al.*, *Chronik zur Geschichte der Arbeiterbewegung in Thüringen 1945 bis 1952*, Beiträge zur Geschichte Thüringens (Erfurt, SED Bezirksleitung Erfurt/Bezirkskommission zur Erforschung der Geschichte der örtlichen Arbeiterbewegung, 1975)

——, *Chronik zur Geschichte der Arbeiterbewegung im Bezirk Erfurt 1952 bis 1961*, Beiträge zur Geschichte Thüringens (Erfurt, SED Bezirksleitung Erfurt/Bezirkskommission zur Erforschung der Geschichte der örtlichen Arbeiterbewegung, 1979)

——, *Chronik zur Geschichte der Arbeiterbewegung im Bezirk Erfurt 1962 bis 1970*, Beiträge zur Geschichte Thüringens (Erfurt, SED Bezirksleitung Erfurt/Bezirkskommission zur Erforschung der Geschichte der örtlichen Arbeiterbewegung/Staatsarchiv Weimar, 1986)

—— (eds), *Dokumente und Materialien zur Geschichte der Arbeiterbewegung in Thüringen 1945–1950*, Beiträge zur Geschichte Thüringens (Erfurt, SED Bezirksleitung Erfurt/Bezirkskommission zur Erforschung der Geschichte der örtlichen Arbeiterbewegung, 1967)

——, *Beiträge zur Geschichte Thüringens* (Erfurt, SED Bezirksleitung Erfurt/Bezirkskommission zur Erforschung der Geschichte der örtlichen Arbeiterbewegung/Rat des Bezirkes, Abteilung Kultur), IV (1984)

Siebert, H., *Das Eichsfeld unter dem Sowjetstern* (Duderstadt, Mecke Druck und Verlag, 1992)

Sorgenicht, K., *et al.* (eds), *Verfassung der Deutschen Demokratischen Republik: Dokumente/Kommentar*, 2 vols (Berlin, Staatsverlag der Deutschen Demokratischen Republik, 1969)

Spittmann, I. and K.W. Fricke (eds), *Der 17. Juni 1953: Arbeiteraufstand in der DDR* (Cologne, Edition Deutschland Archiv/Verlag Wissenschaft und Politik, 1982)

Staritz, D., *Geschichte der DDR 1949–1985* (Frankfurt/Main, Suhrkamp, 1985)

——, *Die Gründung der DDR*, 2nd edn (Munich, Deutscher Taschenbuch Verlag, 1987)

——, *Was war: Historische Studien zu Geschichte und Politik der DDR* (Berlin, Metropol Verlag, 1994)

Stössel, F.T., *Positionen und Strömungen in der KPD/SED 1945–1954* (Cologne, Verlag Wissenschaft und Politik, 1985)

Thiel, V., *Christen Thüringens in der Bewährung: Aus der Geschichte des Landesverbandes*

Thüringen der Christlich-Demokratischen Union Deutschlands, Christlich-Demokratische Union Deutschlands: Beiträge zur Geschichte (Halle/Saale, Sekretariat des Hauptvorstandes der CDU, 1970)

Tracey, D. 'The Development of the National Socialist Party in Thuringia 1924–30', *Central European History*, 8 (1975), 23–50

——, 'Reform in the Early Weimar Republic: The Thuringian Example', *Journal of Modern History*, 44 (1972), 195–212

Die Verfassung des sozialistischen Staates deutscher Nation: 7. Tagung der Volkskammer der Deutschen Demokratischen Republik ([Berlin], Volkskammer der Deutschen Demokratischen Republik/Nationalrat der Nationalen Front des demokratischen Deutschland [1968])

Weber, H., *DDR: Grundriß der Geschichte 1945–1990* (Hanover, Fackelträger Verlag, 1991)

——, *Geschichte der DDR* (Munich, dtv, 1985)

——, ed., *DDR: Dokumente zur Geschichte der Deutschen Demokratischen Republik 1945–1985* (Munich, dtv, 1986)

——, *Parteiensystem zwischen Demokratie und Volksdemokratie: Dokumente und Materialien zum Funktionswandel der Parteien und Massenorganisationen in der SBZ/DDR 1945–1950* (Cologne, Wissenschaft und Politik, 1982)

Weber, J., ed., *Der SED-Staat: Neues über eine vergangene Diktatur* (Munich, Olzog Verlag, 1994)

Welsh, H., *Revolutionärer Wandel auf Befehl? Entnazifizierungs- und Personalpolitik in Thüringen und Sachsen 1945–1948* (Munich, Oldenbourg, 1989)

Wenzel, G., *Eisenach 1945–1952*, Eisenacher Schriften zur Heimatkunde, 42 (1989)

Wietstruk, S., *Geschichte des Staates und des Rechts der DDR: Dokumente 1949–1961* (Berlin, Staatsverlag der Deutschen Demokratischen Republik, 1984)

Zimmermann, H., H. Ulrich and M. Fehlauer (eds), *DDR Handbuch*, 3rd edn, 2 vols (Cologne, Verlag Wissenschaft und Politik, 1985)

Dissertations

Kachel, S., 'Das Wiedererwachen der Arbeiterbewegung und die thüringische Sozialdemokratie' (unpublished master's dissertation, Universität Leipzig, 1993)

Wahl, V., 'Der Beginn der antifaschistisch-demokratischen Umwälzung in Thüringen: Die Organisierung der gesellschaftlichen Kräfte und der Neuaufbau der Landesverwaltung 1945' (unpublished doctoral dissertation, Friedrich-Schiller-Universität Jena, 1976)

INDEX